T0214494

Lecture Notes in Computer Science 11664

More information about this series at http://www.springer.com/series/7408

Shiva Nejati · Gregory Gay (Eds.)

Search-Based Software Engineering

11th International Symposium, SSBSE 2019
Tallinn, Estonia, August 31 – September 1, 2019
Proceedings

Springer

Editors
Shiva Nejati
SnT/University of Luxembourg
Luxembourg, Luxembourg

Gregory Gay 🆔
University of South Carolina
Columbia, SC, USA

ISSN 0302-9743 ISSN 1611-3349 (electronic)
Lecture Notes in Computer Science
ISBN 978-3-030-27454-2 ISBN 978-3-030-27455-9 (eBook)
https://doi.org/10.1007/978-3-030-27455-9

LNCS Sublibrary: SL2 – Programming and Software Engineering

This Springer imprint is published by the registered company Springer Nature Switzerland AG
The registered company address is: Gewerbestrasse 11, 6330 Cham, Switzerland

Foreword

Message from the General Chair

It is a great pleasure for me to welcome you to the proceedings of the 11th Symposium on Search-Based Software Engineering (SSBSE) 2019 held in Tallinn, Estonia. SSBSE is a premium place to discuss novel ideas and practical applications of search-based software engineering suitable for researchers at any stage of their career. More recently, SSBSE has also witnessed an increased number of industrial participants sharing their experience with other participants. Moreover, SSBSE also provides a forum for PhD students to discuss their PhD topics with the leading experts in the area.

I would like to especially thank our chairs of the various tracks for their tremendous efforts in creating an exciting conference program—(1) Research Track: Shiva Nejati and Gregory Gay; (2) Journal-First Track: Fuyuki Ishikawa; (3) Short and Students Track: Raluca Lefticaru and Muhammad Zohaib Iqbal; (4) Challenge Track: Ruchika Malhotra and Michail Papadakis. Besides, our publicity chairs, Aitziber Iglesias, Ning Ge, Aldeida Aleti, and Ali Ouni, did a fantastic job in advertising the symposium through various channels. Our Web chair, Tiexin Wang, did a great job in setting up the website and carrying out numerous updates efficiently. Last but not least, these proceedings would not have been possible without our publication chair, Bruno Lima. A huge thanks to him for his splendid efforts.

I would also like to thank Kadri Joeruut and Reelika Allemann from Reisiekspert for professionally handling all the local arrangements.

Finally, I would like to thank our sponsors, Facebook and the Research Council of Norway, for their generous support for the conference.

June 2019   Shaukat Ali

Message from the Program Chairs

On behalf of the SSBSE 2019 Program Committee, it is our pleasure to present the proceedings of the 11th International Symposium on Search-Based Software Engineering, held in Tallinn, Estonia. Estonia is a self-described "digital society," where Internet access is a human right and digital access to public services is the norm rather than the exception. We can think of few better places to have held the symposium, and hope that the participants left the symposium inspired by both the program we assembled and the culture we presented it in.

The field of search-based software engineering (SBSE) has grown by leaps and bounds, and although research in this field is presented at almost every software engineering conference, SSBSE continues to bring together the international SBSE community to present innovations, discuss new ideas, and to celebrate progress.

This year, 28 papers were submitted, across four tracks: 16 full research papers, nine short and student papers, two journal-first papers, and one challenge paper. In total, 79 authors from 17 countries submitted their work to the symposium, with submissions from authors located in: Austria, Belgium, Brazil, Canada, China, Germany, Ireland, Italy, Luxembourg, The Netherlands, Pakistan, Romania, Spain, Sweden, Switzerland, UK, and the USA. We would like to thank the authors for their submissions, and express our appreciation for their efforts in advancing the SBSE field.

Following a strict review process, where each submission received three reviews, we accepted 15 papers: nine papers to the research track (with four having been improved through a shepherding process and undergoing a second round of review), three to the short and student paper track (one shepherded), one to the challenge track, and two to the journal-first track. We would like to thank the members of the SSBSE Program Committees for each track. Their dedicated work and support makes this symposium possible, and results in a stronger community.

We would also like to thank the general chair, Shaukat Ali, and the rest of the organization team for their efforts in organizing this conference. We additionally would like to thank the chairs of the short and student paper track—Raluca Lefticaru and Muhammad Zohaib Iqbal—the challenge track—Ruchika Malhotra and Michail Papadakis—and the chair of the journal-first track—Fuyuki Ishikawa. Their efforts made this symposium possible.

In addition to a full program of research talks, SSBSE 2019 attendees had the opportunity to attend two outstanding keynotes. The first keynote was presented by Dr. Thomas Bäck of the Leiden Institute of Advanced Computer Science (LIACS), Leiden University, The Netherlands. Dr. Bäck discussed automatic configuration and learning for evolutionary computation, a strategy for analyzing optimization results using data-driven approaches, resulting in a better understanding of the search mechanism. The second keynote was presented by Dr. Federica Sarro of the Department of Computer Science, University College London. Dr. Sarro discussed the use of predictive analytics for software engineering and the use of search-based heuristics to tackle long-standing SE prediction problems. A tutorial from Nadia Alshahwan of Facebook on testing Android applications allowed attendees to gain hands-on experience with SBSE techniques.

For those who were able to attend the symposium, we hope you enjoyed and were inspired by this year's program. For those unable to attend—or those just now discovering these proceedings—we hope you find the work contained in this volume enlightening and applicable. We are proud of the program assembled this year, and are thankful for the opportunity to present these proceedings to the SBSE research community.

June 2019   Gregory Gay
                                                                              Shiva Nejati

Organization

Organizers

General Chair

Shaukat Ali   Simula Research Laboratory, Norway

Program Chairs

Gregory Gay   Chalmers|University of Gothenburg, Sweden
Shiva Nejati   SnT/University of Luxembourg, Luxembourg

Journal-First Chair

Fuyuki Ishikawa   National Institute of Informatics, Tokyo, Japan

Short and Student Papers Track Chairs

Muhammad Zohaib Iqbal National University of Computer and Emerging
            Sciences, Pakistan
Raluca Lefticaru   University of Sheffield, UK

Challenge Track Chairs

Ruchika Malhotra   Delhi Technological University, India
Michail Papadakis   University of Luxembourg, Luxembourg

Publicity Chairs

Aldeida Aleti   Monash University, Australia
Ning Ge   Beihang University, China
Aitziber Iglesias   IK4-Ikerlan, Spain
Ali Ouni   University of Quebec, Canada

Web Chair

Tiexin Wang   Nanjing University of Aeronautics and Astronautics,
            China

Publication Chair

Bruno Lima   University of Porto and INESC TEC, Portugal

SSBSE Steering Committee

Gregory Gay	Chalmers|University of Gothenburg, Sweden
Lars Grunske	Humboldt University Berlin, Germany
Marouane Kessentini	University of Michigan, USA
Phil McMinn	University of Sheffield, UK
Tim Menzies	North Carolina State University, USA
Annibale Panichella	University of Luxembourg, Luxembourg
Federica Sarro	University College London, UK
Mohamed Wiem Mkaouer	Rochester Institute of Technology, YUSA
Shin Yoo	KAIST, South Korea

Technical Program Committee

Aldeida Aleti	Monash University, Australia
Wesley Assuncao	Federal University of Technology Parana, Brazil
Rami Bahsoon	University of Birmingham, UK
Jose Campos	University of Washington, USA
Carlos Cetina	San Jorge University, Spain
Betty H.C. Cheng	Michigan State University, USA
Thelma E. Colanzi	State University of Maringa, Brazil
Robert Feldt	Blekinge Institute of Technology, Sweden
Erik M. Fredericks	Oakland University, USA
Lars Grunske	Humboldt University of Berlin, Germany
Hadi Hemmati	University of Calgary, Canada
Gregory Kapfhammer	Allegheny College, USA
Marouane Kessentini	University of Michigan, USA
Fitsum Meshesha Kifetew	Fondazione Bruno Kessler, Italy
Anne Koziolek	Karlsruhe Institute of Technology, Germany
Leandro Minku	University of Leicester, UK
Annibale Panichella	Delft University of Technology, The Netherlands
Mike Papadakis	University of Luxembourg, Luxembourg
Pasqualina Potena	RISE SICS Västerås AB, Sweden
Jose Miguel Rojas	University of Leicester, UK
Christopher Simons	University of the West of England, UK
Paolo Tonella	Fondazione Bruno Kessler, Italy
Silvia Vergilio	UFPR, Brazil
Tanja Vos	Universitat Politècnica de València, Spain

Challenge Track Program Committee

Xavier Devroey	Delft University of Technology, The Netherlands

Short and Student Papers Track Program Committee

José Campos	University of Washington, USA
Thelma E. Colanzi	State University of Maringá, Brazil
Florentin Ipate	University of Bucharest, Romania
Anne Koziolek	Karlsruhe Institute of Technology, Germany
Annibale Panichella	Delft University of Technology, The Netherlands
Pasqualina Potena	RISE Research Institutes of Sweden AB, Sweden
José Miguel Rojas	University of Leicester, UK
Paolo Tonella	Università della Svizzera Italiana, Switzerland
Tanja Vos	Open Universiteit, The Netherlands, and Universitat Politècnica de València, Spain
Neil Walkinshaw	University of Sheffield, UK

Sponsoring Institutions

1. Research Council of Norway
2. Facebook

Contents

Keynote

Research Papers

Short and Student Papers

Challenge Paper

Keynote

Search-Based Predictive Modelling for Software Engineering: How Far Have We Gone?

Federica Sarro[✉]

Department of Computer Science, University College London, London, UK
f.sarro@ucl.ac.uk
http://www0.cs.ucl.ac.uk/staff/F.Sarro/

Abstract. In this keynote I introduce the use of Predictive Analytics for Software Engineering (SE) and then focus on the use of search-based heuristics to tackle long-standing SE prediction problems including (but not limited to) software development effort estimation and software defect prediction. I review recent research in Search-Based Predictive Modelling for SE in order to assess the maturity of the field and point out promising research directions. I conclude my keynote by discussing best practices for a rigorous and realistic empirical evaluation of search-based predictive models, a *condicio sine qua non* to facilitate the adoption of prediction models in software industry practices.

Keywords: Predictive analytics · Predictive modelling ·
Search-based software engineering · Machine learning ·
Software analytics

1 Introduction

Nowadays software pervades almost every aspect of our life. This allows the production and collection of a large amount of information about people's decisions and behaviours. Predictive Analytics exploits such information through intelligent systems which are able to identify patterns and predict future outcomes and trends. Applied to Software Engineering, predictive analytics helps us better understand software processes, products and customers in order to maximise product quality, users' satisfaction, and revenues [27].

One of the most important use of Predictive Analytics for Software Engineering is building prediction systems to estimate crucial software aspects and support engineers throughout the software production life-cycle (a.k.a Predictive Modelling for Software Engineering). Examples of software engineering prediction problems are: estimating the amount of effort likely required to develop or maintain software [11,25], estimating the successes of mobile applications [29]

This paper provides an outline of the keynote talk given by Dr. Federica Sarro at SSBSE 2019, with pointers to the literature for details of the results covered.

© Springer Nature Switzerland AG 2019
S. Nejati and G. Gay (Eds.): SSBSE 2019, LNCS 11664, pp. 3–7, 2019.
https://doi.org/10.1007/978-3-030-27455-9_1

and identifying software that will most likely contain defects [12], cause crashes [33] or fail tests [19].

Predictive Modelling for Software Engineering has been an important and active research field that can be dated back to 1971, when the first attempt to estimate the number of software defects was made [18]. Since then, predictive systems of various nature have been proposed ranging from statistical models and analogy-based techniques to machine learning and search-based methods. In particular, over the past 10 years, search-based prediction systems have been specifically devised to tackle long-standing software engineering prediction problems such as software development effort, defect proneness, maintainability and change proneness [14, 21]. These systems are either stand-alone systems able to build optimal prediction models [6, 10, 25] or ones that are used in combination with other (usually machine learning-based) estimators [3–5, 20, 24]. A variety of meta-heuristics based on both local and global search techniques (e.g., Simulated Annealing, Tabu Search, Genetic Algorithm, Genetic Programming) has been used, with the latter being definitively the most studied [8, 21, 26] and with Multi-Objective Evolutionary Algorithm usually resulting in the most effective approach for different prediction tasks (see e.g. [2, 25]).

In this keynote I explain how to use search-based heuristics to tackle software engineering prediction problems. I also highlight their strengths and weaknesses with respect to more traditional statistical or machine learning-based estimators. Some of these are the possibility to use one or multiple desired measures as a fitness function to evolve optimal prediction models [2, 7, 25, 28] and the need of scalable solutions [9, 23]. I review the most promising results in this field and also envisage novel applications of search-based heuristics to predictive modelling for SE; this includes using them to analyse interesting trade-offs (e.g. models' predictive quality vs. interpretability) and to test machine learning-based predictors, both of which are challenges currently faced by the wider SE community. I conclude my keynote by discussing best practices for a rigorous [1, 16, 22, 30, 31] and realistic [13, 15, 17, 32] empirical assessment and evaluation of search-based predictive models, which is a *condicio sine qua non* to grow this field and to facilitate the adoption of prediction models in software industry practices.

References

1. Arcuri, A., Briand, L.C.: A hitchhiker's guide to statistical tests for assessing randomized algorithms in software engineering. STVR **24**(3), 219–250 (2014)
2. Canfora, G., De Lucia, A., Di Penta, M., Oliveto, R., Panichella, A., Panichella, S.: Multi-objective cross-project defect prediction. In: Proceedings of the IEEE 6th International Conference on Software Testing, Verification and Validation, ICST 2013, pp. 252–261 (2013). https://doi.org/10.1109/ICST.2013.38
3. Corazza, A., Di Martino, S., Ferrucci, F., Gravino, C., Sarro, F., Mendes, E.: How effective is Tabu search to configure support vector regression for effort estimation? In: Proceedings of the International Conference on Predictive Models in Software Engineering, PROMISE 2010, pp. 4:1–4:10 (2010). https://doi.org/10. 1145/1868328.1868335

4. Corazza, A., Di Martino, S., Ferrucci, F., Gravino, C., Sarro, F., Mendes, E.: Using tabu search to configure support vector regression for effort estimation. Empir. Softw. Eng. **18**(3), 506–546 (2013). https://doi.org/10.1007/s10664-011-9187-3

5. Di Martino, S., Ferrucci, F., Gravino, C., Sarro, F.: A genetic algorithm to configure support vector machines for predicting fault-prone components. In: Caivano, D., Oivo, M., Baldassarre, M.T., Visaggio, G. (eds.) PROFES 2011. LNCS, vol. 6759, pp. 247–261. Springer, Heidelberg (2011). https://doi.org/10.1007/978-3-642-21843-9_20

6. Ferrucci, F., Gravino, C., Oliveto, R., Sarro, F.: Using Tabu search to estimate software development effort. In: Abran, A., Braungarten, R., Dumke, R.R., Cuadrado-Gallego, J.J., Brunekreef, J. (eds.) IWSM 2009. LNCS, vol. 5891, pp. 307–320. Springer, Heidelberg (2009). https://doi.org/10.1007/978-3-642-05415-0_22

7. Ferrucci, F., Gravino, C., Oliveto, R., Sarro, F.: Genetic programming for effort estimation: an analysis of the impact of different fitness functions. In: Proceedings of the 2nd International Symposium on Search Based Software Engineering, SSBSE 2010, pp. 89–98 (2010). https://doi.org/10.1109/SSBSE.2010.20

8. Ferrucci, F., Harman, M., Sarro, F.: Search-based software project management. In: Ruhe, G., Wohlin, C. (eds.) Software Project Management in a Changing World, pp. 373–399. Springer, Heidelberg (2014). https://doi.org/10.1007/978-3-642-55035-5_15

9. Ferrucci, F., Salza, P., Sarro, F.: Using hadoop MapReduce for parallel genetic algorithms: a comparison of the global, grid and island models. Evol. Comput. **26**, 1–33 (2017). https://doi.org/10.1162/evco_a_00213

10. Ferrucci, F., Gravino, C., Oliveto, R., Sarro, F., Mendes, E.: Investigating Tabu search for web effort estimation. In: Proceedings of EUROMICRO Conference on Software Engineering and Advanced Applications, SEAA 2010, pp. 350–357 (2010)

11. Ferrucci, F., Mendes, E., Sarro, F.: Web effort estimation: the value of cross-company data set compared to single-company data set. In: Proceedings of the 8th International Conference on Predictive Models in Software Engineering, pp. 29–38. ACM (2012)

12. Hall, T., Beecham, S., Bowes, D., Gray, D., Counsell, S.: A systematic literature review on fault prediction performance in software engineering. IEEE Trans. Softw. Eng. **38**(6), 1276–1304 (2012). https://doi.org/10.1109/TSE.2011.103

13. Harman, M., Islam, S., Jia, Y., Minku, L.L., Sarro, F., Srivisut, K.: Less is more: temporal fault predictive performance over multiple hadoop releases. In: Le Goues, C., Yoo, S. (eds.) SSBSE 2014. LNCS, vol. 8636, pp. 240–246. Springer, Cham (2014). https://doi.org/10.1007/978-3-319-09940-8_19

14. Harman, M.: The relationship between search based software engineering and predictive modeling. In: Proceedings of the 6th International Conference on Predictive Models in Software Engineering, PROMISE 2010, pp. 1:1–1:13 (2010). https://doi.org/10.1145/1868328.1868330

15. Jimenez, M., Rwemalika, R., Papadakis, M., Sarro, F., Le Traon, Y., Harman, M.: The importance of accounting for real-world labelling when predicting software vulnerabilities. In: Proceedings of the 27th ACM SIGSOFT International Symposium on the Foundations of Software Engineering, ESEC/FSE 2019 (2019)

16. Langdon, W.B., Dolado, J.J., Sarro, F., Harman, M.: Exact mean absolute error of baseline predictor, MARP0. Inf. Softw. Technol. **73**, 16–18 (2016). https://doi.org/10.1016/j.infsof.2016.01.003

17. Lanza, M., Mocci, A., Ponzanelli, L.: The tragedy of defect prediction, prince of empirical software engineering research. IEEE Softw. **33**(6), 102–105 (2016). https://doi.org/10.1109/MS.2016.156

18. Menzies, T., Zimmermann, T.: Software analytics: so what? IEEE Softw. **30**(4), 31–37 (2013). https://doi.org/10.1109/MS.2013.86
19. Najafi, A., Rigby, P., Shang, W.: Bisecting commits and modeling commit risk during testing. In: Proceedings of the 27th ACM SIGSOFT International Symposium on the Foundations of Software Engineering, ESEC/FSE 2019 (2019)
20. Braga, P.L., Oliveira, A.L.I., Meira, S.R.L.: A GA-based feature selection and parameters optimization for support vector regression applied to software effort estimation. In: Proceedings of the ACM Symposium on Applied Computing, SAC 2008, pp. 1788–1792 (2008)
21. Ruchika, M., Megha, K., Rajeev, R.R.: On the application of search-based techniques for software engineering predictive modeling: a systematic review and future directions. Swarm Evol. Comput. **32**, 85–109 (2017)
22. Russo, B.: A proposed method to evaluate and compare fault predictions across studies. In: Proceedings of the 10th International Conference on Predictive Models in Software Engineering, PROMISE 2014, pp. 2–11. ACM (2014). https://doi.org/10.1145/2639490.2639504
23. Salza, P., Ferrucci, F., Sarro, F.: Elephant56: design and implementation of a parallel genetic algorithms framework on hadoop MapReduce. In: Proceedings of the 2016 on Genetic and Evolutionary Computation Conference, GECCO 2016, pp. 1315–1322 (2016). https://doi.org/10.1145/2908961.2931722
24. Sarro, F., Di Martino, S., Ferrucci, F., Gravino, C.: A further analysis on the use of genetic algorithm to configure support vector machines for inter-release fault prediction. In: Proceedings of the 27th Annual ACM Symposium on Applied Computing, SAC 2012, pp. 1215–1220 (2012). https://doi.org/10.1145/2245276.2231967
25. Sarro, F., Petrozziello, A., Harman, M.: Multi-objective software effort estimation. In: Proceedings of the 38th International Conference on Software Engineering, ICSE 2016, pp. 619–630 (2016). https://doi.org/10.1145/2884781.2884830
26. Sarro, F.: Search-based approaches for software development effort estimation. In: Proceedings of the 12th International Conference on Product Focused Software Development and Process Improvement, PROFES 2011, pp. 38–43 (2011). https://doi.org/10.1145/2181101.2181111
27. Sarro, F.: Predictive analytics for software testing: keynote paper. In: Proceedings of the 11th International Workshop on Search-Based Software Testing, SBST 2018, p. 1 (2018). https://doi.org/10.1145/3194718.3194730
28. Sarro, F., Ferrucci, F., Gravino, C.: Single and multi objective genetic programming for software development effort estimation. In: Proceedings of the 27th Annual ACM Symposium on Applied Computing, SAC 2012, pp. 1221–1226 (2012). https://doi.org/10.1145/2245276.2231968
29. Sarro, F., Harman, M., Jia, Y., Zhang, Y.: Customer rating reactions can be predicted purely using app features. In: Proceedings of 26th IEEE International Requirements Engineering Conference, RE 2018, pp. 76–87 (2018). https://doi.org/10.1109/RE.2018.00018
30. Sarro, F., Petrozziello, A.: Linear programming as a baseline for software effort estimation. ACM Trans. Softw. Eng. Methodol. **27**(3), 12:1–12:28 (2018). https://doi.org/10.1145/3234940
31. Shepperd, M.J., MacDonell, S.G.: Evaluating prediction systems in software project estimation. Inf. Sofw. Technol. **54**(8), 820–827 (2012). https://doi.org/10.1016/j.infsof.2011.12.008

32. Sigweni, B., Shepperd, M., Turchi, T.: Realistic assessment of software effort esti-
    mation models. In: Proceedings of the 20th International Conference on Evaluation
    and Assessment in Software Engineering, EASE 2016, pp. 41:1–41:6. ACM (2016).
    https://doi.org/10.1145/2915970.2916005
33. Xia, X., Shihab, E., Kamei, Y., Lo, D., Wang, X.: Predicting crashing releases of
    mobile applications. In: Proceedings of the 10th ACM/IEEE International Sym-
    posium on Empirical Software Engineering and Measurement, ESEM 2016, pp.
    29:1–29:10 (2016). https://doi.org/10.1145/2961111.2962606

Research Papers

A Systematic Comparison of Search Algorithms for Topic Modelling—A Study on Duplicate Bug Report Identification

Annibale Panichella[✉]

Delft University of Technology, Delft, The Netherlands
a.panichella@tudelft.nl

Abstract. Latent Dirichlet Allocation (LDA) has been used to support many software engineering tasks. Previous studies showed that default settings lead to sub-optimal topic modeling with a dramatic impact on the performance of such approaches in terms of precision and recall. For this reason, researchers used search algorithms (e.g., genetic algorithms) to automatically configure topic models in an unsupervised fashion. While previous work showed the ability of individual search algorithms in finding near-optimal configurations, it is not clear to what extent the choice of the meta-heuristic matters for SE tasks. In this paper, we present a systematic comparison of five different meta-heuristics to configure LDA in the context of duplicate bug reports identification. The results show that (1) no master algorithm outperforms the others for all software projects, (2) random search and PSO are the least effective meta-heuristics. Finally, the running time strongly depends on the computational complexity of LDA while the internal complexity of the search algorithms plays a negligible role.

Keywords: Topic modeling · Latent Dirichlet Allocation · Search-based Software Engineering · Evolutionary Algorithms · Duplicate Bug Report

1 Introduction

Topic model techniques have been widely used in software engineering (SE) literature to extract textual information from software artifacts. Textual information is often used support software engineers to semi-automated various tasks, such as traceability link retrieval [2], identify bug report duplicates [27], automated summary generator [30,34], source code labeling [11], and bug localization [22]. Latent Dirichlet Allocation (LDA) is a topic model techniques, which has received much attention in the SE literature due to its ability to extract topics (cluster or relevant words) from software documents. LDA needs to set a number of hyper-parameters. For instance, the Gibbs sampling generative model requires to choose the number of topics K, the number of iteration N, and two hyper-parameters α and β affecting the topic distributions across documents

© Springer Nature Switzerland AG 2019
S. Nejati and G. Gay (Eds.): SSBSE 2019, LNCS 11664, pp. 11–26, 2019.
https://doi.org/10.1007/978-3-030-27455-9_2

and terms. However, there are no optimal hyper-parameter values that produce "good" LDA models for any dataset. In fact, a prior study showed that untuned LDA can lead to suboptimal performance and can achieve lower accuracy than simple heuristics based on identifier analysis [11,12].

To address the tuning challenge, researchers have proposed different strategies over the years [1,16,17,28,35]. While early attempts focused on the number of topics K as the only parameter to tune, Panichella et al. [28] proposed a search-based approach to tune the LDA hyper-parameters. More specifically, the external performance (e.g., the accuracy) of LDA with a given configuration $[K, N, \alpha, \beta]$ can be indirectly estimated looking at internal cluster quality metrics. In their study, the author used the silhouette coefficient as the driving metric (i.e., the fitness function) to guide genetic algorithms towards finding (near) optimal LDA configurations automatically. Their empirical study showed that LDA settings found with GA dramatically improve the performance of LDA, outperform "off-the-shelf" setting used in previous studies.

Based on the results in [28], Agrawal et al. [1] further investigated search algorithms for tuning LDA. They used Differential Evolution (DE) as alternative meta-heuristic and showed through an extensive study that it often achieves more stable LDA configurations, leading to better topic models than GAs. Besides, they provided further evidence about the usefulness of search-based topic models over "off-the-shelf" LDA settings. Among other results, Agrawal et al. [1] advocated the use of DE as superior meta-heuristics for tuning LDA.

In this paper, we aim to investigate further and compare the performances of multiple meta-heuristics (not only GA and DE) to understand whether there is one meta-heuristic (the "master" algorithm) that constantly dominates all the others. To this aim, we consider the case of *duplicate bug report identification*, which has been often addressed with topic modeling. Duplicate reports are bug reports that describe the same issues but that are submitted by different users to bug tracking systems. Duplicate reports lead to a considerable extra overhead for developers who are in charge of checking and solving the reported issues [20].

We selected seven Java projects from the Bench4BL datasets and compared five different meta-heuristics, namely DE, GA, Particle Swarm Optimization (PSO), Simulated Annealing (SA) and Random Search (Ran). Our results show that there is no "master" (dominant) algorithm in search-based topic modeling, although Ran and PSO are significantly less effective than the other meta-heuristics. Besides, DE does not outperforms GA (in terms of both accuracy and running time) when the three meta-heuristics use the same number of fitness evaluations and the stability of LDA is improved using *restarting strategies*.

2   Background and Related Work

Document Pre-processing. Applying IR methods requires to perform a sequence of pre-processing steps aimed to extract relevant words from software artifacts (bug reports in our case). The first step is the *term extraction*, in which non-relevant characters (e.g., special characters and numbers) are removed, and compound identifiers are split (e.g., camel-case splitting) [14]. In the second step, a *stop-word list* is used to remove terms/words that do not contribute to the conceptual context of a given artifact, such as prepositions, articles, auxiliary verbs, adverbs, and language keywords. Besides, the *stop-word function* removes words that are shorter than a given threshold (e.g., words with less than three characters). In the last steps, a *stemming* algorithm (e.g., Porter stemmer for English) transform words into their root forms (e.g., verb conjugations). The resulting pre-processed documents are then converted into a *term-by-document matrix* (M). The rows of the matrix denote the terms in the vocabulary after pre-processing (m terms) while the columns denote the documents/artifacts in the corpora (n documents). A generic $M(i,j)$ denotes the weight of the i-th term in the j-th document [3]. The basic weight of each term corresponds to its frequency in a given document (tf = term frequency). However, prior studies suggested using tf-idf (terms frequency with inverse document frequency) which gives lower weights (relevance) to words that appear in most of the documents [5]. The *term-by-document matrix* is then used as input for an algebraic (e.g., Vector Space Model) or probabilistic model (PLSI) to compute the textual similarities among the documents. Such similarities are used differently depending on the SE task to solve. For example, similarities are used to detect duplicated reports with the idea that similar bug reports likely discuss the same bug/issue.

In this paper, we use the following pre-processing steps suggested in the literature [3,5,10]: (1) punctuation characters and numbers are removed; (2) splitting compound identifiers with camel-case and snake-case regular expression; (3) a stop-word list for English Language and Java code; (4) stop-word function with a threshold of two characters; (5) words are transformed into their root forms using the Porter stemmer; (6) tf-idf as the weighting schema.

Identifying Duplicate Bug Report. The term-by-document matrix (or its low-dimensional approximation produced by LDA) is then used to compute the Euclidean distance for each pair of documents (bug reports in our case) and compute the ranked list of duplicate bug reports. More specifically, each bug report is used as a query to retrieve the corresponding duplicated reports. The candidate list for each query is therefore determined using the Euclidean distance and sorting the documents in ascending order of distances. Effective IR-methods or topic model should assign better rankings to duplicate reports over non-duplicates. For example, Nguyen et al. [27] combined information retrieval and topic models to detect duplicate reports in an automated fashion. Hindle et al. [20] showed that continuously querying bug reports helps developers to discover duplicates at the time of submitting new bug reports.

Topic Modeling with LDA. Latent Dirichlet Allocation (LDA) [8] is a generative probabilistic model for a collection of textual documents (corpora). More specifically, it is a three-level hierarchical Bayesian model which associates documents with multiple topics [8]. In LDA, a topic is a cluster of relevant words in the corpora. Therefore, documents correspond to finite mixtures over a set of K topics. The input of LDA is the term-by-document ($m \times n$) matrix generated using the pre-processing steps described above. LDA generates two distributions of probabilities, one associated with the documents and the other one related the terms in the corpora. The first distribution is the *topic-by-document matrix* (Θ): a $K \times n$ matrix, where K is the number of topics, n is the number of documents, and the generic entry $\Theta(i, j)$ denotes the probability of the jth document to be relevant to the ith topic. The second distribution is the *word-by-topic matrix* (Φ): an $m \times K$ matrix, where m is the number of words in the corpora, K is the number of topics, and the generic entry $\Phi(i, j)$ denotes the probability of the ith word to belong to the jth topic.

LDA can also be viewed as a dimensional reduction techniquesif the number of topics K is lower than the number of words m in the corpora. Indeed, the term-by-document matrix is decomposed using LDA as follows:

$$\underset{m \times n}{M} \approx \underset{m \times K}{\Phi} \times \underset{K \times n}{\Theta} \tag{1}$$

where K is typically smaller than m. Using Θ, documents can be clustered based on the topics they share based on the corresponding topic probabilities. Documents associated with different topics belong to different topic clusters. Vice versa, documents sharing the same topics belong to the same cluster.

There exist multiple mathematical methods to infer LDA for a given corpora. VEM is the applies a deterministic variational EM method using expectation maximization [25]. The fast collapsed Gibbs sampling generative model is an iterative process that applied a Markov Chain Monte Carlo algorithm [37]. In this paper, we focus on Gibbs-sampling as prior studies showed that it much faster [31], and it can achieve more stable results [17] and better convergence towards the global optimum than VEM [1] in SE documents.

There are four hyper-parameters to set when using the Gibbs sampling generative model for LDA [7,28]:

- the number of topics K to generate from the corpora;
- α influences the distribution of the topics per document. Smaller α values lead to fewer topics per documents.
- β influences the term distribution in each topic. Smaller β values lead to topics with fewer words.
- the number of Gibbs iterations N; this parameter is specific to the Gibbs sampling generative model.

Stability of the Generated Topics. LDA is a probabilistic model and, as such, it can produce slightly different models (topics and mixtures) when executed multiple times for the same corpora. Furthermore, different document orderings may lead to different topic distributions [1] (ordering effect). Previous studies (e.g., [1,21]) suggested different strategies to increase LDA stability, including using random seeds and applying multiple Gibb restarts.

The Gibbs sampling generative method is a stochastic method that performs random samples of the corpora. As any random sampler, the Gibbs method generates random sampling using a random number generator and a starting seed. An easy way to achieve the same topics and mixtures consists in using the same initial **seed** when running LDA with the same hyper-parameters and for the same corpora. Another well-known strategy to improve the stability of LDA is restarting the Gibbs sampling to avoid converging toward local optima. For example, Hughes et al. [21] proposed a sparsity-promoting restart and observed dramatic gains due to the restarting. Binkley et al. [6] ran run the Gibbs sampler multiple times suggesting that it reduces the probability of getting stuck in local optima. Recently, Mantyla et al. [24] performed multiple LDA runs and combined the results of different runs through clustering.

In this paper, we use both fixed **seeds** for the sampling and the restarting strategy. More details are provided in Sect. 3.1.

Automated Tuning for LDA. A general problem when using LDA is deciding the hyper-parameters values to adopt when applying it to a specific dataset. Researchers from different communities agree that there is no universal setting that works well for any dataset (e.g., [6,21,28]). Different heuristics have been proposed by researchers to find (near) optimal hyper-parameters for a given task [1,16,17,28,35]. Most of the early approaches focused on the number of topics K to set while using fixed values for α, β and N [16,17,35].

Panichella et al. [28] used an internal metric for cluster quality analysis to estimate the fitness of LDA configurations based on the idea that LDA can also be seen as a clustering algorithm. More specifically, they used the silhouette coefficient as the fitness function to guide genetic algorithms, which were used to find LDA hyper-parameters that increased the coefficient values. The *silhouette coefficient* is defined as [28]:

$$s(C) = \frac{1}{n} \sum_{i=1}^{n} s(d_i) \quad \text{with} \quad s(d_i) = \frac{b(d_i) - a(d_i)}{\max{(a(d_i), b(d_i))}} \tag{2}$$

In the equation above, $s(d_i)$ denotes the silhouette coefficient for the document d_i in the corpora; $a(d_i)$ measures the maximum distance of the document d_i to the other documents in the same cluster (cluster cohesion); $b(d_i)$ measures the minimum distance between of the document d_i to another document in a different cluster (cluster separation); $s(C)$ measure the overall silhouette coefficient as the arithmetic mean of the coefficients $s(d_i)$ for all documents in the corpora. $s(C)$ takes values in $[-1, +1]$; larger values indicate better clusters because (on average) the separation is larger than the cohesion of the clusters. While the silhouette coefficient is an internal cluster quality metric, Panichella et al. [28] showed that hyper-parameters that increased the silhouette coefficient also lead to better external performances, such as the accuracy in traceability recovery. Besides, the LDA configurations found with GAs achieve performance that is pretty close to the global optimum. The silhouette coefficient and GA were also used in a later study [29] to configure the whole IR process (including the pre-processing) automatically.

Recently, Agrawal et al. [1] further investigated the challenges of configuring LDA with search algorithms. They showed than Differential Evolution (DE) can generate optimal hyper-parameter values which lead to more stable LDA models (topic and mixtures). Besides, Agrawal et al. also used a different fitness function. An empirical comparison between GA and DE showed that the latter needs fewer generations and produces more stable LDA models than the former. However, in [1] GA and LDA were configured with different termination criteria: a few dozens of fitness evaluations for DE and thousands of fitness evaluations for GA. Besides, Agrawal et al. [1] did not use standard strategies (e.g., restarting strategies) to produce stable results for both GA and DE. Based on the results in [1], Mantyla et al. [24] used DE in combination with multiple LDA runs to achieve even more stable topics.

While prior studies argued about the superiority of DE over other meta-heuristics for topic modeling, *more research is needed to assess how different meta-heuristics perform when using the same number of fitness evaluations* (e.g., the same termination criteria) *and using random restarting to achieve stable results.* This paper sheds lights on this open question and compares the performance of five different meta-heuristics (not only DE and GA) when configuring LDA for duplicate bug report identification. For the sake of our analysis, we use the silhouette coefficient as the fitness function for all meta-heuristics.

3   Empirical Study

The following research questions steer our study:

- **RQ1:** *Do different meta-heuristics find equally good LDA configurations?* Different meta-heuristics may produce different LDA configurations. Our first research question aims to investigate whether configurations produced by alternative meta-heuristics achieves or not the same accuracy.
- **RQ2:** *Does the running time differ across the experimented meta-heuristics?* Priori study [1] advocated the usage of Differential Evolution (DE) over other meta-heuristics because it requires less running time. With our second research question, we aim to compare the running time of different meta-heuristics when configured with the same number of fitness evaluations.

Benchmark. The benchmark of our study consists of seven datasets from the Bench4BL dataset [22] and publicly available in GitHub[1]. The benchmark has been used by Lee et al. to perform a comprehensive reproduction study of state-of-the-art IR-based bug localization techniques. For our study, we selected seven Java project from Bench4BL: four projects from the *apache commons library*[2], two projects from Spring[3], and one project from JBoss[4]. The characteristics of the selected projects are reported in Table 1. We chose these seven projects because they have been widely used in the SBSE literature (e.g., [9]) and are well-managed together with issue tracking systems.

For each project, the Bench4BL contains (i) issues (from their issue tracking systems) that are explicitly labeled as bug by the original developers, and (ii) the

---

[1] https://github.com/exatoa/Bench4BL.
[2] http://www.apache.org/.
[3] https://spring.io/.
[4] http://www.jboss.org/.

corresponding patches/fixes [22]. Each bug report/issue contains (i) the summary (or title), (ii) the description, and (iii) the reporter. Besides, `Bench4BL` also provides the list of duplicated bug reports for each system in the dataset. The percentage of duplicated bug reports ranges between 3% for *apache commons math* and 56% for *Spring SPR*.

Table 1. Characteristics of the projects in our study

System	#Files	#Bug Reports	#Duplicates
Apache commmons collections	525	92	16 (17%)
Apache commons io	227	91	7 (8%)
Apache commons lang	305	217	23 (11%)
Apache commons math	1,617	245	8 (3%)
Spring Datacmns	604	158	15 (9%)
Spring SPR	6,512	130	73 (56%)
JBoss WFly	8,990	984	27 (3%)

Meta-Heuristic Selection. We selected the following meta-heuristics:

(1) *Genetic Algorithms* (GAs) have been used in a prior study to configure LDA [28] and the whole IR process [29]. GA is population-based meta-heuristic that evolves a pool of randomly-generated solutions (LDA configurations) through sub-sequent generations. In each generation, solutions are selected based on their fitness values (silhouette coefficient) using the *binary tournament selection*. Fittest solutions (parents) are combined using *binary-simulated crossover* and *gaussian mutation* to form new solutions (offspring). Then, the population for the new generation is formed by selecting the best solutions among parents and offspring (*elitism*).

(2) *Differential Evolution* (DE) is an evolutionary algorithm used by Agrawal et al. [1]. DE is also a population-based meta-heuristic with μ randomly generated solutions. The key difference in DE is that new solutions are generated in each generation by using *differential operators* rather than *genetic operators*. A new solution (LDA configuration) is generated by (1) randomly selecting three solutions a, b, and c from the population; (2) a new solution is generated with the formula: $y_i = a_i + f \times (b_i - c_i)$, where f is the differential weight $\in [0; 2]$; a_i, b_i and c_i denote the i-th elements of the three selected solutions (i.e., the i-th LDA hyper-parameters). The differential operator is applied with a probability $p_c \in [0; 1]$ (crossover probability).

(3) *Particle Swarm Optimization (PSO)* is a population-based meta-heuristic proposed by Eberhart and Kennedy [13]. Similarly to DE and GA, PSO iteratively updates the pool of initial particles (solutions) with initial positions (x), inertia (w), and velocity (v). However, unlike GA and DE that uses crossover (and mutation with GA), PSO updates the solutions toward the best solution in the pool by updating their *positions* and *velocity*.

(4) *Simulated Annealing* (SA) is a meta-heuristic that involves only one solution at a time [36]. One randomly-generated solution x (LDA configuration) is updated through random mutation (neighborhood). If the mutated solution x' improves the fitness function (i.e., $fit(x') < fit(x)$) then SA selects x' as new current solution. If the fitness function decreases with x', the current solution x is still replaced with a probability $\exp^{-\Delta D/T}$, where ΔD is the difference between the cost function for x' and x while T is the temperature. The probability of accepting worst solutions decreases exponentially with ΔD: the higher the difference between the two solutions, the lower the probability of accepting the worst one. Usually, the parameter T decreases in each iteration to strengthen the exploitation ability of SA.

(5) *Random Search* (Ran) is the simplest search algorithm to implement. It tries K random samples and selects as the final solution (LDA configuration) the one with the best fitness value across all generated trials. Despite its simplicity, random search can outperform more sophisticated meta-heuristics for specific problems [4] and it is often used as a baseline in SSBSE.

Parameter Settings. For the search, we opt for the standard parameter setting and search operators suggested in the literature [1,28]. In particular, for GA we use the following parameter values: population size of 10 LDA configurations; crossover probability $p_c = 0.9$; mutation probability $p_m = 0.25$ (i.e., $1/n$, where n is the number of hyper-parameters for LDA). For DE, we use the following setting: population size $\mu = 10$; differential weight factor $f = 0.7$; crossover probability $p_c = 0.9$. SA was configured as follows: neighbors are generated using the Gaussian mutation; the number of steps per temperature $ns = 10$; the number of temperatures $nt = 5$. For PSO, we apply the following setting: population size $\mu = 10$; inertia weight $w_i = 0.9$; search weights $c_1 = c_2 = 1$. The only parameter to set for random search is the number of random solutions to generate.

Termination Criteria. To allow a fair comparison, we set all algorithms with the same *stopping criterion*: the search terminates when the maximum number of fitness evaluations (FEs) is reached. Previous studies in search-based topic modeling suggested different values for FEs: Panichella et al. [28] used GA with 100 individuals and 100 generations, corresponding to 10K FEs; Agrawal et al. [1] used DE with 10 individuals and 3 generations, corresponding to 30 FEs. Agrawal et al. [1] argued that fewer FEs are sufficient to achieve good and stable LDA configurations. In addition, too many FEs dramatically impact the overall running time since each LDA execution (individual) is very expensive for large corpora. Based on the motivation by Agrawal et al. [1], we use FEs = 50 since it provides a good compromise between performances (TOP_k metrics) and running time in our preliminary experiments. However, we use the same FEs for all meta-heuristics while prior studies [1] used fewer FEs only for DE.

Implementation. For LDA, we use its implementation available in the package `topicmodels` in R [18]. We chose this implementation over other implementations (e.g., `Mallet`[5] in Java) because it provides an interface to the original LDA implementation in C code by Blei et al. [8]. Furthermore, Binkley et al. [6] showed that the R implementation is less sensitive to local optima compared to `Mallet`. The R implementation was also used in a prior study concerning LDA configurations for SE tasks [28] and support strategies (e.g., random restarts) to achieve stable LDA models. For the meta-heuristics, we also used their implementation available in R: (1) real-coded genetic algorithms from the package `GA` [33]; (2) differential evolution from the package `DEoptim` [26]; (3) random search from the package `randomsearch` [32]; (4) Simulated-Annealing [38], and Particle Swarm Optimization from the package `NMOF` [23].

The R scripts and datasets used in our experiment are publicly available at the following link: https://apanichella.github.io/tools/ssbse-lda/.

3.1 Experimental Methodology

For each project, we run each meta-heuristic 30 times. In each run, we collected the running time needed to reach the stop condition (see the parameter setting) and the performance metric TOP_k. At the end of each run, we use the LDA configuration produced by the meta-heuristic under analysis, and we generated the corresponding LDA model, and the *topic-by-document matrix* (Θ) in particular.

To answer RQ1, we use the TOP_k metric, which measures the performance of an IR-method by checking whether a duplicate bug report to a given query is retrieved within the top k candidate reports in the ranked list. For example, TOP_5 is equal to one if the first duplicate report for a given query q is retrieved within the first top $k = 5$ positions in the ranked list. The overall TOP_k metric for a given project is the average of the TOP_k scores achieved for all target reports in the project. More formally, let $|Q|$ be the number of queries (reports) in a given dataset, the TOP_k metric is defined as [20]:

$$TOP_k(Q) = \frac{1}{|Q|} \sum_{q \in Q} in_k(i) \qquad (3)$$

where $in_k(i)$ is equal to one if the first duplicated report for the query q is retrieved within the first k positions in the corresponding ranked list. The higher the TOP_k, the better the performance of LDA with a given configuration. In this paper, we consider four values of k, i.e., TOP_5, TOP_{10}, TOP_{15}, and TOP_{20}.

To answer RQ2, we compare the running time required by the different meta-heuristics to terminate the search process in each independent run. For our analysis, we compare the arithmetic mean for the running time across the 30 independent runs and the corresponding standard deviation.

To assess the statistical significance, we use the Friedman test to compare the performance (TOP_k and running time) of the assessed meta-heuristics over six projects and five different metrics (four TOP_k and the running time). Each meta-heuristic produced 4 (TOP_k metrics) × 6 (projects) × 30 (runs) = 720 data points. For statistical analysis, we consider the average (arithmetic mean)

---

[5] http://mallet.cs.umass.edu.

of the TOP_k metrics across the 30 runs, resulting in 24 average scores per meta-heuristic. The five distributions (one for each meta-heuristic) are then compared using the Friedman test [15], which is used to assess whether the performance achieved by alternative meta-heuristics significantly differ from one another. Then, to better understand which meta-heuristics performs better, we use the Wilcoxon rank sum test to compare pairs of meta-heuristics. To draw our conclusions, we use the significance level 0.05 for both the Friedman and Wilcoxon tests. Given the large number of pair comparisons with the Wilcoxon tests, we report the number of times (i.e., pair of software projects and TOP_k metrics) a meta-heuristic A performs significantly better than another meta-heuristic B.

Strategies to Achieve Stable Topic Modeling. In this paper, we address the stability problem using two standard strategies: seeding and random restart. When evaluating each LDA configuration (individual), we store both the silhouette coefficient (fitness function) and the random **seed** used to generate the LDA model. Therefore, when the search terminates, LDA is re-run using the best solution (configuration) found across the generation/iterations and using the corresponding random **seed** previously stored. This allows obtaining the same results (silhouette score, topics, and mixtures) even when LDA is re-run multiple times with the same hyper-parameters. Besides, we also used random restarting to improve the stability of the results and reducing the likelihood of reach a local optimum when using the Gibb-sampling method. In particular, the Gibb sampling procedure is restarted $n = 5$ times (independent runs), and the generated topics and mixtures are obtained by averaging the results achieved across the independent results.

4   Empirical Results

Table 2 shows the average (mean) and the standard deviation performance scores (TOP_5, TOP_{10}, TOP_{15}, and TOP_{20}) achieved by the different algorithms in the comparison over 30 independent runs. First, we can notice that there is no "master" (dominant) meta-heuristic that outperforms the others for all software projects. DE, GA, and SA produce the best (largest) TOP_k scores for different projects and with different k values. DE achieves the highest TOP_5 only for two out of seven projects and in only one project for TOP_{10}. However, in all three cases, DE and GA achieve the same performance score. For all the other projects and metrics, it does not outperform nor compete with other meta-heuristics. Therefore, *our results indicate that DE is not superior to other meta-heuristics* as argued in prior studies.

GA achieves the best scores in 17 cases (six projects with different TOP_k metrics). For the projects io, math, and wfly, GA outperforms all other meta-heuristics according to all TOP_k scores. The differences with the second highest scores range between 2% (math with TOP_5) and 21% (wfly with TOP_5). It is worth noting that these three projects present the lowest percentages of duplicated bug reports ($<=8\%$) compared to the other projects (see Table 1). These results suggest that GA is likely more effective on projects with very few

Table 2. Mean and standard deviation of the performance scores achieved by the evaluated meta-heuristics

System	Metric	DE		GA		Ran		SA		PSO	
		Mean	S.d	Mean	S.d	Mean	S.d	Mean	S.d	Mean	S.d
Collections	TOP_5	0.87	0.09	0.90	0.08	0.90	0.07	**0.95**	0.05	0.80	0.07
	TOP_{10}	0.88	0.10	0.90	0.07	0.91	0.08	**0.95**	0.05	0.84	0.07
	TOP_{15}	0.89	0.10	0.90	0.07	0.91	0.08	**0.96**	0.04	0.84	0.07
	TOP_{20}	0.90	0.08	0.90	0.07	0.91	0.08	**0.96**	0.04	0.85	0.07
Datacmns	TOP_5	0.44	0.10	**0.47**	0.10	0.41	0.12	0.37	0.05	0.28	0.09
	TOP_{10}	0.52	0.12	**0.54**	0.11	0.51	0.12	0.52	0.07	0.39	0.13
	TOP_{15}	0.54	0.13	0.57	0.11	0.53	0.15	**0.61**	0.13	0.42	0.14
	TOP_{20}	0.56	0.13	0.58	0.11	0.55	0.14	**0.63**	0.15	0.46	0.13
IO	TOP_5	0.51	0.12	**0.54**	0.11	0.45	0.16	0.41	0.17	0.22	0.05
	TOP_{10}	0.55	0.12	**0.61**	0.12	0.50	0.18	0.54	0.27	0.36	0.07
	TOP_{15}	0.56	0.11	**0.64**	0.10	0.54	0.15	0.55	0.28	0.44	0.07
	TOP_{20}	0.61	0.12	**0.68**	0.10	0.61	0.15	0.56	0.26	0.52	0.05
Lang	TOP_5	**0.58**	0.11	**0.58**	0.05	0.57	0.05	0.50	0.05	0.38	0.13
	TOP_{10}	0.62	0.12	0.62	0.06	0.64	0.05	**0.68**	0.07	0.45	0.09
	TOP_{15}	0.65	0.11	0.64	0.06	0.67	0.05	**0.69**	0.05	0.48	0.09
	TOP_{20}	0.67	0.12	0.65	0.06	0.69	0.04	**0.71**	0.05	0.49	0.10
Math	TOP_5	0.45	0.09	**0.47**	0.12	0.45	0.14	0.43	0.04	0.38	0.19
	TOP_{10}	0.51	0.11	**0.57**	0.12	0.50	0.16	0.48	0.10	0.41	0.19
	TOP_{15}	0.51	0.10	**0.58**	0.12	0.50	0.16	0.50	0.10	0.42	0.19
	TOP_{20}	0.51	0.10	**0.58**	0.12	0.51	0.15	0.50	0.11	0.44	0.18
Spr	TOP_5	**0.62**	0.04	**0.62**	0.06	0.58	0.06	0.53	0.08	0.53	0.12
	TOP_{10}	**0.65**	0.04	**0.65**	0.05	0.61	0.06	**0.65**	0.03	0.57	0.11
	TOP_{15}	0.67	0.05	0.67	0.05	0.63	0.07	**0.72**	0.09	0.61	0.10
	TOP_{20}	0.69	0.04	0.69	0.04	0.66	0.06	**0.76**	0.10	0.63	0.09
WFly	TOP_5	0.31	0.08	**0.53**	0.10	0.30	0.09	0.44	0.10	0.13	0.03
	TOP_{10}	0.33	0.08	**0.53**	0.09	0.31	0.10	0.48	0.09	0.15	0.03
	TOP_{15}	0.33	0.09	**0.53**	0.09	0.32	0.10	0.50	0.10	0.16	0.02
	TOP_{20}	0.33	0.09	**0.53**	0.09	0.32	0.10	0.51	0.09	0.16	0.02

duplicate bug reports. For the projects datacmns, lang, and spr, GA achieves the best TOP_k scores only for $k = 5$ (for both projects) and $k = 10$ (for spr). For larger k values, SA produces the best TOP_k scores among the five meta-heuristics.

In general, SA achieves the best TOP_k scores in 12 cases (four projects with different TOP_k metrics). Independently from the TOP_k metric, SA is the best meta-heuristic for collections, which is the smallest projects (<100 bug reports) in our benchmark. The differences with the second best meta-heuristic vary between 4% and 5%. For other three projects, namely datacmns, lang, and spr, SA achieves the best results only for larger values of k.

Random search never produces the best TOP_k scores. However, it does produce better average TOP_k scores than DE and GA for collections and lang. Finally, PSO produces the lowest TOP_k scores than all other meta-heuristics and for all projects in our study. Therefore, it is not a suitable meta-heuristic for topic models, at least in the context of duplicate bug report identifications.

The differences among the different meta-heuristics are statistically significant according to the Friedman test, whose resulting p-value is 3.79×10^{-10}. To better understands which meta-heuristics performs statistically better (or worse) than others, Tables 3(a)–(d) report the number of projects in which each meta-heuristic (rows in the tables) significantly outperforms another meta-heuristic (columns in the tables) according to the Wilcoxon test. Instead, Table 4 reports the ranking produces by the Friedman tests. According to the statistical results, GA is ranked first, followed by SA and DE, respectively. Instead, Random search and PSO are the bottom two meta-heuristics. While GA was ranked first, we can notice that it does not significantly outperform all other meta-heuristics for

Table 3. Number of projects in which one meta-heuristic (row) statistically outperforms another one meta-heuristic (column) according to the Wilcoxon test.

(a) TOP_5

Vs.	DE	GA	Ran	SA	PSO
DE	-	0	3	3	7
GA	1	-	4	5	7
Ran	0	0	-	2	7
SA	2	1	2	-	7
PSO	0	0	0	0	-

(b) TOP_{10}

Vs.	DE	GA	Ran	SA	PSO
DE	-	0	2	1	7
GA	3	-	4	1	7
Ran	1	0	-	0	6
SA	3	1	3	-	7
PSO	0	0	0	0	-

(c) TOP_{15}

Vs.	DE	GA	Ran	SA	PSO
DE	-	0	1	1	7
GA	3	-	4	1	7
Ran	0	1	-	0	6
SA	3	2	4	-	7
PSO	0	0	0	0	-

(d) TOP_{20}

Vs.	DE	GA	Ran	SA	PSO
DE	-	0	1	1	7
GA	3	-	4	2	7
Ran	0	1	-	0	6
SA	3	1	5	-	7
PSO	0	0	0	0	-

Table 4. Ranking produced by the Friedman Tests

Meta-heuristic	Ranking
GA	2.085714
SA	2.457143
DE	2.571429
Random	3.457143
PSO	4.428571

all projects. However, it significantly outperforms Random Search and PSO in most of the projects. It outperforms SA in most of the projects only for $PTOP_5$ while for $k > 5$, the two meta-heuristics are comparable. DE (that is ranked third) never outperforms GA according to the Wilcoxon test. Vice versa, GA significantly outperforms DE in three out of seven projects for $POS_{k>5}$.

> *There is no "master" (dominant) meta-heuristic when configuring topic models for duplicate bug report identification. GA and SA perform better than other meta-heuristics but not consistently across projects. Random search and PSO are the least effective meta-heuristics.*

Table 5. Mean and standard deviation of the running time required by the evaluated meta-heuristics to perform 50 fitness evaluations

System	DE		GA		Ran		SA		PSO	
	Mean	S.d	Mean	S.d	Mean	S.d	Mean	S.d	Mean	S.d
Collections	14	2.34	11	2.05	7	5.15	6	0.60	14	1.25
Datacmns	91	14.53	72	14.19	46	32.66	72	36.82	85	15.36
Io	15	2.69	11	1.91	9	6.07	9	1.90	15	0.98
Math	118	16.40	96	24.97	66	47.61	138	85.66	129	20.24
Lang	92	8.83	72	11.98	48	34.14	82	58.55	80	14.81
Spr	64	12.02	58	8.00	37	26.35	85	66.07	71	10.28
WFly	6554	62.36	5196	130.78	3653	262.42	5124	501.38	6433	94.56

Table 5 reports the mean (and the standard deviation) running time required by the evaluated meta-heuristics to reach the same stopping criterion (50 FEs) across 30 independent runs. As expected, random search is the fastest among all meta-heuristics since it does not involve any solution selection and update (e.g., mutation). For what regards the other meta-heuristics, we can notice that their running does not differ substantially. On average, the difference between each pair of meta-heuristics is lower than 10%, and this small difference is mostly due to the computational complexity of the different individual operators. For example, GA is faster than SA in three projects but slower in three other projects. DE and PSO are instead slightly slower than GA and SA, although the differences are small and in some cases almost negligible (e.g., few additional seconds for the project *collections*). These results contradict what reported by Agrawal et al. [1], who used fewer fitness evaluations with DE and many more with GA. In this study, we use the same number of fitness evaluations for all meta-heuristics to allow a fair comparison. When using the same stopping criterion, DE is slightly slower than GA. This confirms previous results in evolutionary computation (e.g., [19]) that showed how the extra overhead in DE is due to the computation complexity of differential operators. Indeed, a single generation of DE is on average four times more expensive than one single generation with GA [19].

> *The running time strongly depends on the number of fitness evaluation per-*
> *formed during the search (time to infer LDA). Instead, the internal complex-*
> *ity of the meta-heuristics is small or negligible.*

Threats to Validity. *Construct validity.* All meta-heuristics are implemented in R and were executed with the same stopping criterion. Furthermore, we use *seeding* and *random restarts* for all meta-heuristics to alleviate the instability of the LDA results. *Internal validity.* We drew our conclusions by executing 30 independent runs to address the random natures of the evaluated meta-heuristics. Besides, we use the Wilcoxon and the Friedman tests to assess the statistical significance of the results. We use TOP_k as the performance metric because it is a standard performance metric in duplicate bug report identification. *External validity.* In our study, we consider seven open source projects from the Bench4BL dataset [22]. Assessing the different meta-heuristics and selecting more projects is part of our future plan.

5   Conclusion and Future Work

In this paper, we empirically compare different meta-heuristics when applied to tune LDA parameters in an automated fashion. We focus on topic-model based identification of bug report duplicates, which is a typical SE task and addressed in prior studies with topic model and IR methods (e.g., [20,27]). Experimental results on seven Java projects and their corresponding bug reports show that multiple meta-heuristics are comparable across different projects, although random search and PSO are least effective than other meta-heuristics. Therefore, *no meta-heuristic outperforms all the others* as advocated in prior studies. However, our conclusions hold for the problem of identifying duplicate bug reports. Therefore, different results may be observed in different SE tasks. Our future work will focus on extending our study by (i) comparing more meta-heuristics, (ii) considering more projects and (iii) evaluating other SE tasks.

References

1. Agrawal, A., Fu, W., Menzies, T.: What is wrong with topic modeling? and how to fix it using search-based software engineering. Inf. Softw. Technol. **98**, 74–88 (2018)
2. Antoniol, G., Canfora, G., Casazza, G., De Lucia, A.: Information retrieval models for recovering traceability links between code and documentation. In: The 16th IEEE International Conference on Software Maintenance, pp. 40–51 (2000)
3. Baeza-Yates, R., Ribeiro-Neto, B.: Modern Information Retrieval. Addison-Wesley, Boston (1999)
4. Bergstra, J., Bengio, Y.: Random search for hyper-parameter optimization. J. Mach. Learn. Res. **13**(2), 281–305 (2012)
5. Binkley, D., Lawrie, D.: Information retrieval applications in software maintenance and evolution. Encycl. Softw. Eng. 454–463 (2009)

6. Binkley, D., Heinz, D., Lawrie, D., Overfelt, J.: Source code analysis with lda. J. Softw. Evol. Process **28**(10), 893–920 (2016)
7. Bird, C., Menzies, T., Zimmermann, T.: The Art and Science of Analyzing Software Data. Elsevier, Amsterdam (2015)
8. Blei, D.M., Ng, A.Y., Jordan, M.I.: Latent dirichlet allocation. J. Mach. Learn. Res. **3**, 993–1022 (2003)
9. Campos, J., Ge, Y., Albunian, N., Fraser, G., Eler, M., Arcuri, A.: An empirical evaluation of evolutionary algorithms for unit test suite generation. Inf. Softw. Technol. **104**, 207–235 (2018)
10. Capobianco, G., De Lucia, A., Oliveto, R., Panichella, A., Panichella, S.: On the role of the nouns in IR-based traceability recovery. In: The 17th IEEE International Conference on Program Comprehension (2009)
11. De Lucia, A., Di Penta, M., Oliveto, R., Panichella, A., Panichella, S.: Using IR methods for labeling source code artifacts: Is it worthwhile? In: The 20th IEEE International Conference on Program Comprehension (ICPC), pp. 193–202 (2012)
12. De Lucia, A., Di Penta, M., Oliveto, R., Panichella, A., Panichella, S.: Labeling source code with information retrieval methods: an empirical study. Empirical Softw. Eng. **19**(5), 1383–1420 (2014)
13. Eberhart, R., Kennedy, J.: A new optimizer using particle swarm theory. In: The 6th International Symposium on Micro Machine and Human Science, pp. 39–43 (1995)
14. Enslen, E., Hill, E., Pollock, L.L., Vijay-Shanker, K.: Mining source code to automatically split identifiers for software analysis. In: The 6th International Working Conference on Mining Software Repositories, pp. 71–80 (2009)
15. García, S., Molina, D., Lozano, M., Herrera, F.: A study on the use of non-parametric tests for analyzing the evolutionary algorithms' behaviour: a case study on the CEC'2005 special session on real parameter optimization. J. Heuristics **15**(6), 617–644 (2009)
16. Grant, S., Cordy, J.R.: Estimating the optimal number of latent concepts in source code analysis. In: The 10th International Working Conference on Source Code Analysis and Manipulation, pp. 65–74 (2010)
17. Griffiths, T.L., Steyvers, M.: Finding scientific topics. Proc. Natl. Acad. Sci. **101**(Suppl. 1), 5228–5235 (2004)
18. Grün, B., Hornik, K.: Topicmodels: an R package for fitting topic models. J. Stat. Softw. **40**(13), 1–30 (2011)
19. Hegerty, B., Hung, C.C., Kasprak, K.: A comparative study on differential evolution and genetic algorithms for some combinatorial problems. In: The 8th Mexican International Conference on Artificial Intelligence, pp. 9–13 (2009)
20. Hindle, A., Onuczko, C.: Preventing duplicate bug reports by continuously querying bug reports. Empirical Softw. Eng. **24**(2), 902–936 (2019)
21. Hughes, M., Kim, D.I., Sudderth, E.: Reliable and scalable variational inference for the hierarchical dirichlet process. In: Artificial Intelligence and Statistics, pp. 370–378 (2015)
22. Lee, J., Kim, D., Bissyandé, T.F., Jung, W., Le Traon, Y.: Bench4bl: reproducibility study on the performance of IR-based bug localization. In: The 27th ACM SIGSOFT International Symposium on Software Testing and Analysis, pp. 61–72. ACM (2018)
23. Manfred Gilli, D.M., Schumann, E.: Numerical Methods and Optimization in Finance (NMOF) (2011)

24. Mantyla, M.V., Claes, M., Farooq, U.: Measuring lda topic stability from clusters of replicated runs. In: The 12th ACM/IEEE International Symposium on Empirical Software Engineering and Measurement, p. 49. ACM (2018)

25. Minka, T., Lafferty, J.: Expectation-propagation for the generative aspect model. In: The 18th Conference on Uncertainty in Artificial Intelligence, pp. 352–359. Morgan Kaufmann Publishers Inc. (2002)

26. Mullen, K., Ardia, D., Gil, D., Windover, D., Cline, J.: Deoptim: an R package for global optimization by differential evolution. J. Stat. Softw. **40**(6), 1–26 (2011)

27. Nguyen, A.T., Nguyen, T.T., Nguyen, T.N., Lo, D., Sun, C.: Duplicate bug report detection with a combination of information retrieval and topic modeling. In: The 27th IEEE/ACM International Conference on Automated Software Engineering, pp. 70–79 (2012)

28. Panichella, A., Dit, B., Oliveto, R., Di Penta, M., Poshyvanyk, D., De Lucia, A.: How to effectively use topic models for software engineering tasks? An approach based on genetic algorithms. In: The International Conference on Software Engineering, pp. 522–531. IEEE Press (2013)

29. Panichella, A., Dit, B., Oliveto, R., Di Penta, M., Poshyvanyk, D., De Lucia, A.: Parameterizing and assembling IR-based solutions for se tasks using genetic algorithms. In: 2016 IEEE 23rd International Conference on Software Analysis, Evolution, and Reengineering (SANER), vol. 1, pp. 314–325. IEEE (2016)

30. Panichella, S., Panichella, A., Beller, M., Zaidman, A., Gall, H.C.: The impact of test case summaries on bug fixing performance: an empirical investigation. In: 2016 IEEE/ACM 38th International Conference on Software Engineering (ICSE), pp. 547–558, May 2016

31. Porteous, I., Newman, D., Ihler, A., Asuncion, A., Smyth, P., Welling, M.: Fast collapsed gibbs sampling for latent dirichlet allocation. In: The 14th ACM SIGKDD international conference on Knowledge discovery and data mining. pp. 569–577. ACM (2008)

32. Richter, J.: Randomsearch: Random Search for Expensive Functions (2019)

33. Scrucca, L.: GA: a package for genetic algorithms in R. J. Stat. Softw. **53**(4), 1–37 (2013)

34. Sridhara, G., Hill, E., Muppaneni, D., Pollock, L.L., Vijay-Shanker, K.: Towards automatically generating summary comments for java methods. In: The 25th IEEE/ACM International Conference on Automated Software Engineering, pp. 43–52. ACM Press (2010)

35. Teh, Y., Jordan, M., Beal, M., Blei, D.: Hierarchical Dirichlet processes. J. Am. Stat. Assoc. **101**(476), 1566–1581 (2006)

36. Van Laarhoven, P.J., Aarts, E.H.: Simulated annealing. In: Simulated annealing: Theory and applications, pp. 7–15, vol 37. Springer, Dordrecht (1987). https://doi.org/10.1007/978-94-015-7744-1_2

37. Wei, X., Croft, W.B.: Lda-based document models for ad-hoc retrieval. In: The 29th Annual International Conference on Research and Development in Information Retrieval, pp. 178–185. ACM (2006)

38. Xiang, Y., Gubian, S., Suomela, B., Hoeng, J.: Generalized simulated annealing for efficient global optimization: the GenSA package for R. R J. **5**(1) (2013)

Constructing Search Spaces
for Search-Based Software Testing
Using Neural Networks

Leonid Joffe[✉] and David Clark

University College London, Gower Street, London WC1E 6BT, UK
leonid.joffe.14@ucl.ac.uk

Abstract. A central requirement for any Search-Based Software Testing (SBST) technique is a convenient and meaningful fitness landscape. Whether one follows a targeted or a diversification driven strategy, a search landscape needs to be large, continuous, easy to construct and representative of the underlying property of interest. Constructing such a landscape is not a trivial task often requiring a significant manual effort by an expert.

We present an approach for constructing meaningful and convenient fitness landscapes using neural networks (NN) – for targeted and diversification strategies alike. We suggest that output of an NN predictor can be interpreted as a fitness for a targeted strategy. The NN is trained on a corpus of execution traces and various properties of interest, prior to searching. During search, the trained NN is queried to predict an estimate of a property given an execution trace. The outputs of the NN form a convenient search space which is strongly representative of a number of properties. We believe that such a search space can be readily used for driving a search towards specific properties of interest.

For a diversification strategy, we propose the use of an autoencoder; a mechanism for compacting data into an n-dimensional "latent" space. In it, datapoints are arranged according to the similarity of their salient features. We show that a latent space of execution traces possesses characteristics of a convenient search landscape: it is continuous, large and crucially, it defines a notion of similarity to arbitrary observations.

Keywords: Search-Based Software Testing · Software engineering · Fitness function · Machine learning · Neural networks

1 Introduction

Search Based Software Testing (SBST) [16,30] methods are widely used in software engineering. They rely on a feedback mechanism that evaluates candidate solutions and directs the search accordingly. The effectiveness of any feedback mechanism depends on the choice of representation and fitness function [15]. In the context of automated search driven testing, an additional choice is that of

© Springer Nature Switzerland AG 2019
S. Nejati and G. Gay (Eds.): SSBSE 2019, LNCS 11664, pp. 27–41, 2019.
https://doi.org/10.1007/978-3-030-27455-9_3

a search strategy. In this paper we focus on constructing a convenient fitness function for a search-based testing process.

According to Harman and Clark, the search space of a good fitness function ought to have a number of desirable characteristics [14]. It needs to be large and approximately continuous, the fitness function needs to have low computational complexity and not have known optimal solutions. Furthermore, they propose that various metrics can be used as fitness functions which implies two further characteristics. First, according to the representation condition, a good metric needs to be truly representative of the property it seeks to denote [38]. Second, a metric imposes an order relation over a set of elements by definition, and for a metric to be useful as a fitness function, the order needs to be meaningful. In this paper we present an approach for constructing fitness functions with desirable characteristics for two fundamental testing strategies – property targeting and diversification driven.

1.1 Property Targeting Search Landscape

A fitness function for an execution property targeting search strategy needs to indicate a "proximity" of a candidate solution to a property of interest (given that the property has not been yet observed). The fitness function therefore needs to be representative of the property of interest, i.e. it needs to meet the representation condition.

Consider an example where a tester aims to exercise a specific program point behind a numeric conditional statement. The numeric difference between the value of a variable and the predicate value of the if statement (branch distance) is the obvious fitness function here [45]. In many interesting "needle in a haystack" testing scenarios however, such an easy fitness function does not exist. For instance, a tester is looking for a crash, but the program has not crashed after a thousand executions produced by mutation of an original input. Can we argue that some of those executions are "closer" to a crash and are therefore better candidates for further mutation?

A neural network trained on execution traces and crash/no crash labels can produce a "suspiciousness" score for each candidate solution. So rather than simply observing a "no crash" output, we query a neural network to say that some inputs exhibited a behaviour or "looks suspiciously like a crash". In this work we show how such a fitness function can be constructed, and that it possesses useful characteristics.

1.2 Diversity Driven Search Landscape

Diversity is widely accepted as beneficial for testing. Various representations have been proposed as targets for diversification, e.g. [2,5,6,10]. Perhaps the most common manifestation is code coverage, yet the effectiveness of coverage driven testing strategies has been disputed [11,17,20,27,40]. This suggests that diversifying over coverage – i.e. preferring dissimilarity of candidate solutions as measured by code coverage – is not ideal.

Regardless of representation, the actual purpose of diversity driven testing is to exercise a maximally diverse range of *behaviours*. To be able to exercise diverse (i.e. dissimilar) behaviours given a representation that is thought to be a good abstraction of program behaviour, we need a notion of similarity. The definition of similarity can then be used to drive a search strategy. A similarity measure requires an order relation, which is a difficult task typically requiring an expert's input [38]. For instance, is *"cat"* < *"dog"*? Lexicographically – yes. By average weight of the animal – usually. By preference as a pet – debatable.

We propose defining an order relation and thus similarity using a neural network architecture called an autoencoder to process execution traces. An autoencoder is trained to reproduce input data on outputs. Its (n-dimensional) intermediate layer forms an encoding of the data known as a *latent* space. The autoencoder arranges the data based on the features that are most important in distinguishing one datapoint from another. The distance in the latent space is thus a measure of similarity of features. Importantly, an autoencoder architecture can be applied to arbitrary data formats. This means that we are not restricted to any particular representation of execution traces. We believe that this notion of similarity can be useful for diversification strategies.

1.3   Contributions and Scope

In this paper we propose an approach to building search landscapes for SBST by using neural networks to process observations of executions. The approach relies on predictor and autoencoder neural networks for property targeting and diversification driven testing strategies respectively. We illustrate the approach with a corpus of small C programs and several real world applications.

Our findings suggest that the landscapes possess a number of useful characteristics. The first is that they are continuous and arbitrarily large. Second, they meet the representation condition. Third, they yield a meaningful order relation to seemingly non-orderable observations. Fourth, the order relation implies a notion of similarity. Lastly, they are created automatically, without analytical effort or domain knowledge.

This work is part of a larger effort in which we intend to integrate these landscapes for use in SBST. The scope of this paper is to present the search landscapes themselves, along with an analysis of their characteristics. Here we do *not* evaluate their effectiveness for discovering properties of interest.

The section following this introduction presents the tools and datasets used in our experiments. Section 3 describes the experiments we carried out. Section 4 reports our findings. Finally, Sect. 5 summarises and concludes the paper.

2   Tools and Datasets

2.1   AFL

We use the American Fuzzy Lop (AFL) [46] fuzzer [33] for two purposes. First, to augment a training corpus of programs with additional inputs. Second, to produce a representation of execution traces to train autoencoders. AFL's representation is the following. Before fuzzing, AFL instruments a program at every decision point. During fuzzing, transitions between these points form a hashmap ("bitmap") of edges and their hit counts. For performance purposes, hit counts are assigned into eight buckets: 0, 1, 2, 3, 4–7, 8–15, 16–31, 32–127, 128+. The bitmap also has a static size of 64K, so the resulting vector of hit counts for small programs tends to be very sparse – most values are 0.

AFL's representation is suitable for our second experiment (described below) for three reasons. First, the bucketisation of the bitmap and the fixed size make it convenient for processing by a neural network. It requires no normalisation or pre-processing. Second, thanks to AFL's blistering speed, it can produce vast numbers of datapoints for a data hungry network. Finally, AFL has a built in notion of "interestingness", defined over the hit counts of a bitmap. All inputs it deems interesting are kept in a persistent queue for further fuzzing.

2.2 Pin

We use the *Pin* instrumentation framework [29] to collect execution traces as sequences of instruction. Raw instruction sequence data is inconvenient for two reasons however. First, the traces are infeasibly large. A single execution of a simple program yields a trace file of size in the order of tens of gigabytes. Second, literal values of instruction arguments become problematic. For instance, the target address in the conditional jump `jle 0x1132` is assigned by the memory manager and is not consistent across program executions. It is also not meaningful over executions of different programs; an execution trace with the value `0x1132` in program A is not meaningful for program B. This is a major problem known as alpha renaming [13].

We bypass the above problems as follows. First, we use *Pin's* built in ability to only instrument the first instance of a block execution. For instance, a loop body is only recorded the first time it is executed. This reduces the sizes of traces dramatically while maintaining information on the sequence of events. The problem of alpha renaming is ignored by discarding any literal data. Thus `jle 0x1132` is only recorded as `jle`. This certainly loses a lot of possibly pertinent information, but attempting to solve alpha renaming is out of scope of this paper. Furthermore, the sequence of op-codes is expected to provide enough information for our purposes.

2.3 Valgrind

Valgrind is a powerful instrumentation framework which tracks every instruction as it executes a program in a simulated environment [34,43]. We use two of its tools, Memcheck and Cachegrind, to record properties of interest (properties that a search aims to discover) for our datasets.

Memcheck reports properties relating to memory management. We record Memcheck's output of illegal reads and writes, use of uninitialised values, definitely lost memory blocks and memory still reachable at the end of execution.

The first three are self explanatory. "Definitely lost" blocks means that no pointer to a memory block can be found, which is typically a symptom of a lost pointer, and ought to be corrected. "Still reachable" is a memory block that has not been properly freed at exit. Neither of these issues are necessarily crucial problems and we include them in our experiments as a proof of concept: that a proximity to a rare, as yet unobserved property – "a needle in a haystack" – can be characterised by features of an execution trace as interpreted by a neural network.

Cachegrind reports the number of reads, writes and misses on different levels of cache. With its default settings of a simulated cache architecture, the values are instruction cache reads (Ir), first and last level instruction cache read misses (I1mr, ILmr), data cache reads and writes (Dr, Dw), first and last level data cache read misses (D1mr, DLmr), and first and last level data cache write misses (D1mw, DLmw).

These values are used as an example of a numeric property which might be the target of optimisation in SBST. As any execution has a numeric value of a cache behaviour (i.e. it is not a rare binary property), the use case here is *not* to build a search space representing the proximity to a rare behaviour. Instead, it may be the case that cache behaviour is difficult to measure and needs to be approximated from an easily observable trace. The values of cache behaviour properties are effectively unbounded which makes them inconvenient for neural networks – training is known to become unstable [37]. We therefore log-normalise them. Not only does this make the values amenable to training a neural network, we believe that an order-of-magnitude estimate of these values is an interesting property.

2.4 Dataset

Our dataset is based on a large repository of simple C programs called Codeflaws [42], and five real world applications.

Codeflaws. Codeflaws is a program repository of thousands of small C programs, along with test cases and automatic fix scripts. Although the intended purpose of Codeflaws is to allow for a "comprehensive investigation of the set of repairable defect classes by various program repair tools", we chose to use it because it provides a vast number of varied programs conveniently arranged.

The neural networks of our approach require large training datasets, so the test cases of the repository were not sufficient. Additional inputs were therefore generated by fuzzing. Each program was fuzzed with AFL to produce a grand total of 365,393 executions across 4714 unique programs. This dataset was then split into training, testing and validation datasets. The number of unique programs and inputs were 3978 and 303,233 for the test set, 587 and 52,092 for the test set, and 149 and 10,068 for the validation set.

Real World Applications. We use five real world programs in our experiments. The first one is *lintxml* from libxml [44]. It processes a string input to determine whether it is valid XML. The second is *cjpeg* from libjpeg [28]. It is used for compressing image files into jpeg format. The third program is *sed-4.5* [31], the Unix stream editor for filtering and transforming text [4]. The fourth program is *sparse* [21], a lightweight parser for C. Finally, *cjson* is a parser for the JSON format. These programs were chosen because they are open source, sufficiently quick to fuzz, and their inputs can be easily interpreted. Furthermore, as we aim to investigate the order relation of a latent space, programs that take string inputs are of interest.

3   Experimental Setup

We conducted two sets of experiments. The first presents a method for constructing a search space for a property targeting search strategy. The second shows an approach for synthesising a search space for a diversification strategy.

Exp. 1: Search Landscape for a Property Targeting Strategy. The search landscape for a property targeting search strategy relies on a regression classifier neural network. During training, it takes a *Pin* trace as input and a ground truth property as the target. During inference, it outputs the likelihood or the estimated value of a ground truth property given an execution trace, for categorical and numeric properties respectively. The setup is illustrated in Fig. 1. The characteristics of the datasets for this experiment are summarised in Table 1.

The network is made up of convolutional and recurrent layers. Sequence data is typically handled with recurrent cells such as the LSTM [18]. Due to the vanishing gradient problem however, LSTMs can only handle sequences of up to several hundred elements. *Pin* traces are thousands of elements long and therefore need to be shortened. This is done with strided convolutional layers [9,22].

The network takes a *Pin* trace as input. The second layer is 64-dimensional embedding [32]. This is followed by a stack of nine convolutional layers with a stride of two. The strides of the convolutional layers halve the sequence length, so the initial sequence length is shortened by a factor of 2^9. The next layer is composed of 500 LSTM cells. Each layer is followed by a dropout to reduce the risk of overfitting [39]. The output layer of the network is a single neuron. For categorical variables, it is sigmoid activated, and the network is trained with binary cross-entropy loss. For numeric values, the network is trained with a mean square error loss. The networks are trained using the Adam optimiser [25]. The parameters were tuned manually by observing the performance on the validation dataset.

Exp. 2: Search Landscape for a Diversity Driven Strategy. We construct a search landscape for a diversification strategy using a variational autoencoder [8,26]. It composed of an encoder and a decoder. The encoder takes AFL's

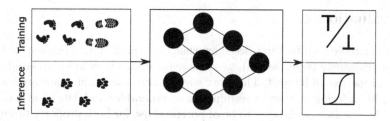

Fig. 1. Illustration of the setup for Exp. 1. A neural network is trained on execution traces of *Pin* instrumented programs as inputs, and properties of interest as prediction targets. During inference, it outputs an estimate of the property as a probability in [0, 1] or a numeric value for categorical and numeric properties respectively.

Table 1. Statistics of the programs and properties of interest in our dataset for Exp. 1.

	CF Train	*CF Test*	*Cjpeg*	*Sparse*	*Cjson*
Total traces	43685	43685	22396	1260	1000
crashes	4458	4458	1722	260	0
deflost_blocks	163	163	0	9	187
illegal_reads	9149	9149	3781	49	0
illegal_writes	626	626	0	0	0
reachable_blocks	1141	1141	16779	0	813
uninit_values	195	195	934	0	0

bitmap representation of an execution trace as input. The hidden layer is a ReLu [23] activated densely connected layer of 2048 neurons. This is followed by a 3-dimensional encoding layer. The decoder has a symmetrical structure to the encoder: the encoding layer is followed by a hidden layer of 2048 neurons, which feeds into the output layer of 65536 (size of AFL's bitmap) neurons on the output. The encoding layer is modelled on work by Kingma et al. [26], with random noise and regularisation. This is intended to force the points close to zero and to provide a continuous landscape for interpolation.

An autoencoder is trained for each real world program in the dataset. The training data is produced by a modified version of AFL. The modified AFL dumps the bitmaps of all executions in its queue, and the bitmap of its current execution into a temporary file. When the temporary file is consumed, AFL dumps the bitmap of the current input again. This way our autoencoder always has training data: the traces of AFL's queue and traces of AFL's latest candidate solutions. During inference, we encode all elements in AFL's queue into the latent space.

4 Evaluation

We present three results. First, we show that the search landscapes are continuous and arbitrarily large. Second, we demonstrate that they are correlated with various properties of interest. Third, we suggest that the latent space produces a meaningful ordering on a set of seemingly non-orderable candidate solutions. We believe these search landscapes to be of potential use for both property targeting and diversification driven search strategies.

4.1 Size and Continuity of Landscapes

Common landscape characterisation techniques like population information content and negative slope coefficient require a notion of a neighbourhood [1]. The neighbourhood of a candidate solution is composed of other candidate solutions within a single *search step*. A step, and hence the neighbourhood, depends on the search operators of the SBST framework. Our landscapes are not defined with respect to search operators, but with respect to a neural network's interpretation of traces. These techniques are therefore inapplicable.

Instead, we argue our claims of continuity and size with the following facts and findings. First, neural networks are continuous by construction [12]. This suggests that the number of possible fitness values is limited by the resolution of the representation. If two candidate solutions can be distinguished in the original representation, they can be mapped to distinct points in the fitness landscape. Second, we observe that in both sets of experiments, the ratio of fitness values

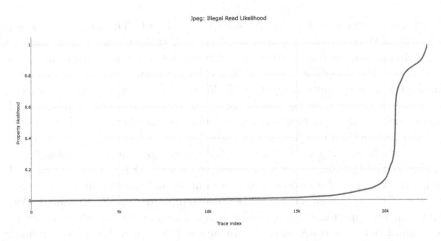

Fig. 2. A plot of the output of a neural network classifier showing its likelihood estimate of whether a trace included an illegal write, for the Jpeg testing dataset. The classifier is trained on the Codeflaws train dataset, with *Pin* execution traces as inputs and an illegal write error as the prediction label output. We suggest that this likelihood can be used as a fitness for a property targeting search strategy. Such a strategy would prioritise candidate solutions that the classifier considers to be more "suspicious".

to the number of unique traces was over 0.95. That is, most distinct traces were mapped to a distinct point in the fitness landscape. Figures 2 and 3 are examples of a property targeting and diversification driven landscape respectively.

4.2   Representation Condition

The neural network classifiers of Exp 1. have a strong predictive power for a range of properties of interest. This means that the landscapes they produce are strongly related to properties of interest, which in turn suggests that they meet the representation condition.

We support this argument with the numeric results of Exp. 1, summarised in Tables 2 and 3. Table 2 shows the Area Under Curve for the Receiver Operator Characteristic (ROC). The ROC is a plot of the false positive versus the true positive rate of a binary classifier. Its main benefit over the use of accuracy is label class size independence [7,19], which makes it a more honest measure of a model's performance.

High values in Table 2 are examples where the model, which was trained on an isolated training dataset of Codeflaws, predicts the property of interest well. In these cases, it has learnt to distinguish and generalise features of execution traces pertinent to properties of interest. Some values are low however. For instance, the presence of reachable blocks in the Jpeg dataset has a low ROC score; the model's understanding of execution trace features indicative of this property is insufficiently general.

Table 3 summarises the networks' predictive ability for cache behaviour values. These are numeric properties, and the results are given as percentage errors from the ground truth. These results give an insight into the fact that the performance of a neural network depends strongly on the training data: they have a strong predictive ability on the test set of Codeflaws programs but poorer performance on others. The Cjson test set is an exception in that the models

Table 2. The predictive ability of a neural network for categorical properties in Exp. 1 by ROC score. The performance is good on an independent test set of programs from the same dataset as the training data. The generalisability to real world applications is limited, but not non-existent. This is evident by the low ROC scores of some test sets. Blanks mean that there were no instances of executions with the property in our dataset.

	CF test	Jpeg	Sparse	Cjson
crash	0.87	0.998	0.794	-
deflost_blocks	0.992	-	0.915	0.772
illegal_reads	0.966	0.885	0.344	-
illegal_writes	0.915	-	-	-
reachable_blocks	0.985	0.251	-	0.187
uninit_values	0.735	0.751	-	-

Table 3. The predictive ability of a neural network for numeric properties in Exp. 1 by percentage error. The results indicate that these numeric properties can be predicted from *Pin* execution traces, and that the prediction meets the representation condition. The generalisation to arbitrary programs is not uniformly good however which can likely be improved with a larger training dataset.

	CF test	Cjpeg	Xmllint	Sparse	Cjson
D1mr	0.151%	10.926%	7.462%	10.854%	1.583%
D1mw	0.817%	13.122%	11.195%	20.587%	0.926%
DLmr	0.747%	4.621%	8.549%	10.805%	0.594%
DLmw	0.008%	6.058%	13.755%	24.374%	2.783%
Dr	1.154%	2.413%	7.580%	16.656%	1.173%
Dw	0.695%	9.011%	3.388%	17.464%	2.326%
I1mr	0.699%	9.037%	22.508%	19.610%	1.607%
ILmr	0.265%	7.865%	16.132%	15.747%	1.586%
Ir	0.578%	13.382%	8.619%	8.808%	1.706%

predict its cache behaviour well. This is likely due to some inherent similarity of Cjson and the programs in Codeflaws. An in depth investigation of these inherent similarities is an interesting direction of future work but out of scope for this paper.

The results presented here are an instantiation of our proposed approach – they are conditional on the representation, the properties of interest and the training dataset. We expect that given a larger, more representative dataset our approach ought to perform better. This is based on the fact that given a sufficient dataset and model size, neural networks are known to avoid local optima [24,35,36,41]. That is, if there is a pattern in the data, a neural network will find it. We recognise the "Deus ex machina" (or rather, "Deus ex data") nature of this argument: *given enough data*, a neural network turns into a silver bullet. Nonetheless, even with the limited dataset, our results demonstrate a clear effectiveness of the technique.

4.3 Meaningful Ordering of Candidate Solutions

The techniques proposed in this work can induce a meaningful ordering given an arbitrary representation. In the case of a property targeting search landscape (Exp. 1), the ordering is obvious – by a classifier's estimate of the property of interest. When there is no explicit property of interest however, an ordering is not apparent. We suggest that a latent space of an autoencoder has a ordering that is meaningful with respect to *features* of observations.

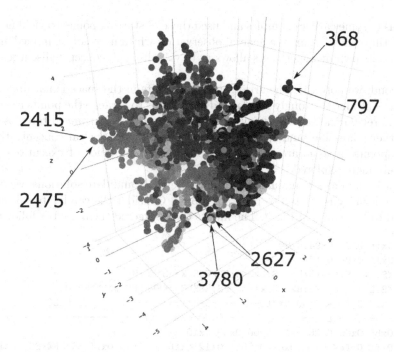

Fig. 3. 3-dimensional latent space encoding of the execution traces of the AFL queue for *xmllint*. The position of each point in the latent space is determined by characteristics of execution traces that the autoencoder found most useful for distinguishing one trace from another. The points are coloured by the sequential index of the queue elements, which allows AFL's search process to be visualised. Whilst the candidate solutions are spread throughout the latent space, there are regions with denser clusters and a diversity driven search strategy could be directed to explore the less populated regions. The numbers are ids of example candidate solutions discussed below. (Color figure online)

Figure 3 is an example of a latent space of candidate solutions for *xmllint*. It is a three dimensional space[1] onto which elements of AFL's fuzzing queue are mapped. The axes themselves do not correspond to any specific feature, they are simply the internal state of the autoencoder. The locality in the latent space represents the similarity of *salient* features of execution traces. The colours correspond to the sequential id of a candidate solution. The earliest candidates are in dark purple, while more recent ones are yellow.

We present several findings of the nature of this landscape. First, the locality in the latent space is correlated with the progression of AFL's search process. This is evident by points of similar colour being grouped into adjacent regions of the space. Early candidate solutions (purple) produced similar traces. As search progressed, novel behaviours (green clusters) were discovered. AFL then turned

---

[1] The dimensionality is arbitrary, three is chosen here so that the space can be plotted for qualitative analysis.

its focus to some earlier examples and used those as starting points to yield newer traces still (yellow). This is a general observation which may not be immediately useful on its own, it nonetheless allows us to visualise and conceptualise a search process.

Second, we note that the arrangement of points in the space is not uniform. The autoencoder is strongly regularised to attempt to arrange the points close to zero (L2 regularisation) and to prevent points from being arranged too close to each other (Gaussian random noise). Despite this, there are clear concentrations of datapoints in some areas. This suggests that some kinds of executions are relatively more explored.

Third, upon closer manual inspection of several candidate solutions, we note that the locality is related to program inputs. Consider the candidate solutions pointed to by arrows in Fig. 3. The inputs that triggered them are the following.

```
 368: 0x1f 0x8b 0x94 0x80
 797: 0x1f 0x8b 0xff
2415: <S:L>><S:F>><S:R>><S:k>><S:FFFFdS:W>>5>M5>M<
2473: <S:L>><S:F>><S:R>><S:k>><S:FS:RSKFS>><FFFFFF:W>>5>Ma>M<
2627: 0xff 0xfe < 0x00 0xff --------C--ii------------ 0x00 0x80 -ii
      --------- L--------------- 0x00 0x80 -ii-------------------- 0x00
      0x80 0x05 0x80 0x10 0x05 0x80 0x10
3780: 0xff 0xfe< 0x00 0xef 0x0b@! 0x12 0xfb @! 0x12 0xff :R>kF@<S@! 0x13
      0x19 >5>M5>M 0x01 \% 0xff 0xff 0x05
```

Ids 368 and 797 are close to each other in the latent space. The strings are short and syntactically similar. 2415 and 2473 are likewise close to each other and their syntactic structure is also similar. They are rather different from the first pair however – both in their position in the latent space and their syntax. Finally, 2627 and 3780 are close in the latent space, and while they share some syntactic features, they are far from identical. The similarity of their traces (and hence proximity in the latent space) may be due to their shared prefix. There happens to be a connection between input strings and latent space locality because the program is a linter whose purpose is to process strings – and exhibit corresponding behaviours. This notion of similarity is much more general however: it captures the innate similarity of features of arbitrary data. Furthermore, its definition requires no manual effort.

We suggest the following implications based on the above observations. First, a latent space representation gives us a way of reasoning about similarity of behaviours given an arbitrary representation: something that was not naturally ordered can now be compared in a convenient, continuous n-dimensional space. In the context of a diversification strategy, we can utilise this notion of similarity to drive a search towards less explored behaviours, i.e. towards less densely populated regions of the latent space[2].

---

[2] Böhme et al. showed that enforcing diversity on AFL's search is beneficial [3]. In future work we intend to investigate how the effectiveness using their notion of diversity compares with that proposed here.

5 Conclusion

The effectiveness of any SBST process depends on a good fitness function. The landscape ought to be large, continuous and representative of the underlying property of interest. Constructing such a landscape is not trivial.

We propose the use of neural networks for constructing search landscapes with convenient characteristics for both property targeting and diversity driven search strategies. We suggest that a property targeting search strategy can use a landscape produced by a classifier neural network, and we illustrate this by experiment. Our results show that the landscape is continuous, arbitrarily large and representative of various properties of interest. For a diversity driven strategy, we propose constructing a search landscape using autoencoders. An autoencoder maps arbitrary observations onto an n-dimensional space where the location is determined by the most distinguishing features of the data. We show how such a space can be created and illustrate that it possesses useful characteristics such as size, continuity and meaningful ordering.

The results and experiments of this paper present the approach of constructing search landscapes, and comment on their characteristics. To the best of our knowledge, our approach is conceptually novel and we believe it to open new directions in SBST. This work is part of ongoing research in which the next steps include evaluating the application of these landscapes for discovery of properties of interest.

References

1. Aleti, A., Moser, I., Grunske, L.: Analysing the fitness landscape of search-based software testing problems. Autom. Softw. Eng. **24**(3), 603–621 (2017)
2. Alshahwan, N., Harman, M.: Coverage and fault detection of the output-uniqueness test selection criteria. In: Proceedings of the 2014 International Symposium on Software Testing and Analysis, pp. 181–192. ACM (2014)
3. Böhme, M., Pham, V.T., Roychoudhury, A.: Coverage-based greybox fuzzing as Markov chain. IEEE Trans. Softw. Eng. **45**, 489–506 (2017)
4. Bonzini, P.: sed(1) - Linux man page (2019). https://linux.die.net/man/1/sed
5. Chen, T.Y., Leung, H., Mak, I.K.: Adaptive random testing. In: Maher, M.J. (ed.) ASIAN 2004. LNCS, vol. 3321, pp. 320–329. Springer, Heidelberg (2004). https://doi.org/10.1007/978-3-540-30502-6_23
6. Ciupa, I., Leitner, A., Oriol, M., Meyer, B.: ARTOO: adaptive random testing for object-oriented software. In: Proceedings of the 30th International Conference on Software Engineering, pp. 71–80. ACM (2008)
7. Cortes, C., Mohri, M.: AUC optimization vs. error rate minimization. In: Advances in Neural Information Processing Systems, pp. 313–320 (2004)
8. Doersch, C.: Tutorial on variational autoencoders. arXiv preprint arXiv:1606.05908 (2016)
9. Dumoulin, V., Visin, F.: A guide to convolution arithmetic for deep learning. arXiv preprint arXiv:1603.07285 (2016)
10. Feldt, R., Poulding, S., Clark, D., Yoo, S.: Test set diameter: quantifying the diversity of sets of test cases. In: 2016 IEEE International Conference on Software Testing, Verification and Validation (ICST), pp. 223–233. IEEE (2016)

11. Gay, G., Staats, M., Whalen, M., Heimdahl, M.P.: The risks of coverage-directed test case generation. IEEE Trans. Softw. Eng. **41**(8), 803–819 (2015)
12. Glasmachers, T.: Limits of end-to-end learning. arXiv preprint arXiv:1704.08305 (2017)
13. Gordon, A.D., Melham, T.: Five axioms of alpha-conversion. In: Goos, G., Hartmanis, J., van Leeuwen, J., von Wright, J., Grundy, J., Harrison, J. (eds.) TPHOLs 1996. LNCS, vol. 1125, pp. 173–190. Springer, Heidelberg (1996). https://doi.org/10.1007/BFb0105404
14. Harman, M., Clark, J.: Metrics are fitness functions too. In: Proceedings of 10th International Symposium on Software Metrics, pp. 58–69. IEEE (2004)
15. Harman, M., Jones, B.F.: Search-based software engineering. Inf. Softw. Technol. **43**(14), 833–839 (2001)
16. Harman, M., Mansouri, S.A., Zhang, Y.: Search-based software engineering: trends, techniques and applications. ACM Comput. Surv. (CSUR) **45**(1), 11 (2012)
17. Heimdahl, M.P.E., George, D., Weber, R.: Specification test coverage adequacy criteria = specification test generation inadequacy criteria. In: Proceedings of Eighth IEEE International Symposium on High Assurance Systems Engineering, pp. 178–186. IEEE (2004)
18. Hochreiter, S., Schmidhuber, J.: Long short-term memory. Neural Comput. **9**(8), 1735–1780 (1997)
19. Huang, J., Ling, C.X.: Using auc and accuracy in evaluating learning algorithms. IEEE Trans. Knowl. Data Eng. **17**(3), 299–310 (2005)
20. Inozemtseva, L., Holmes, R.: Coverage is not strongly correlated with test suite effectiveness. In: Proceedings of the 36th International Conference on Software Engineering, pp. 435–445. ACM (2014)
21. Jones, D.: Sparse - a semantic parser for C (2019). https://sparse.wiki.kernel.org/index.php/Main_Page
22. Kalchbrenner, N., Grefenstette, E., Blunsom, P.: A convolutional neural network for modelling sentences. arXiv preprint arXiv:1404.2188 (2014)
23. Karpathy, A.: Cs231n convolutional neural networks for visual recognition (2016). http://cs231n.github.io/neural-networks-1/
24. Kawaguchi, K.: Deep learning without poor local minima. In: Advances in Neural Information Processing Systems, pp. 586–594 (2016)
25. Kingma, D.P., Ba, J.: Adam: a method for stochastic optimization. arXiv preprint arXiv:1412.6980 (2014)
26. Kingma, D.P., Welling, M.: Auto-encoding variational bayes. arXiv preprint arXiv:1312.6114 (2013)
27. Kochhar, P.S., Thung, F., Lo, D.: Code coverage and test suite effectiveness: empirical study with real bugs in large systems. In: 2015 IEEE 22nd International Conference on Software Analysis, Evolution and Reengineering (SANER), pp. 560–564. IEEE (2015)
28. Lane, T., et al.: libjpeg 6b (1998). http://libjpeg.sourceforge.net/
29. Luk, C.K., et al.: Pin: building customized program analysis tools with dynamic instrumentation. In: ACM SIGPLAN Notices, vol. 40, pp. 190–200. ACM (2005)
30. McMinn, P.: Search-based software test data generation: a survey. Softw. Test. Verif. Reliab. **14**(2), 105–156 (2004)
31. Meyering, J., Gordon, A.: GNU sed (2019). https://www.gnu.org/software/sed/
32. Mikolov, T., Chen, K., Corrado, G., Dean, J.: Efficient estimation of word representations in vector space. arXiv preprint arXiv:1301.3781 (2013)
33. Miller, B.P., Fredriksen, L., So, B.: An empirical study of the reliability of unix utilities. Commun. ACM **33**(12), 32–44 (1990)

34. Nethercote, N., Seward, J.: Valgrind: a framework for heavyweight dynamic binary instrumentation. In: ACM SIGPLAN Notices, vol. 42, pp. 89–100. ACM (2007)
35. Nguyen, Q., Hein, M.: The loss surface of deep and wide neural networks. arXiv preprint arXiv:1704.08045 (2017)
36. Nguyen, Q., Hein, M.: Optimization landscape and expressivity of deep CNNs. In: International Conference on Machine Learning, pp. 3727–3736 (2018)
37. Salimans, T., Kingma, D.P.: Weight normalization: a simple reparameterization to accelerate training of deep neural networks. In: Advances in Neural Information Processing Systems, pp. 901–909 (2016)
38. Shepperd, M.: Fundamentals of Software Measurement. Prentice-Hall, Upper Saddle River (1995)
39. Srivastava, N., Hinton, G., Krizhevsky, A., Sutskever, I., Salakhutdinov, R.: Dropout: a simple way to prevent neural networks from overfitting. J. Mach. Learn. Res. 15(1), 1929–1958 (2014)
40. Staats, M., Gay, G., Whalen, M., Heimdahl, M.: On the danger of coverage directed test case generation. In: de Lara, J., Zisman, A. (eds.) FASE 2012. LNCS, vol. 7212, pp. 409–424. Springer, Heidelberg (2012). https://doi.org/10.1007/978-3-642-28872-2_28
41. Swirszcz, G., Czarnecki, W.M., Pascanu, R.: Local minima in training of neural networks. arXiv preprint arXiv:1611.06310 (2016)
42. Tan, S.H., Yi, J., Mechtaev, S., Roychoudhury, A., et al.: Codeflaws: a programming competition benchmark for evaluating automated program repair tools. In: Proceedings of the 39th International Conference on Software Engineering Companion, pp. 180–182. IEEE Press (2017)
43. VP Users (2017). http://valgrind.org/gallery/users.html
44. Veillard, D.: The XML C parser and toolkit of Gnome (2019). http://xmlsoft.org/
45. Wegener, J., Baresel, A., Sthamer, H.: Evolutionary test environment for automatic structural testing. Inf. Softw. Technol. 43(14), 841–854 (2001)
46. Zalewski, M.: American fuzzy lop (2007). http://lcamtuf.coredump.cx/afl/

A Review of Ten Years of the Symposium on Search-Based Software Engineering

Thelma Elita Colanzi[1(✉)], Wesley Klewerton Guez Assunção[2],
Paulo Roberto Farah[3,4], Silvia Regina Vergilio[4], and Giovani Guizzo[5]

[1] DIN - State University of Maringa, Maringa, Brazil
thelma@din.uem.br
[2] Federal University of Technology - Paraná, Toledo, Brazil
wesleyk@utfpr.edu.br
[3] Santa Catarina State University, Ibirama, Brazil
paulo.farah@udesc.br
[4] DInf - Federal University of Parana, Curitiba, Brazil
silvia@inf.ufpr.br
[5] CREST Centre, University College London, London, UK
giovaniguizzo@gmail.com

Abstract. The year 2018 marked the tenth anniversary of the Symposium on Search Based Software Engineering (SSBSE). In order to better understand the characteristics and evolution of papers published in SSBSE, this work reports results from a mapping study targeting the ten proceedings of SSBSE. Our goal is to identify and to analyze authorship collaborations, the impact and relevance of SSBSE in terms of citations, the software engineering areas commonly studied as well as the new problems recently solved, the computational intelligence techniques preferred by authors and the rigour of experiments conducted in the papers. Besides this analysis, we list some recommendations to new authors who envisage to publish their work in SSBSE. Despite of existing mapping studies on SBSE, our contribution in this work is to provide information to researchers and practitioners willing to enter the SBSE field, being a source of information to strengthen the symposium, guide new studies, and motivate new collaboration among research groups.

Keywords: Systematic mapping · SBSE · Bibliometric analysis

1 Introduction

The year 2018 marked the tenth anniversary of the Symposium on Search Based Software Engineering (SSBSE), the premier event on Search Based Software Engineering (SBSE). SBSE is the research field that formulates Software Engineering (SE) problems as search problems. In this way, heuristic techniques are used to reach optimal solutions to efficiently solve a large variety of problems associated to different SE tasks. Over the past ten years, the symposium has drawn attention of researchers, academics and practitioners alike, contributing

This work was funded by CNPq (Grants 428994/2018-0 and 408356/2018-9) and by the ERC Advanced Grant 2016, ID 741278, Evolving Program Improvement PE6 London Collaborators (EPIC).

© Springer Nature Switzerland AG 2019
S. Nejati and G. Gay (Eds.): SSBSE 2019, LNCS 11664, pp. 42–57, 2019.
https://doi.org/10.1007/978-3-030-27455-9_4

to strengthen the field and to integrate the SBSE community, gathering a large body of studies that serve as reference for researchers. To obtain and understand a big picture of SSBSE, we synthesized this ten-year history of research through a systematic mapping [9] conducted over all the SSBSE proceedings.

In the literature we can find surveys in the SBSE field [5–7] reporting applications of search-based algorithms on software bug fixing, project management, planning and cost estimation, software comprehension, refactoring, software slicing, service-oriented software engineering, compiler optimization, quality assessment, etc. Such surveys analyze the most used search-based algorithms and also point out research directions on SBSE. de Freitas et al. [3] present a bibliometric analysis of the SBSE field. Such works show a growing number of SBSE papers, and an increasing number of addressed SE activities.

Our work also analyzes the addressed SE tasks and used Computational Intelligence (CI) techniques, similarly to aforementioned SBSE studies. But, differently from related work, our focus is the SSBSE. In this way, we provide different analysis regarding the composition of steering and program committees, submission tracks, paper acceptance rate, and impact of the papers published. Such analysis allows a deeper view of SSBSE and contributes to comprehend how the symposium has been evolving along the years.

In our mapping[1], we adopted the guidelines of Petersen et al. [9] and the following Research Questions (RQ):

RQ1: What are the basic SSBSE numbers? To answer this RQ we provide a quantitative analysis of the event: number of submitted and published papers along the years, acceptance rate, authors and committees characteristics, research groups and collaborations.

RQ2: What is the external impact of SSBSE? To answer this RQ we provide a citation analysis of the SSBSE papers, in order to evaluate the visibility and importance of publishing in the symposium.

RQ3: What are the most common addressed SE areas and CI techniques? To answer this question we provide a quantitative analysis of the addressed SE areas and number of papers in each, as well as the employed CI techniques. Besides, we analyze possible changes and trends over time.

RQ4: How have the SBSE approaches been evaluated? To answer this question we provide an analysis of the experimental evaluation carried out in the papers, identifying applied statistical tests and subjects. The main idea is to analyze experimental rigour employed in the studies published in the symposium and if such a rigour has changed over time.

In this way, the main contributions of this work are: (i) to ascertain the impact and relevance of SSBSE, by reporting its main numbers and performing a citation analysis of the published works; (ii) to devise a co-authorship network and depict the most prolific research groups and researchers, as well as the participation of the industry; (iii) to point out the software engineering areas

---

[1] Raw data at https://wesleyklewerton.github.io/SSBSE2019-DataCollection.ods.

that have been most subjected to investigation as well as the ones that need more attention; (iv) to identify the main CI techniques; and (v) to analyze how SBSE approaches have been evaluated.

Studies like ours are important to corroborate the importance of the symposium and if it has been following up the main changes pointed out by the existing surveys and mappings of the SBSE field, as well as to evaluate its representativeness. Besides, we list some recommendations to new authors who envisage to publish their work in SSBSE, providing information to researchers and practitioners willing to enter the SBSE field, being a source of information to strengthen the symposium, guide new studies, and motivate new collaboration among research groups. In Sects. 2 to 5 we answered each posed RQ. Section 6 presents some recommendations to new authors. Section 7 concludes the paper.

2   RQ1 – SSBSE in Numbers

The first edition of SSBSE occurred in 2009, in Windsor, United Kingdom (UK), and since then the symposium took place in six different countries in Europe, South America (2014), and North America (2016). Some editions were co-located with ESE/FSE, and with other events such as ICSME and ASE.

The symposium attracts researchers, students, lecturers and members from industry. Each SSBSE edition had the honor of having at least two keynotes, one from SE and other from the optimization field, in a total of 25 keynotes, as well as 11 tutorials and 4 panels.

Committee Characteristics. Regarding the committee composition, the number of committee members varies from a minimum of 23 in 2017 to a maximum of 43 in 2014 (see Fig. 1(a)). Such members are from different countries, but we do not observe a great variation in the number of represented countries along the editions (minimum number of countries is 9, in 2009 and maximum number is 14, in 2014), average of 11.5.

A greater variation and significant gender imbalance are observed when we consider the percentage of women in the committee[2]. This percentage varies from a minimum of 5% (2009) to a maximum of 25% (2017). The gender imbalance has been decreasing in the last years. Considering the steering committee (Fig. 1(b)) such imbalance has also been decreasing. Such committee was composed for the first time in 2011. In the first four editions it had only 1 woman in a total of 9 members (percentage of 11%). The maximum percentage of women is 30% (2016). The number of countries represented in such committee has been kept almost constant (around 5, with a maximum number of 8 in 2012).

In spite of this gender imbalance, the percentage of women researchers in leadership positions in SSBSE is greater regarding other conferences and the

---

[2] We manually checked the gender of committee members and authors by doing a web search in their profiles by using Google Scholar, Microsoft Academic, Research Gate, Linkedin, etc. We didn't find name and affiliation of two authors only; we used Genderize.io API and both were defined as females.

Computer Science area [1]. We had a total of 43 chairs, 14 of which are women (33%). If we consider only the main track, this percentage is similar (35%), 7 women out of 20 chairs. This imbalance has been decreasing in the last five years. Considering the main track, we observe a perfect balance since 2014; a woman and a man have been chosen for chairs since then.

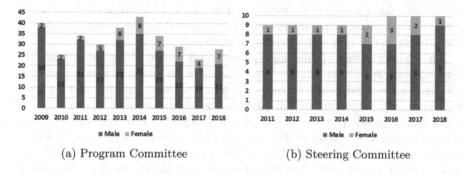

(a) Program Committee   (b) Steering Committee

Fig. 1. Committee characteristics - gender imbalance

Table 1. SSBSE in Numbers. (COU: number of different countries submitting papers. TSUB: number of submissions including all tracks. SUB: number of submissions. ACC: number of accepted papers. Rate: percentage of acceptance. "-" means unknown or 0.)

Year	COU	TSUB	Full			Short/F.Abstract			Student			Challenge		
			SUB	ACC	Rate	SUB	ACC	Rate	SUB	ACC	Rate	SUB	ACC	Rate
2009	14	26	-	9		-	5	-	3	-	-	-	-	-
2010	-	36	-	14		-	-	-	3	-	-	-	-	-
2011	21	43	37	15	40.5	-	8	-	6	3	50	-	-	-
2012	20	38	34	15	44.1	-	3	-	4	2	50	-	-	-
2013	24	50	39	14	35.9	-	6	-	9	6	66.6	4	2	50
2014	19	51	32	14	43.7	3	1	33.3	8	3	37.1	8	4	50
2015	15	51	26	12	46.1	8	4	50	4	2	50	13	13	100
2016	20	48	25	13	52	9	4	44.4	7	4	57.1	7	7	100
2017	14	32	26	7	26.9	2	5	-	2	2	100	4	4	100
2018	10	13	12	12	100	8[a]	6	75	-	-	-	1	1	100

[a] with Hot of the Press Track

Number of Submissions and Acceptance Rate. SSBSE has provided different tracks in its ten editions. Some statistics about such tracks are presented in Table 1. The main track of full research papers and the student track occurred in all editions with independent chairs. We can see that the total number of submitted papers considering all tracks is greater in the period of 2013–2016. A similar fact can be observed considering the number of submitted papers for the full research papers and the student track.

Regarding the main track of full research papers, the number of accepted papers varies from 7 (in 2016) to 15 (in 2011 and 2012). The acceptance rate of the main track falls in the range of 27% (2017) to 100% in (2018). These last two years are outliers. In 2018, a shepherding phase was added in the reviewing process, which may justify 100% of acceptance. In fact, we do not observed great variations in the acceptance rate before 2016, considering 2011–1016 the mean rate is 43%. After a period of growing and boom, we observed a decrease in the number of submitted papers, what might be justified by the recent inclusion of SBSE in the list of topics of several conferences.

The characteristics of the short papers track varied along the editions. In most editions, separated calls for short papers or fast abstracts were provided, with or without independent chairs. In some editions accepted short papers were originally submitted as full papers. The challenge track started only in 2013. Thus it is not possible to analyze the acceptance rate over the ten years of both tracks. The edition of 2017 included a journal-first papers track with 2 papers, and the last edition, in 2018, a Hot of the Press track that also included short/student papers with 6 papers. Including all tracks, we had a corpus of 220 papers, 125 associated to the full track, published by IEEE in the first two editions, and by Springer since the third one. Because of this variety in the tracks, the analysis conducted to answer our research questions includes only the 125 papers of the full research track collected from all the SSBSE proceedings.

Table 2. Most prolific authors

Name	Country	P	C
Andrea Arcuri	Norway, Luxembourg	8	250
Gordon Fraser	Germany, UK	7	208
Paolo Tonella	Italy, Switzerland	7	120
Shin Yoo	UK, Korea	6	176
Mark Harman	UK	6	157
Marouane Kessentini	USA	6	119
Jerffeson T. de Souza	Brazil	5	136
Giuliano Antoniol	Canada	5	67
Yann-Gaël Guéhéneuc	Canada	5	64
Enrique Alba	Spain	4	84
Ruilian Zhao	China	4	42
Silvia R. Vergilio	Brazil	4	34
Thelma E. Colanzi	Brazil	4	34
Betty H.C. Cheng	USA	4	30
Annibale Panichella	Netherlands, Luxembourg	4	14

Table 3. Author's churn

Year	New	Rep.	Left	Total	Churn
2009	24	0	0	24	0.0
2010	32	6	18	38	133.3
2011	34	8	30	42	89.4
2012	34	16	26	50	80.9
2013	34	8	42	42	68.0
2014	39	5	37	44	92.8
2015	35	4	40	39	79.5
2016	39	6	33	45	100.0
2017	13	3	42	16	28.9
2018	31	4	12	35	193.7

Authorship. In 125 full papers, we found 271 distinct authors. Then we analyzed their affiliations, and identified the most prolific authors and collaborations. Table 2 presents a ranking of authors that have published at least four papers, ordered by number of papers and number of citations. The third and the fourth columns present the number of published papers and the total number of citations received of all published papers, respectively. Andrea Arcuri is the author with the greatest number of publications and citations. Another aspect to highlight is that greater productivity does not mean higher citations as some authors have fewer SSBSE papers and more citations (see also Sect. 3).

We can see that the great majority of authors (256 out 271 (94.5%)) published less than 4 papers. Table 3 quantifies unique authors who are new or returned to publish at SSBSE with at least one year without publication (column New), authors that published in the year before and maintained their position publishing at least one paper in the event (column Rep) and authors who did not publish anymore and left the event (Left). Additionally, we calculated the yearly churn rate, presented in the last column. The results indicate that few authors keep publishing along the years, 2012 was the edition with highest number of unique authors and 2017 was the year with the lowest. Churn rate is very high, the highest value was obtained for 2018 and the lowest for 2017.

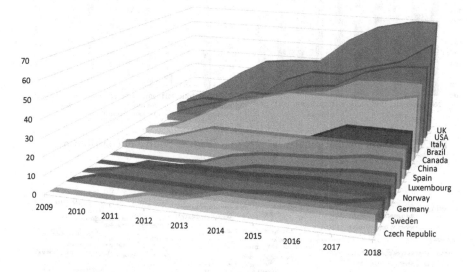

Fig. 2. Contribution by countries

We also investigated the number of countries represented by the authors. To this end we identified the country of all affiliations presented in the papers. Thus, if an author was affiliated to two countries, both were counted in our analysis. The analysis revealed that 24 different countries contributed to SSBSE. The top 3 countries (12.5%) had a contribution of 44.6% and the top 5 countries (20.8%) had a contribution of 64.7%. Figure 2 shows cumulative number of contributions of 12 country affiliations (50%). We can observe that authors from the UK contributed considerably more than other countries over the ten years. Next, there are four countries that have been disputing the second position in the period: USA, Italy, Brazil and Canada. The USA have been maintaining the second place since 2013, tied with other countries in some years. Following, there is a third block, composed by: China, Spain, Luxembourg, Norway, the Netherlands, Germany, Sweden and Czech Republic. There are some interesting aspects about theses countries. First, the number of authors from China did a big jump in years 2015 and 2016, which made them lead the number of contributions of this third group. We can also highlight the fact that Spanish authors participated actively only in the first four years of the event and, since 2014, nobody from Spain has published any other paper. Authors from Germany presented a similar behaviour, 81.8% of the contributions were published in 2010 and 2011. Another important aspect of this group is that we observed an increase in the number of papers from Norway and Luxembourg, maybe due to collaborations with other countries. Norway collaborated with other countries in 41.6% of published papers and Luxembourg in 30%.

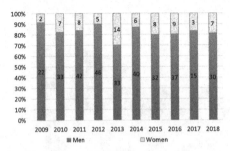

Fig. 3. Authors gender imbalance   **Fig. 4.** Source of contributions

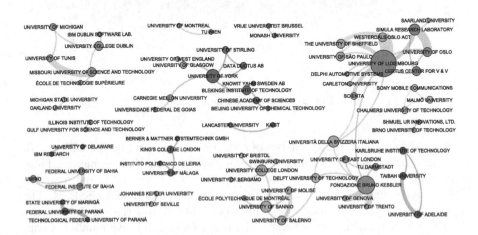

Fig. 5. Collaboration network.

Another analysis shown in Fig. 3 presents the percentage of women that published papers. It varies from 8.3% in 2009 to 29% in 2013. The results show a big gender imbalance that has not been decreasing along the years.

Some authors belong to more than one kind of institution. Figure 4 displays the percentage of authors from universities, research foundations and industry. We can observe clearly that the great majority are from universities. One interesting point is that the research foundation Fondazione Bruno Kessler contributed in almost all editions, except 2013 and 2015. The percentage of papers exclusively from universities is 87.7%, exclusively from industry and also exclusively from research foundations is 4.3%, from universities in collaboration with industry is 3.3% and from universities and research foundations is 0.5%. We noticed a modest participation of the industry.

Collaborations. We observed that 47.2% of papers have external collaboration, that is, were published by authors from different institutions, and in 28.8% the institutions are from different countries. To better identify the main SSBSE groups and collaborations we constructed a co-authorship network (Fig. 5). We observed that the University of Luxembourg formed the main group, collaborating with 11 different institutions. Fondazione Bruno Kessler collaborated with 6, University of York with 5 and University College London, University of Sannio, Simula Research Laboratory and Università Della Svizzera Italiana with 4. Moreover, there are many other collaborations with fewer connections.

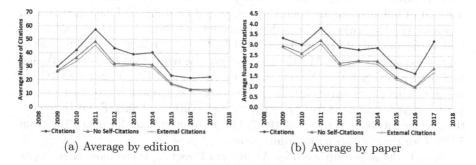

(a) Average by edition   (b) Average by paper

Fig. 6. Average number of citations per year.

3 RQ2 – Citations Analysis and External Impact

This section presents results regarding the total number of citations of SSBSE papers and citations by papers in order to evaluate the impact of the symposium.

The number of citations was collected from Google Scholar (GS) on 14th and 15th of March, 2019. All papers were individually evaluated, for which we collected their total number of citations (tagged as "Citations"), total number of citations excluding self-citations (tagged as "No Self-Citations"), and total number of citations excluding self-citations and citations by other SSBSE papers (tagged "External Citations")[3]. Our citation analysis does not encompass the last edition of SSBSE, because by the time we collected this data, the citations of 2018 papers had not been computed by Google Scholar yet.

In the past 10 years, SSBSE papers have received a total of 2,080 citations, of which 1,692 (81.4%) account for no self-citations and 1,599 (76.9%) represent external citations. However, the difference between the number of no self-citations and external citations is only 93 (4.5%), i.e., there are only 93 citations of SSBSE papers by different SSBSE authors and the remaining citations are all from different authors in different venues.

Figure 6 depicts the average number of citations the papers received per year since they have been published. Figure 6(a) shows the average citations by edition, whereas Fig. 6(b) shows the average by paper. Each SSBSE edition receives on average 35.5 citations per year (39 median), of which 27.9 are no self-citations (31.4 median), and 26.5 are external citations (29.4 median). Papers of SSBSE'11 are the most cited, considering both total number of citations and citations per year, with a total of 458 citations and 57.5 citations per year.

Next we present some statistics by paper. On average, each SSBSE paper has received 18.41 citations (11 median), of which 14.97 are no self-citations (8 median), and 14.15 are external citations (8 median). Moreover, each paper receives on average 2.83 citations per year of its publication (2.17 median), of which 2.22 are no self-citations (1.5 median) and 2.10 are external citations (1.44 median). As it happened to the cumulative number of citations of each SSBSE edition, SSBSE'11 has the most cited papers on average with 3.82 citations per year of publication, 3.23 of which are no self-citations and 3.05 are external citations. However, when we consider the median, SSBSE'11 is only the 8th in the rank with a median of 1.63, while SSBSE'17 gets the 1st position with a median of 3.00. This can be explained by the 135 citations the paper "On Parameter Tuning in Search Based Software Engineering" by Arcuri and Fraser [2] on SSBSE'11 has got. This paper single-handedly drags the average number of citations by paper per year from 2.88 to 3.82 considering all editions of SSBSE. Furthermore, the average citations per year of the 2011 edition would go down to 40.38 from 57.25 if we remove this paper from the average pool.

In fact, the paper authored by Arcuri and Fraser [2] is the most cited paper of the symposium. Table 4 shows the 10 most cited papers from all editions. It is worth mentioning that these 10 papers have 678 citations (32% of all SSBSE papers combined). Another interesting observation is that 5 of these papers are focused on Testing. This greater frequency of citations for testing papers can be explained by the greater number of testing papers in general (see Sect. 4).

Another interesting information is regarding SSBSE h-index and h5-index values [8]. The h-index counts the maximum number of h papers that have been cited at least h times. Similarly, the h5-index compute the h-index for the papers

---

[3] To ease this task, we used Publish or Perish (https://harzing.com/resources/publish-or-perish), a tool that helps researchers look up information about papers, conferences, journals and others researchers in several repositories, including GS.

Table 4. Ranking of the 10 most cited SSBSE papers. (C: citations, NS: no self-citations, E: external citations.)

Year	Title	Authors	C	NS	E
2011	On Parameter Tuning in Search Based Software Engineering	Arcuri and Fraser	135	121	112
2009	An Improved Meta-Heuristic Search for Constrained Interaction Testing	Garvin et al.	82	75	73
2012	Evolving Human Competitive Spectra-Based Fault Localisation Techniques	Yoo	69	56	52
2011	Highly Scalable Multi Objective Test Suite Minimisation Using Graphics Cards	Yoo et al.	68	59	56
2011	Ten Years of Search Based Software Engineering: A Bibliometric Analysis	de Freitas and Souza	59	58	55
2012	Putting the Developer in-the-Loop: An Interactive GA for Software Re-modularization	Bavota et al.	57	54	52
2009	A Study of the Multi-Objective Next Release Problem	Durillo et al.	56	51	47
2012	Reverse Engineering Feature Models with Evolutionary Algorithms: An Exploratory Study	Lopez-Herrejon et al.	52	35	33
2009	Search-Based Testing of AjaxWeb Applications	Marchetto and Tonella	51	47	46
2010	Genetic Programming for Effort Estimation: an Analysis of the Impact of Different Fitness Functions	Ferrucci et al.	49	39	37

published in the last 5 complete years (we consider the 5 years between 2013 and 2017). The SSBSE h-index is 26 and the h5-index is 15. As a matter of comparison, according to GS, the h5-index of ACM/IEEE International Conference on Software Engineering (ICSE) is 74, IEEE Transactions on Software Engineering (TSE) is 56, IEEE Software is 37, IEEE/ACM International Conference on Automated Software Engineering (ASE) is 35 and ACM Transactions on Software Engineering and Methodology (TOSEM) is 31. Considering only external citations, the SSBSE h-index and h5-index values are respectively 23 and 13.

This close gap between no self-citations and external citations (both count and h-index) may indicate that the SSBSE papers have got some substantial external visibility, as most of the citations are from different venues. Furthermore, this can also imply that such papers might have been used as source of inspiration for further research by the SE community.

We reported the number of citations as a measure of impact, however this might not be very accurate. As Ghezzi [4] stated in his keynote during the 31st edition of ICSE, the most cited papers will not always represent the most influential ones. Sometimes a paper is reported to be directly influenced by another paper, while having more citations. This can also be observed when comparing the rank of papers by citations count to the rank of most influential papers judged by the experts of the field. As shown by Ghezzi [4], the 8 most cited papers in their ICSE editions were elected as the most influential papers of that same year, but further down the rank, the most cited papers were not always selected as the most influential ones by experts.

This phenomenon actually happened for SSBSE. During the 10th edition of the symposium in 2018, the community was asked to vote on the most influential paper of the past 10 years. The award was given to "The Human Competitiveness of Search Based Software Engineering" by de Souza et al. [10]. However, the award-winning paper is only the 11th most cited paper (46 citations).

All in all, the number of citations seemed to be the best metric of impact in the context of our work. This metric can be of some value, as a greater number of citations can tell more than smaller numbers, even though only about the visibility of papers. The best approach to evaluate the external impact of SSBSE papers would be to actually check the experts opinion, however, that is not a trivial task. Indeed, this could be done in future work with a more carefully designed impact evaluation with experts of top-tier software engineering venues.

4   RQ3 – Software Engineering Areas and Tasks

SE Areas. To answer RQ3, the papers were grouped by SE areas[4] as depicted in Fig. 7. 54.4% of the papers are from Software Defect Analysis, which includes software testing and debugging, and 45.6% tackled some task related to software testing. Test data generation was addressed by papers in every SSBSE edition.

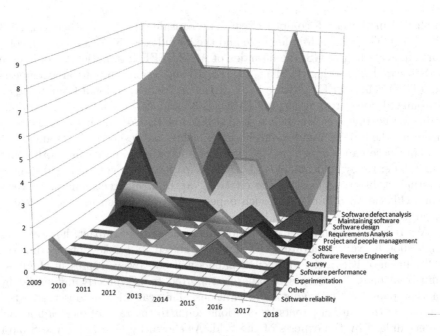

Fig. 7. Amount of papers published by software engineering area

---

[4] We used the four first levels of the 2012 ACM Computing Classification System (https://www.acm.org/publications/class-2012).

Defect prediction, test case evaluation and test management were tackled only in the first two editions. The last three editions contained papers on regression testing, stress testing, interaction testing and test suite minimization. Papers on tasks related to debugging addressed fault localization and program analysis over time and, more recently (2016 and 2017), program repair.

Requirements Analysis, Software Design and Maintenance represent, respectively, 8.8%, 12% and 8% of the SSBSE papers. The Next Release Problem is the most addressed Requirements task, although the last publication about this task was in 2015. More recently, papers have focused on detection of incomplete requirements and non-functional requirements optimization. Regarding Software Design, most papers deal with architecture definition and model transformation (MDE), followed by automatic software configuration, architecture improvement and software modularization. After two years without publications in this area, three papers addressing MDE were published in 2018. Maintenance papers appeared between 2012–2016 and 55% of them addressed refactoring.

The other SE areas were focused in less than 5% of the papers. Most papers on Project and People Management deal with business process reduction and software project planning. Three surveys were published from 2011 to 2015. They addressed SBSE research analysis, metrics to search-based refactoring and software requirement selection and prioritization problems. Four papers treat SBSE over time, in the following order: SBSE evaluation, SBSE scalability, project decision making and online experimentation. Reverse engineering was applied to the software product line approach in 3 published papers. SE Areas such as Software Performance, Software Reliability, Experimentation and source-code authorship definition (identified as Other in Fig. 7) had only one paper each.

Finally, tasks that have emerged in the last 4 years are the ones related to non-functional properties (software performance, software reliability, non-functional properties optimization and non-functional requirements optimization), as well as program repair, stress testing, MDE and experimentation.

CI Techniques. Figure 8 shows the CI techniques used in the SSBSE papers over time. 76% of the papers applied (mono or multi-objective) evolutionary algorithms. 24% applied local search, such as Hill-Climbing, Greedy, Simulated Annealing and Tabu Search. 4.8% used swarm intelligence algorithms (ACO and PSO). The category named Other (almost 10% of the papers) includes algorithms such as Mathematical Optimization, Mixed Integer Linear programming, Error-Correcting Graph Matching algorithm, Constraint Programming, Artificial Immune Recognition Systems, Random Search, etc. 3.2% of papers have also applied Machine Learning algorithms (Artificial Neural Network, Greedy Agglomerative Clustering or Multiple Regression).

19 out 125 papers used more than one CI technique. In some cases, different algorithms were used to compare which one has the best performance to solve the addressed problem. In other cases, algorithms from different CI techniques were combined to better solve a problem, which happened with the 4 papers that combined evolutionary algorithms and machine learning. Each one

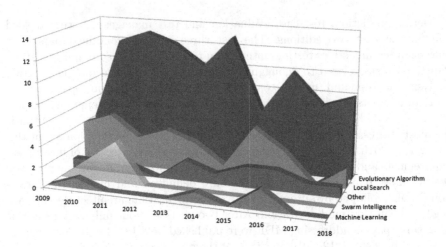

Fig. 8. Amount of papers published by CI technique

addressed the following tasks: refactoring, test data generation, test management and automatic generation of maximally diversified versions.

As seen in Fig. 8, since 2012 swarm intelligence has not been applied in SSBSE papers. The application of evolutionary algorithms have also decreased over time. On the other hand, other CI techniques and machine learning algorithms have been increasingly used.

5   RQ4 – Experimental Rigour

In this section, we discuss some aspects of the evaluations carried out in the SSBSE papers. We observed that 121 papers (96.6%) present evaluation results and among them 57.8% perform a statistical analysis. Almost all papers evaluate their proposed solution with a wide range of subjects and the attention on using statistical tests. Mainly in the last years, we can attest that the experimental rigour has been taken into account by SSBSE authors. Further details about subjects and statistical tests, are presented next.

Subjects. A wide range of different subjects are used. Some of them are small computer programs typically used for educational purposes or proof of concept. Arcade Game Maker, Microwave Oven Software, and Service and Support System are examples of academic subjects. Other used subjects are real-world software, allowing an evaluation of how SBSE solutions work in practice. Such systems are in platforms like desktop (Microsoft Word and ReleasePlanner), Web (Tudu, Oryx and Softslate Commerce), mobile (Sony Mobile and Android programs), embedded software (Adaptive headlight control, door lock control and electric windows control modules), and MATLAB Simulink models. Open source projects are widely used in SSBSE papers. These projects are taken mainly from repositories such as SourceForge, GitHub, SPLOT, and Google Play. Examples of open source projects are Eclipse, Mozilla, Apache Commons project, Apache Ant, ArgoUML, Azureus, Xerces-J, JHotDraw, AJHSQLDB, Health Watcher, Toll System, JFreeChart, Rhino, and GanttProject.

Publicly available datasets and benchmarks also appeared in the evaluations. Example of a benchmark set is the one with faulty programs originally developed by Siemens: print_tokens, replace, schedule, schedule2, tcas, tot_info, and SF110 dataset. We also observed the use of synthetic data, non-real artifacts, sometimes randomly generated, used to represent difficult problems or large artifacts, allowing to expose the power of SBSE solutions.

Statistical Tests and Effect Size Measures. Considering that SBSE approaches rely on CI techniques, which employ randomness in their search process, commonly proposed approaches are executed many times to identify a standard behaviour. The collected data results are evaluated with statistical tests to assess whether there are significant difference among results or not. Table 5 presents the Statistical tests and Effect size measures that were applied in at least 2 SSBSE papers. The last column of the table shows the number of papers using the tests. Among the 17 found tests/measures, Mann-Whitney-Wilcoxon U-test, Wilcoxon Ranked Sum Test, and Vargha-Delaney A12 effect size were by far the most commonly used. In Table 6 we can see the percentage of papers along the years which used those tests/measures. Tests and measures have been used since 2009, however, we can observe that after 2014 they have been used more frequently. In 2017 all papers used these tests/measures.

Table 5. Statistical tests and Effect size measures used

Test/Measure	#Papers
Mann-Whitney-Wilcoxon U-test	26
Wilcoxon Ranked Sum Test	25
Vargha-Delaney A12 effect size	22
Student's T-test	5
Cliff's Delta	3
Kolmogorov-Smirnov test	3
Spearman's RC coefficient	3
Friedman test	2
Kruskal-Wallis	2
Two-Tailed Test	2

Table 6. Percentage of papers that apply statistical tests or Effect size per year

Year	Percentage
2009	11.1
2010	64.3
2011	46.7
2012	26.7
2013	28.6
2014	85.7
2015	83.3
2016	69.2
2017	100
2018	75

6   Recommendations to Future SSBSE Authors

During the screening of the 125 papers, we have realized that some pieces of information are not presented in several papers, what makes the SBSE approaches not completely clear to readers. Following, we present some recommendations to future SSBSE authors aiming at helping them to develop high quality studies, to improve text readability and to enable study replication.

- Make it clear the ingredients of SBSE approaches that enable the application of CI techniques to solve the corresponding SE problem: problem representation and fitness function(s). Some (meta)heuristics also need operators to modify candidate solutions, which should also mentioned in the text;
- Illustrative examples so that readers can easily understand the problem and the proposed solution.
- Make it clear which are the CI techniques and algorithms used, not just mention the tool or framework name;
- For the evaluation, authors should prefer using real-word systems from different domains and sizes. This would make the findings more general;
- To avoid threats regarding randomness of CI techniques, run your approaches many times (at least 30 runs) and assess the results with statistical tests and effect size measures;
- Make the experimental package available providing, as much as possible, ways to other authors replicate your study and/or to ease comparison.

7   Conclusion

In this paper we presented an overview of the ten-year history of SSBSE as well as results from a systematic mapping involving all full papers of the ten proceedings. Our findings allow us to state that SSBSE papers have made some external impact on the SE research community. We found that most of the citations are from different venues and identified a close gap between no self-citations and external citations. This indicates SSBSE papers have got some substantial external visibility.

The women SSBSE leadership participation is rather good, but authorship is low. Gender bias is a major concern in software engineering discipline. Gender diversity is important because it can help sharing different skills, points of view and experiences, bringing and incorporating gender aspects of the customers and users in software engineering, expanding potential talents, among other aspects. Hence, increasing the participation of women in the symposium is of great value.

Regarding the area of SE problems solved with CI techniques, software testing is still the main addressed task, but other problems have emerged, mostly related to non-functional requirements, program repair, MDE and experimentation. Evolutionary algorithms remained the most used CI technique.

We could observe along the ten years a wide range of subjects used by authors to evaluate their approaches. These subjects can also be used in new research.

Besides, in recent years authors are paying more attention to the use of statistical tests to better evaluate their results. But it is important to increase industry participation and the creation of repositories containing benchmarks regarding the different SBSE sub-areas.

To call attention and guide new authors willing to publish their papers and to participate in SSBSE, we presented a set of recommendations to improve their publications on understandability, replicability, and experimentation soundness. However, the recommendations are limited to what we observed during the papers screening. Also, our findings are limited to SSBSE editions and they were not compared to other venues, which might be done in future studies.

SSBSE has been a representative venue to divulge studies and put together academics, researchers and practitioners to discuss SBSE. Currently, the SBSE field is explicitly listed as a topic of interest of important conferences and journals. Given what we reported and discussed in this paper, we can state that SSBSE has helped increase the popularity of SBSE in the SE research community and plays an important role to strengthen SBSE over the past ten years.

References

1. Agarwal, S., Mittal, N., Katyal, R., Sureka, A., Correa, D.: Women in computer science research: what is the bibliography data telling us? SIGCAS Comput. Soc. **46**(1), 7–19 (2016)
2. Arcuri, A., Fraser, G.: On parameter tuning in search based software engineering. In: Cohen, M.B., Ó Cinnéide, M. (eds.) SSBSE 2011. LNCS, vol. 6956, pp. 33–47. Springer, Heidelberg (2011). https://doi.org/10.1007/978-3-642-23716-4_6
3. de Freitas, F.G., de Souza, J.T.: Ten years of search based software engineering: a bibliometric analysis. In: Cohen, M.B., Ó Cinnéide, M. (eds.) SSBSE 2011. LNCS, vol. 6956, pp. 18–32. Springer, Heidelberg (2011). https://doi.org/10.1007/978-3-642-23716-4_5
4. Ghezzi, C.: Reflections on 40+ years of software engineering research and beyond an insider's view (2009). https://www.cs.uoregon.edu/events/icse2009/keynoteSpeakers/ICSEkeynote.pdf
5. Harman, M., Jia, Y., Zhang, Y.: Achievements, open problems and challenges for search based software testing. In: International Conference on Software Testing, Verification and Validation (2015)
6. Harman, M., Mansouri, S.A., Zhang, Y.: Search based software engineering: a comprehensive analysis and review of trends techniques and applications. Technical report, Department of Computer Science, King's College London (2009)
7. Harman, M., Mansouri, S.A., Zhang, Y.: Search-based software engineering: trends, techniques and applications. ACM Comput. Surv. **45**(1), 1–61 (2012)
8. Hirsch, J.E.: An index to quantify an individual's scientific research output. Natl. Acad. Sci. **102**(46), 16569–16572 (2005)
9. Petersen, K., Vakkalanka, S., Kuzniarz, L.: Guidelines for conducting systematic mapping studies in software engineering: an update. Inf. Softw. Technol. **64**, 1–18 (2015)
10. Souza, J.T., Maia, C.L., de Freitas, F.G., Coutinho, D.P.: The human competitiveness of search based software engineering. In: SSBSE, pp. 143–152 (2010)

Does Diversity Improve the Test Suite Generation for Mobile Applications?

Thomas Vogel$^{(\boxtimes)}$, Chinh Tran, and Lars Grunske

Software Engineering Group, Humboldt-Universität zu Berlin, Berlin, Germany
{thomas.vogel,grunske}@informatik.hu-berlin.de, mail@chinhtran.de

Abstract. In search-based software engineering we often use popular heuristics with default configurations, which typically lead to suboptimal results, or we perform experiments to identify configurations on a trial-and-error basis, which may lead to better results for a specific problem. To obtain better results while avoiding trial-and-error experiments, a fitness landscape analysis is helpful in understanding the search problem, and making an informed decision about the heuristics. In this paper, we investigate the search problem of test suite generation for mobile applications (apps) using SAPIENZ whose heuristic is a default NSGA-II. We analyze the fitness landscape of SAPIENZ with respect to genotypic diversity and use the gained insights to adapt the heuristic of SAPIENZ. These adaptations result in SAPIENZ^{div} that aims for preserving the diversity of test suites during the search. To evaluate SAPIENZ^{div}, we perform a head-to-head comparison with SAPIENZ on 76 open-source apps.

Keywords: Fitness landscape analysis · Diversity · Test generation

1 Introduction

In search-based software engineering and particularly search-based testing, popular heuristics (*e.g.*,[17]) with best-practice configurations in terms of operators and parameters (*e.g.*,[7]) are often used. As this out-of-the-box usage typically leads to suboptimal results, costly trial-and-error experiments are performed to find a suitable configuration for a given problem, which leads to better results [4]. To obtain better results while avoiding trial-and-error experiments, fitness landscape analysis can be used [16,23]. The goal is to analytically understand the search problem, determine difficulties of the problem, and identify suitable configurations of heuristics that can cope with these difficulties (*cf.* [16,19]).

In this paper, we investigate the search problem of test suite generation for mobile applications (apps). We rely on SAPIENZ that uses a default NSGA-II to generate test suite for apps [17]. NSGA-II has been selected as it "is a widely-used multiobjective evolutionary search algorithm, popular in SBSE research" [17, p. 97], but without adapting it to the specific problem (instance). Thus, our goal is to analyze the fitness landscape of SAPIENZ and use the insights for adapting the heuristic of SAPIENZ. This should eventually yield better test results.

© Springer Nature Switzerland AG 2019
S. Nejati and G. Gay (Eds.): SSBSE 2019, LNCS 11664, pp. 58–74, 2019.
https://doi.org/10.1007/978-3-030-27455-9_5

Our analysis focuses on the global topology of the landscape, especially how solutions (test suites) are spread in the search space and evolve over time. Thus, we are interested in the genotypic diversity of solutions, which is considered important for evolutionary search [30]. According to our analysis, SAPIENZ lacks diversity of solutions so that we extend it to SAPIENZ^{div} that integrates four diversity promoting mechanisms. Therefore, our contributions are the descriptive study analyzing the fitness landscape of SAPIENZ (Sect. 3), SAPIENZ^{div} (Sect. 4), and the empirical study with 76 apps evaluating SAPIENZ^{div} (Sect. 5).

2   Background: SAPIENZ and Fitness Landscape Analysis

SAPIENZ is a multi-objective search-based testing approach [17]. Using NSGA-II, it automatically generates test suites for end-to-end testing of Android apps. A test suite t consists of m test cases $\langle s_1, s_2, ..., s_m \rangle$, each of which is a sequence of up to n GUI-level events $\langle e_1, e_2, ..., e_n \rangle$ that exercise the app under test. The generation is guided by three objectives: (i) maximize fault revelation, (ii) maximize coverage, and (iii) minimize test sequence length. Having no oracle, SAPIENZ considers a crash of the app caused by a test as a fault. Coverage is measured at the code (statement coverage) or activity level (skin coverage). Given these objectives, the fitness function is the triple of the number of crashes found, coverage, and sequence length. To evaluate the fitness of a test suite, SAPIENZ executes the suite on the app under test deployed on an Android device or emulator.

A *fitness landscape analysis* can be used to better understand a search problem [16]. A fitness landscape is defined by three elements (*cf.* [28]): (1) A search space as a set X of potential solutions. (2) A fitness function $f_k : X \to \mathbb{R}$ for each of the k objectives. (3) A neighborhood relation $N : X \to 2^X$ that associates neighbor solutions to each solution (*e.g.*, using basic operators, or distances of solutions). Based on these three elements, various metrics have been proposed to analyze the landscape [16, 23]. They characterize the landscape, for instance, in terms of the global topology (*i.e.*, how solutions and the fitness are distributed), local structure (*i.e.*, ruggedness and smoothness), and evolvability (*i.e.*, the ability to produce fitter solutions). The goal of analyzing the landscape is to determine difficulties of a search problem and identify suitable configurations of search algorithms that can cope with these difficulties (*cf.* [16, 19]).

3   Fitness Landscape Analysis of SAPIENZ

3.1   Fitness Landscape of SAPIENZ

At first, we define the three elements of a fitness landscape (*cf.* Sect. 2) for SAPIENZ: (1) The search space is given by all possible test suites t according to the representation of test suites in Sect. 2. (2) The fitness function is given by the triple of the number of crashes found, coverage, and test sequence length (*cf.* Sect. 2). (3) As the neighborhood relation we define a genotypic distance metric for two test suites (see Algorithm 1). The distance of two test suites t_1 and t_2 is the sum of the distances between their ordered test sequences, which is obtained by comparing all sequences s_i^{t1} of t_1 and s_i^{t2} t_2 by index i (lines 2–4). The distance of two sequences is the difference of their lengths (line 5) increased by 1 for each different event at index j (lines 6–9). Thus, the distance is based on the differences of ordered events between the ordered sequences of two test suites.

This metric is moti-vated by the basic mutation operator of SAPIENZ shuffling the order of test sequences within a suite, and the order of events within a sequence. It is com-mon that the neighbor-hood relation is based on operators that make small changes to solutions [19].

Algorithm 1. $dist(t_1, t_2)$: compute distance between two test suites t_1 and t_2.

Input: Test suites t_1 and t_2, max. suite size $suite_{max}$, max. sequence length seq_{max}
Output: Distance between t_1 and t_2
1: distance ← 0;
2: for i ← 0 to $suite_{max}$ do   ▷ iterate over all $suite_{max}$ test sequences
3:      s_i^{t1} ← $t_1[i]$;   ▷ i^{th} test sequence of test suite t_1
4:      s_i^{t2} ← $t_2[i]$;   ▷ i^{th} test sequence of test suite t_2
5:      distance ← distance + abs($|s_i^{t1}|$ − $|s_i^{t2}|$); ▷ length difference as distance
6:      for j ← 0 to seq_{max} do   ▷ iterate over all seq_{max} events
7:          if $|s_i^{t1}|$ ≤ j or $|s1_i^{t2}|$ ≤ j then break;
8:          if $s_i^{t1}[j]$ ≠ $s_i^{t2}[j]$ then   ▷ event comparison by index j
9:              distance ← distance + 1;   ▷ events differ at index j in both seqs.
10: return distance;

3.2 Experimental Setup

To analyze the fitness landscape of SAPIENZ, we extended SAPIENZ with metrics that characterize the landscape. We then executed SAPIENZ on five apps, repeat each execution five times, and report mean values of the metrics for each app.[1]

The five apps we selected for the descriptive study are part of the 68 F-Droid benchmark apps [6] used to evaluate SAPIENZ [17]. We selected *aarddict*, *Munch-Life*, and *passwordmanager* since SAPIENZ did not find any fault for these apps, and *hotdeath* and *k9mail*[2], for which SAPIENZ did find faults [17]. Thus, we con-sider apps for which SAPIENZ did and did not reveal crashes to obtain potentially different landscape characteristics that may present difficulties to SAPIENZ.

We configured SAPIENZ as in [17]. The crossover and mutation rates are set to 0.7 and 0.3 respectively. The population and offspring size is 50. An individual (test suite) contains 5 test sequences, each constrained to 20–500 events. Instead of 100 generations [17], we observed in initial experiments that the search stag-nates earlier so that we set the number of generation to 40 (stopping criterion).

3.3 Results

The results of our study provide an analysis of the fitness landscape of SAPIENZ with respect to the global topology, particularly the diversity of solutions, how the solutions are spread in the search space, and evolve over time. According to Smith *et al.* [27, p. 31], "No single measure or description can possibly charac-terize any high-dimensional heterogeneous search space". Thus, we selected 11 metrics from literature and implemented them in SAPIENZ, which characterize (1) the Pareto-optimal solutions, (2) the population, and (3) the connectedness

---

[1] All experiments were run on single 4.0 Ghz quad-core PC with 16 GB RAM, using 5 Android emulators (KitKat 4.4.2, API level 19) in parallel to test one app.
[2] We used ver. 5.207 of k9mail and not ver. 3.512 as in the 68 F-Droid apps benchmark.

of Pareto-optimal solutions, all with a focus on diversity. These metrics are computed after every generation so that we can analyze their development over time. In the following, we discuss these 11 metrics and the results of the fitness landscape analysis. The results are shown in Fig. 1 where the metrics (y-axis) are plotted over the 40 generations of the search (x-axis) for each of the five apps.

(1) Metrics for Pareto-Optimal Solutions

• *Proportion of Pareto-optimal solutions (ppos).* For a population P, *ppos* is the number of Pareto-optimal solutions P_{opt} divided by the population size: $ppos(P) = \frac{|P_{opt}|}{|P|}$. A high and especially strongly increasing *ppos* may indicate that the search based on Pareto dominance stagnates due to missing selection pressure [24]. A moderately increasing *ppos* may indicate a successful search.

For SAPIENZ and all apps (see Fig. 1(a)), *ppos* slightly fluctuates since a new solution can potentially dominate multiple previously non-dominated solutions. At the beginning of the search, *ppos* is low (0.0–0.1), shows no improvement in the first 15–20 generations, and then increases for all apps except of *password-manager*. Thus, the search seems to progress while the enormously increasing *ppos* for MunchLife and hotdeath might indicate a stagnation of the search.

• *Hypervolume (hv).* To further investigate the search progress, we compute the *hv* after each generation. The *hv* is the volume in the objective space covered by the Pareto-optimal solutions [10,31]. Thus, an increasing *hv* indicates that the search is able to find improved solutions, otherwise the *hv* and search stagnate.

Based on the objectives of SAPIENZ (max. crashes, max. coverage, and min. sequence length), we choose the nadir point (0 crashes, 0 coverage, and sequence length of 500) as the reference point for the *hv*. In Fig. 1(b), the evolution of the *hv* over time rather than the absolute numbers are relevant to analyze the search progress of SAPIENZ. While the *hv* increases during the first 25 generations, it stagnates afterwards for all apps; for k9mail already after 5 generations. For aarddict, MunchLife, and hotdeath the *hv* stagnates after the *ppos* drastically increases (*cf.* Fig. 1(a)), further indicating a stagnation of the search.

(2) Population-Based Metrics

• *Population diameter (diam).* The *diam* metrics measure the spread of all population members in the search space using a distance metric for individuals, in our case Algorithm 1. The maximum *diam* computes the largest distance between any two individuals of the population P: $maxdiam(P) = \max_{x_i,x_j \in P} dist(x_i, x_j)$ [5,20], showing the absolute spread of P. To respect outliers, we can compute the average *diam* as the average of all pairwise distances between all individuals [5]:

$$avgdiam(P) = \frac{\sum_{i=0}^{|P|} \sum_{j=0,j\neq i}^{|P|} dist(x_i, x_j)}{|P|(|P| - 1)} \tag{1}$$

Additionally, we compute the minimum diameter to see how close individuals are in the search space, or even identical: $mindiam(P) = \min_{x_i,x_j \in P} dist(x_i, x_j)$.

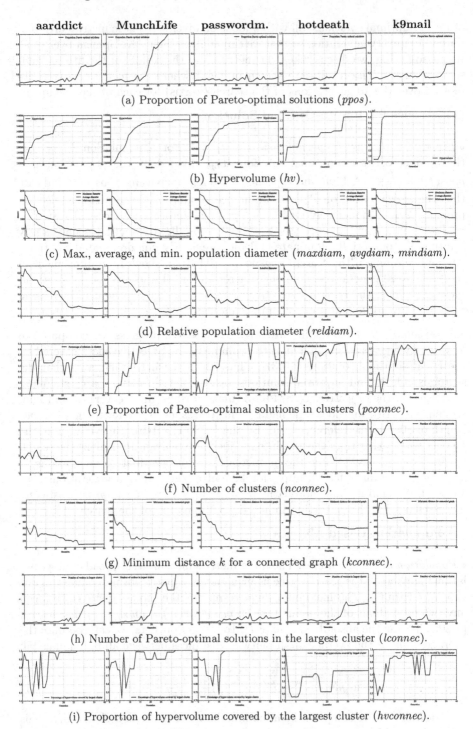

| aarddict | MunchLife | passwordm. | hotdeath | k9mail |

(a) Proportion of Pareto-optimal solutions (*ppos*).

(b) Hypervolume (*hv*).

(c) Max., average, and min. population diameter (*maxdiam, avgdiam, mindiam*).

(d) Relative population diameter (*reldiam*).

(e) Proportion of Pareto-optimal solutions in clusters (*pconnec*).

(f) Number of clusters (*nconnec*).

(g) Minimum distance *k* for a connected graph (*kconnec*).

(h) Number of Pareto-optimal solutions in the largest cluster (*lconnec*).

(i) Proportion of hypervolume covered by the largest cluster (*hvconnec*).

Fig. 1. Fitness landscape analysis results for SAPIENZ.

Concerning each plot for SAPIENZ and all apps (see Fig. 1(c)), the upper, middle, and lower curve are respectively *maxdiam*, *avgdiam*, and *mindiam*. For each curve, we see a clear trend that the metrics decrease over time, which is typical for genetic algorithms due to the crossover. However, the metrics drastically decrease for SAPIENZ in the first 25 generations. The *avgdiam* decreases from >1500 to eventually <200 for each app. The *maxdiam* decreases similarly but stays higher for hotdeath and k9mail than for the other apps. The development of the *avgdiam* and *maxdiam* indicates that all individuals are continuously getting closer to each other in the search space, thus becoming more similar. The population even contains identical solutions as indicated by *mindiam* reaching 0.

• *Relative population diameter (reldiam).* Bachelet [5] further proposes the relative population diameter, which is the *avgdiam* in proportion to the largest possible distance d: $reldiam(P) = \frac{avgdiam(P)}{d}$. This metric is indicative of the concentration of the population in the search space. A small *reldiam* indicates that the population members are grouped together in a region of the space [5].

For SAPIENZ, the largest possible distance d between two test suites is 2500, in which case they differ in all events (up to 500 for a test sequence) for all of their five individual test sequences. For $d = 2500$ and all apps (*cf.* Fig. 1(d)), *reldiam* starts at a high level of around 0.9 indicating that the solutions are spread in the search space. Then, it decreases in the first 25 generations to around 0.4 (aarddict, MunchLife, and passwordmanager), and below 0.3 (hotdeath and k9mail) indicating a grouping of the solutions in one or more regions of the search space.

(3) Metrics Based on the Connectedness of Pareto-Optimal Solutions

The following metrics analyze the *connectedness* and thus, clusters of Pareto-optimal solutions in the search space [9,22]. For this purpose, we consider a graph in which Pareto-optimal solutions are vertices. The edges connecting the vertices are labeled with weights δ, which are the number of moves a neighborhood operator has to make to reach one vertex from another [22]. This results in a graph of fully connected Pareto-optimal solutions. Introducing a limit k on δ and removing the edges whose weights δ are larger than k leads to varying sizes of connected components (clusters) in the graph. This graph can be analyzed by metrics to characterize the Pareto-optimal solutions in the search space [12,22].

In our case, the weights δ are determined by the distance metric for test suites based on the mutation operator of SAPIENZ (*cf.* Algorithm 1). We determined k experimentally to be 300 investigating values of 400, 300, 200, and 100. While a high value results in a single cluster of Pareto-optimal solutions, a low value results in a high number of singletons (*i.e.*, clusters with one solution). Thus, two test suites (vertices) are connected (neighbors) in the graph if they differ in less than 300 events across their test sequences as computed by Algorithm 1.

• *Proportion of Pareto-optimal solutions in clusters (pconnec).* This metric divides the number of vertices (Pareto-optimal solutions) that are members of clusters (excl. singletons) by the total number of vertices in the graph [22]. A high *pconnec* indicates a grouping of the Pareto-optimal solutions in the search space.

As shown in Fig. 1(e), *pconnec* is relatively low during the first generations before it increases for all apps. For MunchLife, passwordmanager, and hotdeath, *pconnec* reaches 1 meaning that all Pareto-optimal solutions are in clusters, while it converges around 0.7 and 0.8 for aarddict and k9mail respectively. This indicates that the Pareto-optimal solutions are grouped in the search space.

● *Number of clusters (nconnec).* We further analyze in how many areas of the search space (clusters) the Pareto-optimal solutions are grouped. Thus, *ncon-nec* counts the number of clusters in the graph [12,22]. A high (low) *nconnec* indicates that the Pareto-optimal solutions are spread in many (few) areas of the search space.

Figure 1(f) plots *nconnec* for SAPIENZ and all apps. The y-axis of each plot denoting *nconnec* ranges from 0 to 6. Initially, the Pareto-optimal solutions are distributed in 2–4 clusters, then grouped in 1 cluster. An exception is k9mail for which there always exists more than 3 clusters. Except for k9mail, this indicates that the Pareto-optimal solutions are grouped in one area of the search space.

● *Minimum distance k for a connected graph (kconnec).* This metric identifies k so that all Pareto-optimal solutions are members of one cluster [12,22]. Thus, *kconnec* quantifies the spread of all Pareto-optimal solutions in the search space.

For SAPIENZ, Fig. 1(g) plots *kconnec* (ranging from 0 to 1400) over the generations. Similarly to the *diam* metrics (*cf.* Fig. 1(c)), *kconnec* decreases, moderately for hotdeath (from initially ≈ 700 to ≈ 600) and k9mail ($\approx 1000 \rightarrow \approx 800$), and drastically for passwordmanager ($\approx 1200 \rightarrow \approx 200$), MunchLife ($\approx 1000 \rightarrow \approx 200$), and aarddict ($\approx 600 \rightarrow \approx 100$). This indicates that *all* Pareto-optimal solutions are getting closer in the search space as the spread of the cluster is decreasing.

● *Number of Pareto-optimal solutions in the largest cluster (lconnec).* It determines the size of the largest cluster by the number of members [12], showing how many Pareto-optimal solutions are in the most dense area of the search space.

Figure 1(h) plots *lconnec* (ranging from 0 to 50 given the population size of 50) over the generations. *lconnec* increases after 15–30 generations to 20 (aarddict and hotdeath) or even 50 (MunchLife) solutions. This indicates that the largest cluster is indeed large so that many Pareto-optimal solutions are grouped in one area of the search space. In contrast, *lconnec* stays always below 10 indicating smaller largest clusters for passwordmanager and k9mail than for the other apps.

● *Proportion of hypervolume covered by the largest cluster (hvconnec).* Besides *lconnec*, we compute the relative size of the largest cluster in terms of hypervolume (hv). Thus, *hvconnec* is the proportion of the overall hv covered by the Pareto-optimal solutions in the largest cluster. It quantifies how this cluster in the search space dominates in the objective space and contributes to the hv.

For SAPIENZ (*cf.* Fig. 1(i)), *hvconnec* varies a lot during the first 10 generations, then stabilizes at a high level for all apps. For aarddict, MunchLife, and passwordmanager, the largest clusters covers 100% of the hv since there is only 1 cluster left (*cf.* *nconnec* in Fig. 1(f)). For hotdeath, *hvconnec* is close to 70% indicating that there is 1 other cluster covering 30% of the hv (*cf.* *nconnec*). For k9mail, *hvconnec* is around 90% indicating that the other 2–3 clusters (*cf. nconnec*) cover only 10% of the *hv*. This indicates that the largest cluster covers the largest proportion of the *hv*, and thus contributes most to the Pareto front.

3.4   Discussion

The results characterizing the fitness landscape of SAPIENZ reveal insights about how SAPIENZ manages the search problem of generating test suites for apps.

Firstly, the development of the proportion of Pareto-optimal solutions (*cf.* Fig. 1(a)) and hypervolume (*cf.* Fig. 1(b)) indicates a stagnation of the search after 25 generations. The drastically increasing proportion of Pareto-optimal solutions in some cases may indicate a problem of *dominance resistance*, *i.e.*, the search cannot produce new solutions that dominate the current, poorly performing but locally non-dominated solutions [24]. In other cases, the proportion remains low, *i.e.*, the search cannot find many non-dominated solutions.

Secondly, the development of the population diameters (*cf.* Fig. 1(c)) indicate a decreasing diversity of *all* solutions during the search. The development of the relative population diameter (*cf.* Fig. 1(d)) witnesses this observation and indicates that the population members are concentrated in the search space [5]. The minimum diameter (*cf.* Fig. 1(c)) even indicates that the population contains duplicates of solutions, which reduces the genetic variation in the population.

Thirdly, the development of the proportion of Pareto-optimal solutions in clusters (*cf.* Fig. 1(e)) indicates a grouping of these solutions in the search space, mostly in one cluster (*cf.* Fig. 1(f)). Another indicator for the decreasing diversity of the Pareto-optimal solutions is the decreasing minimum distance k required to form one cluster of all these solutions (*cf.* Fig. 1(g)). Additionally, the largest cluster is often indeed large in terms of number of Pareto-optimal solutions (*cf.* Fig. 1(h)), and hypervolume covered by these solutions (*cf.* Fig. 1(i)). Even if there exist multiple clusters of Pareto-optimal solutions, the largest cluster still contributes most to the overall hypervolume and thus, to the Pareto front.

In summary, the fitness landscape analysis of SAPIENZ indicates a stagnation of the search while the diversity of all solutions decreases in the search space.

4   SAPIENZ^{div}

Given the fitness landscape analysis results, SAPIENZ suffers from a decreasing diversity of solutions in the search space over time. It is known that the performance of genetic algorithms is influenced by diversity [21,30]. A low diversity may lead the search to a local optimum that cannot be escaped easily [30]. Thus, diversity is important to address dominance resistance so that the search can produce new solutions that dominate poorly performing, locally non-dominated solutions [24]. Moreover, Shir *et al.* [26, p. 95] report that promoting diversity in the search space does not hamper "the convergence to a precise and diverse Pareto front approximation in the objective space of the original algorithm".

Therefore, we extended SAPIENZ to SAPIENZ^{div} by integrating mechanisms into the search algorithm that promote the diversity of the population in the search space.[3] We developed four mechanisms that extend the SAPIENZ algorithm at different steps: at the initialization, before and after the variation, and at the selection. Algorithm 2 shows the extended search algorithm of SAPIENZ^{div} and highlights the novel mechanisms in blue. We now discuss these mechanisms.

Diverse initial population. As the initial population may effect the results of the search [13], we assume that a diverse initial population could be a better start for the exploration. Thus, we extend the generation of the initial population P_{init} to promote diversity. Instead of generating $|P| = size_{pop}$ solutions, we generate $size_{init}$ solutions where $size_{init} > size_{pop}$ (line 7 in Algorithm 2). Then, we select those $size_{pop}$ solutions from P_{init} that are most distant from each other using Algorithm 1, to form the first population P (line 8).

Adaptive diversity control. This mechanism dynamically controls the diversity if the population members are becoming too close in the search space relative to the initial population. It further makes the algorithm adaptive as it uses feedback of the search to adapt the search (*cf.* [30]).

To quantify the diversity div_{pop} of population P, we use the average population diameter (*avgdiam*) defined in Eq. 1. At the beginning of each generation, div_{pop} is calculated (line 13) and compared to the diversity of the initial population div_{init} (line 14) calculated once in line 10. The comparison checks whether div_{pop} has decreased to less than $div_{limit} \times div_{init}$. For example, the condition is satisfied for the given threshold $div_{limit} = 0.4$ if div_{pop} has decreased to less than 40% of div_{init}.

Algorithm 2. Overall algorithm of SAPIENZ^{div}

Input: AUT A, crossover probability p, mutation probability q, max. generation g_{max}, population size $size_{pop}$, offspring size $size_{off}$, size of the large initial population $size_{init}$, diversity threshold div_{limit}, number of diverse solutions to include n_{div}

Output: UI model M, Pareto front PF, test reports C

```
 1: M ← K_0; PF ← ∅; C ← ∅;                              ▷ initialization
 2: generation g ← 0;
 3: boot up devices D;              ▷ prepare devices/emulators that will run the app
 4: inject MOTIFCORE into D;     ▷ install SAPIENZ component for hybrid exploration
 5: static analysis on A;       ▷ for seeding strings to be used for text fields of A
 6: instrument and install A; ▷ app under test is instrumented and installed on D
 7: initialize population P_init of size size_init;        ▷ large initial population
 8: P = selectMostDistant(P_init, size_pop);   ▷ select size_pop most distant individuals
 9: evaluate P with MOTIFCORE and update (M, PF, C);
10: div_init = calculateDiversity(P);     ▷ diversity of the initial population (Eq. 1)
11: while g < g_max do
12:    g ← g + 1;
13:    div_pop = calculateDiversity(P); ▷ diversity of the current population (Eq. 1)
14:    if div_pop ≤ div_limit × div_init then       ▷ check decrease of diversity
15:       Q ← generate offspring of size size_off;  ▷ ≈ generate a population
16:       evaluate Q with MOTIFCORE and update (M, PF, C);
17:       P = selectMostDistant(P ∪ Q, |P|);        ▷ selection based on distance
18:    else
19:       Q ← wholeTestSuiteVariation(P, p, q);      ▷ create offspring
20:       evaluate Q with MOTIFCORE and update (M, PF, C);
21:       PQ ← removeDuplicates(P ∪ Q);            ▷ duplicate elimination
22:       F ← sortNonDominated(PQ, |P|);
23:       P' ← ∅;                              ▷ non-dominated individuals
24:       for each front F in F do
25:          if |P'| ≥ |P| then break;
26:          assignCrowdingDistance(F);
27:          for each individual f in F do
28:             P' ← P' ∪ f;
29:       P' ← sorted(P', ≺_c);
30:       P ← P'[0 : (size_pop − n_div)]; ▷ take best (size_pop − n_div) solution from P'
31:       P_div = selectMostDistant(PQ, n_div); ▷ select n_div most distant solutions
32:       P = P ∪ P_div;                         ▷ next population
33: return (M, PF, C);
```

---

[3] SAPIENZ^{div} is available at: https://github.com/thomas-vogel/sapienzdiv-ssbse19.

In this case, the offspring Q is obtained by generating new solutions using the original SAPIENZ method to initialize a population (line 15). The next population is formed by selecting the $|P|$ most distant individuals from the current population P and offspring Q (line 17). In the other case, the variation operators (crossover and mutation) of SAPIENZ are applied to obtain the offspring (line 19) followed by the selection. Thus, this mechanism promotes diversity by inserting new individuals to the population, having an effect of restarting the search.

Duplicate elimination. The fitness landscape analysis found duplicated test suites in the population. Eliminating duplicates is one technique to maintain diversity and improve search performance [25,30]. Thus, we remove duplicates after reproduction and before selection in the current population and offspring (line 21). Duplicated test suites are identified by a distance of 0 computed by Algorithm 1.

Hybrid selection. To promote diversity in the search space, the selection is extended by dividing it in two parts: (1) The non-dominated sorting of NSGA-II is performed as in SAPIENZ (lines 22–29 in Algorithm 2) to obtain the solutions P' sorted by domination rank and crowding distance. (2) From P', the best $(size_{pop} - n_{div})$ solutions form the next population P where $size_{pop}$ is the size of P and n_{div} the configurable number of diverse solutions to be included in P (line 30). These n_{div} diverse solutions P_{div} are selected as the most distant solutions from the current population and offspring PQ (line 31) using the distance metric of Algorithm 1. Finally, P_{div} is added to the next population P (line 32).

While the NSGA-II sorting considers the diversity of solutions in the objective space (crowding distance), the selection of SAPIENZ^{div} also considers the diversity of solutions in the search space, which makes the selection hybrid.

5   Evaluation

We evaluate SAPIENZ^{div} in a head-to-head comparison with SAPIENZ to investigate the benefits of the diversity-promoting mechanisms. Our evaluation targets five research questions (RQ) with two empirical studies similarly to [17]:

RQ1. How does the coverage achieved by SAPIENZ^{div} compare to SAPIENZ?
RQ2. How do the faults found by SAPIENZ^{div} compare to SAPIENZ?
RQ3. How does SAPIENZ^{div} compare to SAPIENZ concerning the length of their fault-revealing test sequences?
RQ4. How does the runtime overhead of SAPIENZ^{div} compare to SAPIENZ?
RQ5. How does the performance of SAPIENZ^{div} compare to the performance of SAPIENZ with inferential statistical testing?

5.1   Experimental Setup

We conduct two empirical studies, Study 1 to answer RQ1–4, and Study 2 to answer RQ5. The execution of both studies was distributed on eight servers[4] while each server runs one approach to test one app at a time using 10 Android emulators (Android KitKat version, API 19). We configured SAPIENZ and SAPIENZ^{div} as in the experiment for the fitness landscape analysis (*cf.* Sect. 3.2) and in [17]. The only difference is that we test each app for 10 generations in contrast to Mao *et al.* [17] who test each app for one hour, since we were not in full control of the servers running in the cloud. However, we still report the execution times of both approaches (RQ4). Moreover, we configured the novel parameters of SAPIENZ^{div} as follows: $size_{init} = 100$, $div_{limit} = 0.5$, and $n_{div} = 15$. For Study 1 we perform one run to test each app over 10 generations by each approach. For Study 2 we perform 20 repetitions of such runs for each app and approach.

5.2   Results

Study 1. In this study we use 66 of the 68 F-Droid benchmark apps[5] provided by Choudhary *et al.* [6] and used to evaluate SAPIENZ [17]. The results on each app are shown in Table 1 where **S** refers to SAPIENZ, **Sd** to SAPIENZ^{div}, **Coverage** to the final statement coverage achieved, **#Crashes** to the number of revealed unique crashes, **Length** to the average length of the minimal fault-revealing test sequences (or '–' if no fault has been found), and **Time (min)** to the execution time in minutes of each approach to test the app over 10 generations.

RQ1. SAPIENZ achieves a higher final coverage for 15 apps, SAPIENZ^{div} for 24 apps, and both achieve the same coverage for 27 apps. Figure 2 shows that a similar coverage is achieved by both approaches on the 66 apps, in average 45.05 by SAPIENZ and 45.67 by SAPIENZ^{div}, providing initial evidence that SAPIENZ^{div} and SAPIENZ perform similarly with respect to coverage.

RQ2. To report about the found faults, we count the total crashes, out of which we also identify the unique crashes (*i.e.*, their stack traces are different from the traces of the other crashes of the app). Moreover, we exclude faults caused by the Android system (*e.g.*, native crashes) and test harness (*e.g.*, code instrumentation).

As shown in Table 2, SAPIENZ^{div} revealed more total (6941 vs 5974) and unique (141 vs 119) crashes, and found faults in more apps (46 vs 43) than SAPIENZ. Moreover, it found 51 unique crashes undetected by SAPIENZ, SAPIENZ found 29 unique crashes undetected by SAPIENZ^{div}, and both found the same 90 unique crashes. The results for the 66 apps provide initial evidence that SAPIENZ^{div} can outperform SAPIENZ in revealing crashes.

---

[4] For each server: 2×Intel(R) Xeon(R) CPU E5-2620 @ 2.00 GHz, with 64 GB RAM.

[5] We exclude *aGrep* and *frozenbubble* as SAPIENZ/SAPIENZ^{div} cannot start these apps.

RQ3. Considering the minimal fault-revealing test sequences (*i.e.*, the shortest of all sequences causing the same crash), their mean length is 244 for SAPIENZ^{div} and 209 for SAPIENZ on the 66 apps (*cf.* Table 2). This provides initial evidence that SAPIENZ^{div} produces longer fault-revealing sequences than SAPIENZ.

RQ4. Considering the mean execution time of testing one app over 10 generation, SAPIENZ^{div} takes 118 and SAPIENZ 101 min for the 66 apps. Figure 3 shows that the diversity-promoting mechanisms of SAPIENZ^{div} cause a noticeable runtime overhead compared to SAPIENZ. This provides initial evidence about the cost of promoting diversity at which an improved fault detection can be obtained.

Study 2. In this study we use the same 10 F-Droid apps as in the statistical analysis in [17]. Assuming no Gaussian distribution of the results, we use the Kruskal-Wallis test to assess the statistical significance ($p<0.05$) and the Vargha-Delaney effect size $\hat{A}_{12}$ to characterize small, medium, and large differences between SAPIENZ^{div} and SAPIENZ ($\hat{A}_{12} > 0.56$, 0.64, and 0.71 respectively).

RQ5. The results are presented by boxplots in Fig. 4 for each of the 10 apps and concern: coverage, #crashes,

Table 1. Results on the 66 benchmark apps.

Subject	Coverage		#Crashes		Length		Time (min)	
	S	Sd	S	Sd	S	Sd	S	Sd
a2dp	33	32	4	3	315	250	95	117
aarddict	14	14	1	1	103	454	69	74
aLogCat	66	67	0	2	–	232	125	140
Amazed	69	69	2	1	193	69	67	78
AnyCut	64	64	2	0	244	–	80	105
baterrydog	65	65	1	1	26	155	82	91
swiftp	13	13	0	0	–	–	88	105
Book-Catalogue	19	24	2	4	273	223	86	98
bites	33	35	1	1	76	39	78	91
battery	79	79	9	10	251	230	109	122
addi	19	18	1	1	39	31	87	133
alarmclock	62	62	6	9	133	279	143	163
manpages	69	69	0	0	–	–	81	92
mileage	34	33	5	6	252	286	100	114
autoanswer	16	16	0	0	–	–	78	90
hndroid	15	16	1	1	27	53	97	111
multimssender	57	54	0	0	–	–	88	102
worldclock	90	91	2	1	266	169	109	132
Nectroid	54	54	1	1	261	243	112	136
acal	21	20	7	7	222	187	140	160
jamendo	32	38	8	5	248	266	91	105
aka	45	44	8	9	234	226	140	171
yahtzee	47	47	1	1	356	215	79	86
aagtl	17	17	5	4	170	123	84	111
CountdownTimer	61	62	0	0	–	–	108	143
sanity	13	13	2	3	236	192	154	149
dalvik-explorer	69	69	2	4	148	272	143	162
Mirrored	42	44	10	9	114	179	219	245
dialer2	41	41	2	0	223	–	123	129
DivideAndConquer	79	81	3	3	75	55	90	94
fileexplorer	50	50	0	0	–	–	142	153
gestures	52	52	0	0	–	–	62	69
hotdeath	61	67	2	2	312	360	80	95
adsdroid	38	34	2	4	210	211	107	161
myLock	31	30	0	0	–	–	87	101
lockpatterngenerator	76	76	0	0	–	–	80	94
mnv	29	32	5	6	222	315	118	131
k9mail	5	6	1	2	445	412	93	113
LolcatBuilder	29	28	0	0	–	–	88	101
MunchLife	67	67	0	0	–	–	72	80
MyExpenses	45	41	2	3	359	309	115	133
LNM	57	58	1	1	292	209	104	120
netcounter	59	61	0	1	–	256	95	106
bomber	72	71	0	0	–	–	63	72
fantastischmemo	25	28	3	6	325	275	86	96
blokish	49	62	2	2	197	204	75	86
zooborns	36	36	0	0	–	–	86	95
importcontacts	41	41	0	1	–	462	94	106
wikipedia	26	31	1	3	95	373	69	88
PasswordMaker	50	49	1	2	86	216	103	112
passwordmanager	15	13	1	1	185	354	121	136
Photostream	30	31	2	3	195	161	143	192
QuickSettings	44	41	0	1	–	307	96	130
RandomMusicPlayer	58	59	0	0	–	–	97	113
Ringdroid	40	23	2	4	126	208	280	188
soundboard	53	53	0	0	–	–	61	67
SpriteMethodTest	59	73	0	0	–	–	63	74
SpriteText	60	60	1	2	116	448	93	101
SyncMyPix	19	19	0	2	–	402	97	143
tippy	70	72	1	1	384	459	84	105
tomdroid	50	52	1	1	152	90	93	111
Translate	48	48	0	0	–	–	82	99
Triangle	79	79	1	0	235	–	93	89
weight-chart	47	49	3	4	171	283	88	109
whohasmystuff	60	66	0	1	–	466	118	139
Wordpress	5	5	1	1	244	223	104	224

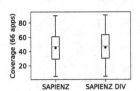

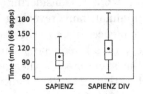

66 benchmark apps		
	SAPIENZ	SAPIENZ^{div}
# App Crashed	43	46
# Total Crashes	5974	6941
# Unique Crashes	119	141
# Disjoint Crashes	29	51
# Intersecting Crashes	90	90
Mean sequence length	209	244

Fig. 2. Coverage.   **Table 2.** Crashes and seq. length.   **Fig. 3.** Time (min).

sequence length, and time (*cf.* Study 1). The $\hat{A}_{12}$ effect size for these concerns are shown in Table 3, which compares SAPIENZ^{div} and SAPIENZ (Sd-S) and emphasizes statistically significant results in bold. SAPIENZ significantly outperforms SAPIENZ^{div} with large effect size on all apps for execution time. The remaining results are inconclusive. SAPIENZ^{div} significantly outperforms SAPIENZ with large effect size on only 3/10 apps for coverage, 2/10 for #crashes, and almost 1/10 for length. The remaining results are not statistically significant or do not indicate large differences.

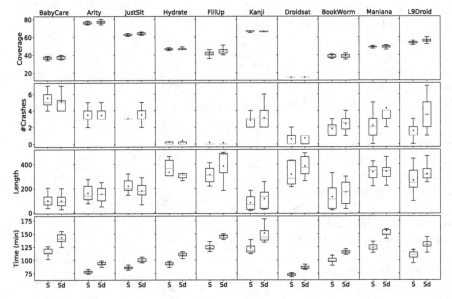

Fig. 4. Performance comparison on 10 apps for SAPIENZ^{div} (Sd) and SAPIENZ (S).

Table 3. Vargha-Delaney effect size (statistically significant results in bold).

App	Ver.	Coverage Sd-S	#Crashes Sd-S	Length Sd-S	Time Sd-S
BabyCare	1.5	0.66	0.46	0.52	**0.15**
Arity	1.27	0.67	0.49	0.54	**0.05**
JustSit	0.3.3	**0.75**	**0.66**	**0.70**	**0.00**
Hydrate	1.5	0.52	0.52	0.64	**0.00**
FillUp	1.7.2	**0.77**	0.47	0.33	**0.00**
Kanji	1.0	0.66	0.56	0.38	**0.09**
Droidsat	2.52	0.55	0.60	0.26	**0.00**
BookWorm	1.0.18	0.58	0.66	0.36	**0.05**
Maniana	1.26	0.66	**0.82**	0.49	**0.00**
L9Droid	0.6	**0.75**	**0.81**	0.32	**0.11**

5.3 Discussion

Study 1 provided initial evidence that SAPIENZ^{div} can find more faults than SAPIENZ while achieving a similar coverage but using longer sequences. Especially, the fault revelation capabilities of SAPIENZ^{div} seemed promising, however, we could not confirm them by the statistical analysis in Study 2. The results of Study 2 are inconclusive in differentiating both approaches by their performance. Potentially, the diversity promotion of SAPIENZ^{div} does not results in the desired effect in the first 10 generations we considered in the studies. In contrast, it might show a stronger effect at later stages since we observed in the fitness landscape analysis that the search of SAPIENZ stagnates after 25 generations.

6 Threats to Validity

Internal validity. A threat to the internal validity is a bias in the selection of the apps we took from [6,17] although the 10 apps for Study 2 were selected by an "unbiased random sampling" [17, p. 103]. We further use the default configuration of SAPIENZ and SAPIENZ^{div} without tuning the parameters to reduce the threat of overfitting to the given apps. Finally, the correctness of the diversity-promoting mechanisms is a threat that we addressed by computing the fitness landscape analysis metrics with SAPIENZ^{div} to confirm the improved diversity.

External validity. As we used 5 (for analyzing the fitness landscape) and 76 Android apps (for evaluating SAPIENZ^{div}) out of over 2.500 apps on F-Droid and millions on Google Play, we cannot generalize our findings although we rely on the well-accepted "68 F-Droid benchmark apps" [6].

7 Related Work

Related work exists in two main areas: approaches on test case generation for apps, and approaches on diversity in search-based software testing (SBST).

Test case generation for apps. Such approaches use random, model-based, or systematic exploration strategies for the generation. Random strategies implement UI-guided test input generators where events on the GUI are selected randomly [3]. Dynodroid [14] extends the random selection using weights and frequencies of events. Model-based strategies such as PUMA [8], DroidBot [11], MobiGUITAR [2], and Stoat [29] apply model-based testing to apps. Systematic exploration strategies range from full-scale symbolic execution [18] to evolutionary algorithms [15,17]. All of these approaches do not explicitly manage diversity, except of Stoat [29] encoding diversity of sequences into the objective function.

Diversity in SBST. Diversity of solutions has been researched for test case selection and generation. For the former, promoting diversity can significantly improve the performance of state-of-the-art multi-objective genetic algorithms [21]. For the latter, promoting diversity results in increased lengths of tests without improved coverage [1], matching our observation. Both approaches witness that diversity promotion is crucial and its realization "requires some care" [24, p. 782].

8   Conclusions and Future Work

In this paper, we reported on our descriptive study analyzing the fitness landscape of SAPIENZ indicating a lack of diversity during the search. Therefore, we proposed SAPIENZ^{div} that integrates four mechanisms to promote diversity. The results of the first empirical study on the 68 F-Droid benchmark apps were promising for SAPIENZ^{div} but they could not be confirmed statistically by the inconclusive results of the second study with 10 further apps. As future work, we plan to extend the evaluation to more generations to see the effect of SAPIENZ^{div} when the search of SAPIENZ stagnates. Moreover, we plan to identify diversity-promoting mechanisms that quickly yield benefits in the first few generations.

Acknowledgments. This work has been developed in the *FLASH* project (GR 3634/6-1) funded by the German Science Foundation (DFG) and has been partially supported by the 2018 Facebook Testing and Verification research award.

References

1. Albunian, N.M.: Diversity in search-based unit test suite generation. In: Menzies, T., Petke, J. (eds.) SSBSE 2017. LNCS, vol. 10452, pp. 183–189. Springer, Cham (2017). https://doi.org/10.1007/978-3-319-66299-2_17
2. Amalfitano, D., Fasolino, A.R., Tramontana, P., Ta, B.D., Memon, A.: Mobiguitar: automated model-based testing of mobile apps. IEEE Softw. **32**(5), 53–59 (2015)
3. Android: Ui/application exerciser monkey (2017)
4. Arcuri, A., Fraser, G.: Parameter tuning or default values? an empirical investigation in search-based software engineering. Emp. Softw. Eng. **18**(3), 594–623 (2013)
5. Bachelet, V.: Métaheuristiques Parallèles Hybrides: Application au Problème D'affectation Quadratique. Ph.D. thesis, Université Lille-I (1999)

6. Choudhary, S.R., Gorla, A., Orso, A.: Automated test input generation for android: are we there yet? In: Proceedings of ASE 2015, pp. 429–440. IEEE (2015)

7. Fraser, G., Arcuri, A.: Whole test suite generation. IEEE Trans. Softw. Eng. **39**(2), 276–291 (2013)

8. Hao, S., Liu, B., Nath, S., Halfond, W.G., Govindan, R.: Puma: programmable ui-automation for large-scale dynamic analysis of mobile apps. In: Proceedings of MobiSys 2014, pp. 204–217. ACM (2014)

9. Isermann, H.: The enumeration of the set of all efficient solutions for a linear multiple objective program. Oper. Res. Q. **28**(3), 711–725 (1977)

10. Li, M., Yao, X.: Quality evaluation of solution sets in multiobjective optimisation: a survey. ACM Comput. Surv. **52**(2), 26:1–26:38 (2019)

11. Li, Y., Yang, Z., Guo, Y., Chen, X.: Droidbot: a lightweight ui-guided test input generator for android. In: Proceedings of ICSE 2017 Companion, pp. 23–26. IEEE (2017)

12. Liefooghe, A., Verel, S., Aguirre, H., Tanaka, K.: What makes an instance difficult for black-box 0–1 evolutionary multiobjective optimizers? In: Legrand, P., Corsini, M.-M., Hao, J.-K., Monmarché, N., Lutton, E., Schoenauer, M. (eds.) EA 2013. LNCS, vol. 8752, pp. 3–15. Springer, Cham (2014). https://doi.org/10.1007/978-3-319-11683-9_1

13. Maaranen, H., Miettinen, K., Penttinen, A.: On initial populations of a genetic algorithm for continuous optimization problems. J. Global Optim. **37**(3), 405–436 (2006)

14. Machiry, A., Tahiliani, R., Naik, M.: Dynodroid: an input generation system for android apps. In: Proceedings of ESEC/FSE 2013. pp. 599–609. ACM (2013)

15. Mahmood, R., Mirzaei, N., Malek, S.: Evodroid: segmented evolutionary testing of android apps. In: Proceedings of FSE 2014. pp. 599–609. ACM (2014)

16. Malan, K.M., Engelbrecht, A.P.: A survey of techniques for characterising fitness landscapes and some possible ways forward. Inf. Sci. **241**, 148–163 (2013)

17. Mao, K., Harman, M., Jia, Y.: Sapienz: multi-objective automated testing for android applications. In: Proceedings of ISSTA 2016. pp. 94–105. ACM (2016)

18. Mirzaei, N., Malek, S., Păsăreanu, C.S., Esfahani, N., Mahmood, R.: Testing android apps through symbolic execution. Softw. Eng. Notes **37**(6), 1–5 (2012)

19. Moser, I., Gheorghita, M., Aleti, A.: Identifying features of fitness landscapes and relating them to problem difficulty. Evol. Comp. **25**(3), 407–437 (2017)

20. Olorunda, O., Engelbrecht, A.P.: Measuring exploration/exploitation in particle swarms using swarm diversity. In: Proceedings of CEC 2008. pp. 1128–1134. IEEE (2008)

21. Panichella, A., Oliveto, R., Penta, M.D., Lucia, A.D.: Improving multi-objective test case selection by injecting diversity in genetic algorithms. IEEE Trans. Software Eng. **41**(4), 358–383 (2015)

22. Paquete, L., Stützle, T.: Clusters of non-dominated solutions in multiobjective combinatorial optimization: an experimental analysis. Multiobjective Programming and Goal Programming. Lecture Notes in Economics and Mathematical Systems, vol. 618, pp. 69–77. Springer, Berlin (2009). https://doi.org/10.1007/978-3-540-85646-7_7

23. Pitzer, E., Affenzeller, M.: A comprehensive survey on fitness landscape analysis. Recent Advances in Intelligent Engineering. Studies in Computational Intelligence, vol. 378, pp. 161–191. Springer, Berlin (2012). https://doi.org/10.1007/978-3-642-23229-9_8

24. Purshouse, R.C., Fleming, P.J.: On the evolutionary optimization of many conflicting objectives. IEEE Trans. Evolut. Comp. **11**(6), 770–784 (2007)

25. Ronald, S.: Duplicate genotypes in a genetic algorithm. In: Proceedings of ICEC 1998. pp. 793–798. IEEE (1998)
26. Shir, O.M., Preuss, M., Naujoks, B., Emmerich, M.: Enhancing decision space diversity in evolutionary multiobjective algorithms. In: Ehrgott, M., Fonseca, C.M., Gandibleux, X., Hao, J.-K., Sevaux, M. (eds.) EMO 2009. LNCS, vol. 5467, pp. 95–109. Springer, Heidelberg (2009). https://doi.org/10.1007/978-3-642-01020-0_12
27. Smith, T., Husbands, P., Layzell, P.J., O'Shea, M.: Fitness landscapes and evolvability. Evol. Comput. **10**(1), 1–34 (2002)
28. Stadler, P.F.: Fitness landscapes. Biological Evolution and Statistical Physics. Lecture Notes in Physics, vol. 585, pp. 183–204. Springer, Berlin (2002). https://doi.org/10.1007/3-540-45692-9_10
29. Su, T., Meng, G., Chen, Y., Wu, K., et al.: Guided, stochastic model-based gui testing of android apps. In: Proceedings of ESEC/FSE 2017. pp. 245–256. ACM (2017)
30. Črepinšek, M., Liu, S.H., Mernik, M.: Exploration and exploitation in evolutionary algorithms: a survey. ACM Comput. Surv. **45**(3), 35:1–35:33 (2013)
31. Wang, S., Ali, S., Yue, T., Li, Y., Liaaen, M.: A practical guide to select quality indicators for assessing pareto-based search algorithms in search-based software engineering. In: Proceedings of ICSE 2016. pp. 631–642. ACM (2016)

PRICE: Detection of Performance Regression Introducing Code Changes Using Static and Dynamic Metrics

Deema Alshoaibi[✉], Kevin Hannigan, Hiten Gupta,
and Mohamed Wiem Mkaouer[✉]

Rochester Institute of Technology, New York, USA
{da3352,kph1958,hg1928,mwmvse}@rit.edu

Abstract. Performance regression testing is highly expensive as it delays system development when optimally conducted after each code change. Therefore, it is important to prioritize the schedule of performance tests by executing them when a newly committed change is most likely to introduce performance regression. This paper introduces a novel formulation of the detection of performance regression introducing code changes as an optimization problem. Static and dynamic metrics are combined to generate a detection rule, which is being optimized in terms of its ability to flag problematic code changes, and avoid false positives. We evaluated our approach using performance issues, extracted from the *Git* project. Results show the effectiveness of our approach in accurately detecting performance regression introducing code changes compared with state-of-the-art techniques. Moreover, our suggested detection rules were found to be robust to the software changes over time, which reduces the overhead of updating them frequently.

Keywords: Performance regression · Multi-objective optimization ·
Software testing · Software quality

1 Introduction

Performance is critical to software quality. Being one of the practices of quality assurance, performance regression testing monitors the software's overall performance during its evolution to ensure least to negligible degradation of time. It mainly detects whether any committed changes may have introduced performance regressions.

Ideally, in order to prevent any code change from negatively impacting the software performance, performance tests, also known as benchmarks, should be executed along with any committed change, as a sanity check. However, in a real-world setting, performance tests are expensive, and with the growth in the number of committed changes, software testers are constantly challenged to find the right trade-off between optimally performance testing newly introduced changes,

© Springer Nature Switzerland AG 2019
S. Nejati and G. Gay (Eds.): SSBSE 2019, LNCS 11664, pp. 75–88, 2019.
https://doi.org/10.1007/978-3-030-27455-9_6

and increasing the development overall productivity [7]. Nevertheless, executing Performance testing after each commit is an expensive and long process that has overhead of resources and delays programmers from further development until the results of testing have been gathered [8]. As a result, performance tests are not conducted after each change on the code because they consume resources [7]. This practice challenges the early finding the performance regression changes. For example, if performance tests are postponed by the end of the Sprint, then developers need to commit their code throughout the cycle and hope that no performance test would fail by the end, otherwise, they have to rewind all previously committed changes to debug them. In this context, various research has been analyzing performance regression inducing code changes to characterize them and allow their early detection to support the prioritization of performance regression i.e., for upcoming changes to commit, if any of them exhibits characteristics that are similar to these known to have induced performance regression, then this may be a trigger for software testers to schedule their performance tests.

To cope with this expensive process, recent studies focus on mining performance regression testing repositories to either support performance analysis [2,6,10], or improve regression strategies [8,9], or to characterize code changes that have introduced regression [3,11]. Characterizing performance regression introducing code changes is complex since it goes beyond the static design of the code e.g., coupling and complexity, and it is reflected by the dynamic nature of the change e.g., excessive calls to external APIs, besides being specific to the projects development practices, and programming languages [12].

This paper defines detecting Performance Regression Introducing Code Changes (PRICE) as an optimization problem. Initially, our approach takes as input a set of commits that are known to be problematic, then analyzes them using static and dynamic metrics, previously used an existing study [11]. Afterward, these commits, with their corresponding metric values, are used as a training set for the Non dominated sorting genetic algorithm (NSGA-II) [5], which evolves the given metrics to generate a detection rule that maximizes the detection of problematic code changes. Our experiments were carried out using *Git* as the system under test. Our findings show the ability of the evolutionary algorithm to generate promising results, in comparison with state-of-art approaches.

2   Methodology

In this section, we give a high-level overview of our approach's workflow, then we explain how we designed NSGA-II for detecting performance regression changes.

2.1   Approach Overview

The goal of our approach is to find the best rule that detects PRICE. The general structure is sketched in Fig. 1.

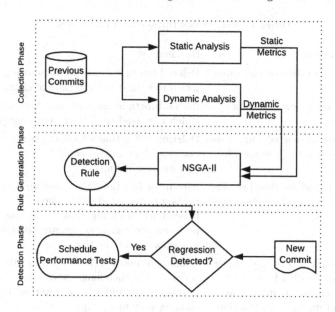

Fig. 1. Approach overview.

Our approach is composed of three phases. Collection phase uses history performance tests data collected from previous commits to calculate metrics. Metrics represent collected data of each commit to the respect of the previous commit. Table 1 lists static and dynamic metrics used in this work. Metrics 1,2,6 are static where the rest are both static and dynamic. The tool used to collect static metrics is Lizard code complexity analyzer. Static data is afterward fed into dynamic analysis process to run benchmarks and calculate dynamic metrics.

The second phase after collecting metrics is generating a detection rule. Finding this rule is a multi-objective optimization problem. A Detection rule should have the highest detection of problematic commits while minimizing the detection of benign commits. The search space contains solutions with different combination of metrics and a value for each metric. In this paper, we considered seven metrics from a previous study [11], which we will also compare our approach with. Once a detection rule is generated, developers can apply it on each commit to detect regression and decide whether to run benchmark testing or not. In case benchmark testing is applied on a commit, dynamic metrics of that commit is stored on the database to help in updating detection rule in the future when rule is no longer providing good predictions.

2.2   Data Collection

We have selected the *Git* project to be the system under test of our study. We have selected *Git* for multiple reasons, including it being open-source, containing a complete set of benchmarks, easy to compile and run (mandatory for our dynamic analysis), besides our familiarity with its commands. We collected data

Table 1. Metrics descriptions and rationales.

#	Description	Rationale
1	Number of deleted functions	Deleted functions indicate refactoring, which may lead to performance changes
2	Number of new functions	Added functions indicate new functionality, which may lead to performance changes
3	Number of deleted Functions reached by the benchmark	Deleting a function which was part of the benchmark execution could lead to a performance change
4	The percent overhead of the top most called function that was changed	Altering a function that takes up a large portion of the processing time of a benchmark has a high risk of causing a performance regression because it is such a large portion of the test
5	The percent overhead of the top most called function that was changed by more than 10% of its static instruction length	Similar to metric 4, however this takes into account that the change affects a reasonable portion of the function in question. Bigger changes may mean higher risk
6	The highest percent static function length change	Large changes to functions are more likely to cause regressions than small ones
7	The highest percent static function length change that is called by the benchmark	The same as for metric 7, but here we guarantee that the functions are actually called by the benchmark in question

for 8798 commits originally. Those commits were chosen by executing the 'git rev-parse' command from the master branch at the time and going back to the first commit we could find which had performance tests. Across that range of commits, there were 202 commits which, for technical reasons, were untestable, so we removed them. Thus in total we considered 8596 commits.

Afterward, for each commit, we run all performance tests, and this is for two reasons: the first one, we need to see whether any test would fail, and if so, we tag the commit under test as problematic. The second reason is to dynamically profile each code change and calculate some of metrics at runtime. To avoid the flakiness of some tests and the stochastic nature of the code, we test each commit 5 times. Running all of the performance tests for a single commit takes a significant amount of time (hence the need for this study), so we parallelized the task across many machines. The results of the *Git* performance tests are reported in wall time, which can be impacted by using machines with different clock speeds, RAM, etc., so to mitigate this we used identical Virtual machines in a proprietary cloud[1]. The dynamic information was collected using Linux perf [4], as for the static information, the list of functions and their location in the

---

[1] https://www.digitalocean.com.

source code, was collected by using the python lizard[2] tool. While intended for calculating cyclomatic complexity, it also provides list of functions identified in all of the source files in the repository for that commit. We provide the dataset and tools we used for reproducibility and extension purposes[3].

2.3 Solution Representation

Our solution is encoded as a tree-based rule. The leaf nodes are termed 'terminals' and internal nodes as 'primitives'. Primitives are logical operators that compares metric value with the threshold assigned to it respectively. Figure 2 illustrates a solution tree that combines five metrics and their threshold values by logical operators AND and OR. Solution tree is strictly typed to assure structure is not broken during the evolution.

2.4 Solution Evaluation

Generated rules are evaluated by two objectives, which are hit and dismiss rates. This subsection defines these objectives and shows how they are conflicted.

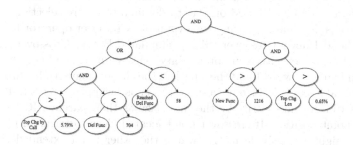

Fig. 2. Solution representation as a tree-based rule.

Hit Rate as an Objective. The Hit rate indicates the number of correctly detected commits to total number of commits encountering regression. In formula 1 H_p is predicted problematic commits while H is actual regression commits. Values of hit rate are between 0.0 and 1.0. Hit rate of 1 means that all commits encounter regression are detected. Hit rate can also be 1 if all commits considered to be problematic which is not proper to this type of problems.

$$|H_p \cap H|/|H| \tag{1}$$

---

[2] http://terryyin.github.io/lizard/.
[3] https://smilevo.github.io/price/.

Dismiss Rate as an Objective. The Dismiss rate is the number of commits classified not to be introducing regression to the total actual number of stable, not problematic, commits. In formula 2 D_p is predicted stable commits while D is actual stable commits. Dismiss rate values are between 0.0 and 1.0. Dismiss rate of value 1 indicates that all non-problematic commits are correctly classified as not introducing regression. Dismiss rate of 1 might indicate that all commits are not problematic. It cannot be used individually as hit rate.

$$|D_p \cap D|/|D| \tag{2}$$

An optimal solution would score a hit and dismiss rate of 1. Since hit and dismiss rates are conflicting, when optimizing one objective, we automatically degrade the other as shown in Fig. 3. Hence, we are searching for near optimal solutions that should deliver a good trade-off between these objectives that are meant to be maximized.

2.5   Solution Variation

The multi-objective evolutionary algorithm used to traverse the search space and find the best solution is Non-dominated Sorting Genetic Algorithm (NSGA-II) [5]. Population is ranked based on Pareto dominance before selection to insure no objective is dominating during the evolution. Crossover operator for NSGA-II is Simulated Binary Crossover (SBX). Simulated Binary Crossover simulates single point crossover with using probability density function. Crossover point is chosen randomly between 1 and the length of the chromosome [1]. In chromosome represented as tree, rule in our case, crossover is swapping tree sub-branches. New trees will not necessarily be the same size as their parents. It depends on crossover point position. If crossover point located close to terminal nodes, one off spring might be a single metric where the other is an extended tree that might have duplicated metrics with different threshold values.

Mutation operator in NSGA-II is Polynomial Mutation. This operator uses polynomial probability distribution to select node to be mutated. Mutation operator depends on node type to insure producing a logical rule. To illustrate, primitive nodes connecting terminal nodes should always be a comparison operator, which are greater than or less than. As a result it will be mutated to different operator than the original.

Choice of the Final Solution. The multi-objective nature of the algorithm allows the choice of multiple Pareto-equivalent solutions that may differ in optimizing one objective in comparison with the other. So, software testers can choose either to prioritize the hit rate over the dismiss rate if the cost of running benchmarks is high or the allowed testing time period is relatively short; or they can favor the dismiss rate if they are afraid of missing any code change introducing a performance regression, at the expense of running extra test cases. For our experiments, we have chosen the solution with the highest F-Measure across various runs.

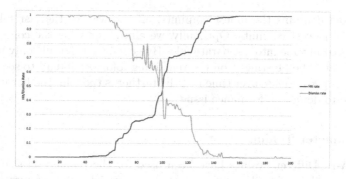

Fig. 3. Hit and dismiss are conflicted objectives.

3   Experimental Setting

3.1   Research Questions

To evaluate the relevance of generated rules in detecting commits introducing regression, we defined the following research questions:

RQ1. To what extent does NSGA-II provide better regression detection compared with other techniques?

To address this research question, we applied the 10-fold cross validation. We initially sort the commits chronologically, then we split them into 10 equal folds where fold 1 contains the earliest (oldest) commits subset, all the way to fold 10, which contains the latest commits subset. The validation is performed using 10 iterations. In each iteration, one fold is used for testing and the rest is used for training. Note that Folds do not necessarily contain same number of problematic commits, but since the majority of folds are used for training, the training set tends to contain significantly more problematic commits, than the testing set, which does simulate real world scenarios. Results are compared with k-Nearest Neighbors algorithm (KNN) and a state-of-the-art approach called Perphecy [11]. We choose KNN to see the results of considering the problem of performance regression as a non-parametric binary classification, where metrics represent the feature space. We also compare with Perphecy since it is available online and known to provide good results. Hit and dismiss rates and F-measurement to compare the performance of the three methods.

RQ2. Do the generated rules continue to perform well with the evolution of the software?

This research question challenges the stability of generated rules over the evolution of the software. As software evolves, with committing a significant amount of code changes, the software may undergo several structural and functional changes, which may change the characteristics that have been previously captured by the metrics. Which may consequently hinder the accuracy of the performance detection. To simulate such scenario, similarly to RQ1, we again sort the commits chronologically, then we split them into 10 equal folds, where the first fold contains the oldest commits, all the way to the last fold which contains the newest commits. Optimally, we aim in splitting the commits that are co-located in time into a separate fold. By generating the rule only using the oldest fold, and then testing it on the remaining folds, we intend to see whether our rule may get *obsolete* over time i.e., the further is the fold, the harder should be the rule to detect performance issues.

3.2   Parameter Tuning

For NSGA-II, Different values have been used for the population size and the maximum number of evaluations, generating a variety of configurations. We use the trial and error and choose the configuration providing better results in terms of hit rate and dismiss rate. We used the following parameters: *Population size = 50, iterations = 10000, Selection = Binary tournament selection without replacement, Simulated Binary Crossover probability = 0.8, Polynomial Mutation probability = 0.5.*

Perphecy combines metrics to find the best rule that better detect performance issues in a deterministic way. Before trying all possible metrics combinations to find the best rule, Perphecy determines each metric threshold value individually. The combination with highest hit and dismiss rate is selected. The authors of Perphecy applied this process for each project separately, as every project has its own characteristics and so the nominated rule differs from project to another. In this context, we did not reuse any existing rules from the previous study and we had to generate a rule for each subset of commits, from *Git* project.

For KNN, we use the gap statistic method to estimate the optimal number of clusters K. Gap statistic is chosen since it provides a statistical procedure to model traditional elbow and silhouette methods. To ensure fairness when compared to NSGA-II and Perphecy, we re-estimate K for each set of input commits.

Since our experiments contain a fold cross validation, we tune the algorithms together once, for the first fold. To ensure fairness, we regenerate a rule representing each algorithm for every training fold, as we will detail later.

4   Results

This section will show results of experiments conducted to answer research questions.

4.1   RQ1. To What Extent Does NSGA-II Provide Better Regression Detection Compared with Other Techniques?

In order to compare performance of NSGA-II with KNN and Perphecy, we plotted hit rate, dismiss rate and F-measure of each technique. In this cross-validation, each fold has been tested with a rule, which was created using the remaining folds as the training set. In Fig. 4, the hit rate represents correctly classified commits while the dismiss rate represents correctly avoided commits. According to Fig. 4 results, KNN's hit rate is very low, and only reached 10% at most, so it highly missclassifies commits with regression in contrast with a more successful dismiss rate where more than 95% of benign commits have been correctly classified. This is due to the imbalance between the two class representations: commits encounter regression are only about 4% of the overall commits. Although, this imbalanced setting represents a challenge for machine learning algorithms, it mimics naturally the real setting for typical software projects, where performance regression tends to be less frequent but critical to software health [8].

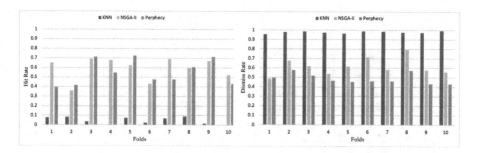

Fig. 4. Hit Rate, and Dismiss Rate of KNN, Perphecy and NSGA-II, on 10-folds.

Perphecy also combines metrics to find the best rule that better detect performance issues in a deterministic way. Before trying all possible metrics combinations to find the best rule, Perphecy determines each metric threshold value individually. The combination with highest hit and dismiss rate is selected. The authors of Perphecy applied this process for each project separately, as every project has its own characteristics and so the nominated rule differs from project to another. In this context we applied Perphecy approach in *Git* project to compare it with our results.

This approach has provided significantly better results than KNN since its hit rate, across folds, varies between 39%, and 72%, as for the dismiss rate, it ranges between 42% and 58%. Perphecy is independent of the naive aggregation of all values, and so it clearly outperforms KNN, since its F-Measure goes up to 68% while KNN achieved an F-Measure of 17% at best.

NSGA-II's performance was competitive to Perphecy, since its hit rate is between 35%, and 69%, which is slightly below Perphecy's hit rate, and for the dismiss rate, it ranges between 48% and 79%, which was slightly above Perphecy's dismiss rate. As for the F-Measure, as shown in Fig. 5, NSGA-II 's values are between 47%, and 68%, and it also outperforms Perphecy, in all folds, expect for the second one. The main difference between NSGA-II and Perphecy is the ability of the latter to change the threshold values while composing the decision

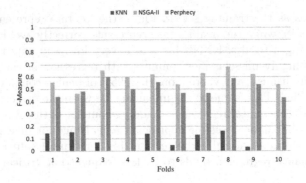

Fig. 5. F-measure of KNN, Perphecy and NSGA-II, on 10-folds.

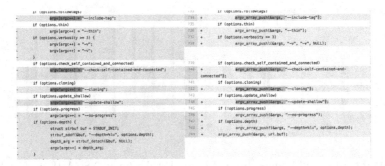

Fig. 6. An example of performance regression introducing code change. (Color figure online)

tree, besides the global exploration of NSGA-II for many possible competing rules during its evolutionary process.

To show a concrete example of one[4] of the problematic commits, Fig. 6 shows its contrast with previous commits. As shown in Fig. 6, the deleted lines of code (in red) is the conventional operation of assigning a value to a particular index of an array which is a least expensive way of adding values in an array. This operation was replaced, as shown in the added lines (in green), by adding the values through a function call and passing the value to be added as an argument. If scheduling regression tests was using a straightforward heuristic like Lines Of Code (LOC), the above-shown code will not trigger any flags as there is no addition of new lines of code. Whereas, the newly introduced statements are expensive, since for each function call, it will traverse a data structure and append the new value. This issue was captured by a rule depicted in Fig. 7 (for visibility we show a subset of the tree).

---

[4] https://bit.ly/2I4khC3d491cf.

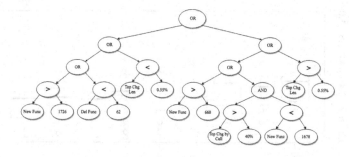

Fig. 7. Subset of a solution extracted from the Pareto front.

4.2 RQ2 Do the Generated Rules Continue to Perform Well with the Evolution of the Software?

To evaluate generated rules stability with the evolution of the software, we used the earliest commits subset for training and the rest nine subsets for testing. Figure 8 contains the boxplot of F-Measure values of the Pareto front solutions during 31 simulation runs. As shown in Fig. 8, no significant difference on median and the 75th percentile presented on f-measure values. This indicates that generated rules were able to offer regression prediction up to the forth fold as good as the second fold. For the remaining folds, we can observe a slight decrease from the seventh until the tenth fold. Characteristics of code changes introducing regression may change with the evolution of the code. This explains the regression in the prediction. Although our rules have shown their ability to maintain a good performance across various code changes, it is recommended to update the prediction regularly.

5 Threats to Validity

Internal Validity. We report on the uncontrolled factors that interfere with causes and effects, and may impact the experimental results. Commits not necessarily sequential: The git project itself uses git as source control, and employs a branching strategy with merges. If the project history branched and then merged, when you view the history linearly you might have two commits next to each other which technically were not developed sequentially when originally committed by the developer. However, since our approach is not dependent to the program's logic, it is a problem to compare out of order commits as long as we can detect any performance regression.

Construct Validity. Herewith we report on certain challenges that validate whether the findings of our study reflect real-world conditions. In order to execute the performance tests for over 8000 commits in a timely manner, the task was parallelized across multiple machines. This could become a threat because the results for the performance tests are given as a time duration, which can vary based on CPU speed, number of cores, and other random variables between

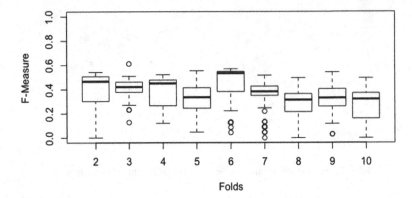

Fig. 8. Boxplots of Pareto front solutions' F-Measure values, trained on fold 1, over 31 runs.

machines. To mitigate this, identical virtual machines were used for all performance test results, which means CPU speed, RAM, and so on were identical. Additionally, we ran each test 5 separate times, such that each execution was at a different time of day on a different virtual machine. This helps mitigate other uncontrollable random noise in the results of the testing.

External Validity. The prediction of performance regression was limited only to one project. The generated predictor does not necessarily give the best results for other projects. We plan on the future to apply our approach to more projects and, if possible, across more programming languages.

6   Related Work

Chen et al. [3] found that performance regression introducing changes is rigorous and associated with complex syndrome. As a result, the study suggests to frequently conduct performance testing rather than defer it until the end of development process. Although executing comprehensive performance testing will ease locating code change introducing performance regression, it is expensive and might delay development process. Many researches have been conducted to overcome this limitation. Huang et al. [8] argue that performance testing should be devoted to only commits counter performance regression rather than all commits. To achieve that they rank commits based on the probability of encountering performance regression based on a static Performance Risk Analysis (PRA). This analysis focuses on how the change is expensive and frequent. After ranking commits, based on the analysis, a comprehensive testing is conducted on risky commits while light testing conducted on the rest. PRA is considered a light approach because it statically estimates the risk of a code change without running the software. Perphecy [11] agrees with PRA [8] that applying comprehensive performance testing on each commit is expensive. Rather than finding the problematic commit and intensively perform regression testing on it, Perphecy insists on testing each commit but with only test suites that would detect performance regression. To determine which test suite can detect performance regression, they have implemented a predictor based on a combination of indicators built up from static and dynamic data collected from previous commits compared with static data of the new commit.

7 Conclusion and Future Work

We presented a novel formulation of the early detection of performance regression as multi-objective optimization problem. We used NSGA-II to generate a detection rule, while maximizing the correctness of *hitting* a regression and maximizing the correctness of *dismissing* a non-regression, as two objectives. We evaluated our detection rule by building a dataset of performance regression, extracted from the *Git* project. As we compare our results to other techniques, we found that our approach provides a competitive detection that improves the state-of-the-art existing results. We plan to extend this study by adding additional metrics, including branch and bound, Cyclomatic complexity, and coupling between objects. We plan on also analyzing more projects to challenge the generalizability of our approach.

Acknowledgement. We would like to sincerely thank the authors of *Perphecy* for providing enough details that allowed its replication. We also thank the members of #git-devel IRC community for answering some of our questions during this work.

References

1. Agrawal, R.B., Deb, K., Agrawal, R.B.: Simulated binary crossover for continuous search space. Complex Syst. **9**(2), 115–148 (1995)
2. Ahmed, T.M., Bezemer, C.P., Chen, T.H., Hassan, A.E., Shang, W.: Studying the effectiveness of application performance management (APM) tools for detecting performance regressions for web applications: an experience report. In: Proceedings of the 13th International Conference on Mining Software Repositories, pp. 1–12. ACM (2016)
3. Chen, J., Shang, W.: An exploratory study of performance regression introducing code changes. In: 2017 IEEE International Conference on Software Maintenance and Evolution (ICSME), pp. 341–352. IEEE (2017)
4. De Melo, A.C.: The new linux 'perf' tools. In: Slides from Linux Kongress, vol. 18 (2010)
5. Deb, K., Agrawal, S., Pratap, A., Meyarivan, T.: A fast elitist non-dominated sorting genetic algorithm for multi-objective optimization: NSGA-II. In: Schoenauer, M., Deb, K., Rudolph, G., Yao, X., Lutton, E., Merelo, J.J., Schwefel, H.-P. (eds.) PPSN 2000. LNCS, vol. 1917, pp. 849–858. Springer, Heidelberg (2000). https://doi.org/10.1007/3-540-45356-3_83
6. Foo, K.C., Jiang, Z.M., Adams, B., Hassan, A.E., Zou, Y., Flora, P.: Mining performance regression testing repositories for automated performance analysis. In: 2010 10th International Conference on Quality Software, pp. 32–41. IEEE (2010)

7. Ghaith, S., Wang, M., Perry, P., Murphy, J.: Profile-based, load-independent anomaly detection and analysis in performance regression testing of software systems. In: 2013 17th European Conference on Software Maintenance and Reengineering (CSMR), pp. 379–383. IEEE (2013)

8. Huang, P., Ma, X., Shen, D., Zhou, Y.: Performance regression testing target prioritization via performance risk analysis. In: Proceedings of the 36th International Conference on Software Engineering, pp. 60–71. ACM (2014)

9. Luo, Q., Poshyvanyk, D., Grechanik, M.: Mining performance regression inducing code changes in evolving software. In: 2016 IEEE/ACM 13th Working Conference on Mining Software Repositories (MSR), pp. 25–36. IEEE (2016)

10. Nguyen, T.H., Adams, B., Jiang, Z.M., Hassan, A.E., Nasser, M., Flora, P.: Automated detection of performance regressions using statistical process control techniques. In: Proceedings of the 3rd ACM/SPEC International Conference on Performance Engineering, pp. 299–310. ACM (2012)

11. Oliveira, A.B.d., Fischmeister, S., Diwan, A., Hauswirth, M., Sweeney, P.F.: Perphecy: performance regression test selection made simple but effective. In: 2017 IEEE International Conference on Software Testing, Verification and Validation (ICST), pp. 103–113. IEEE (2017)

12. Ostermueller, E.: Troubleshooting Java Performance: Detecting Anti-Patterns with Open Source Tools, 1st edn. Apress, Berkely (2017)

General Program Synthesis Using Guided Corpus Generation and Automatic Refactoring

Alexander Wild[✉] and Barry Porter

Lancaster University, Lancaster, UK
{a.wild3,b.f.porter}@lancaster.ac.uk

Abstract. Program synthesis aims to produce source code based on a user specification, raising the abstraction level of building systems and opening the potential for non-programmers to synthesise their own bespoke services. Both genetic programming (GP) and neural code synthesis have proposed a wide range of approaches to solving this problem, but both have limitations in generality and scope. We propose a hybrid search-based approach which combines (i) a genetic algorithm to autonomously generate a training corpus of programs centred around a set of highly abstracted hints describing interesting features; and (ii) a neural network which trains on this data and automatically refactors it towards a form which makes a more ideal use of the neural network's representational capacity. When given an unseen program represented as a small set of input and output examples, our neural network is used to generate a rank-ordered search space of what it sees as the most promising programs; we then iterate through this list up to a given maximum search depth. Our results show that this approach is able to find up to 60% of a human-useful target set of programs that it has never seen before, including applying a clip function to the values in an array to restrict them to a given maximum, and offsetting all values in an array.

1 Introduction

The ever-increasing complexity of writing software – in design, implementation, and ongoing maintenance – has led researchers to consider how programs can be synthesised automatically from a given specification. This could allow system designers to operate at a higher level of abstraction, defining and verifying functionality rather than implementing the fine details, and also has the potential to allow non-programmers to create custom software.

The state of the art in code synthesis has generally considered the problem for domain-specific languages, such as string manipulation, and also tends to restrict the scope of the problem to programs without loops. DeepCoder, for example, uses these restrictions to demonstrate that neural network training over a randomly sampled corpus can find speed versus exhaustive search for a simple language [1]. FlashFill, meanwhile, demonstrates that inductive programming can follow user examples to propose possible functions for Excel data

© Springer Nature Switzerland AG 2019
S. Nejati and G. Gay (Eds.): SSBSE 2019, LNCS 11664, pp. 89–104, 2019.
https://doi.org/10.1007/978-3-030-27455-9_7

transformations within a limited set of operators [8]. Despite these promising results, the limitations of domain specificity and linear logic result in significant restrictions on the kinds of program that can be constructed by code synthesis.

We propose a programming-by-example approach which uses neural-network-based program prediction to operate on a simplified *general-purpose* programming language, with a current focus on integer manipulation, which is capable of producing functions that contain loops and conditional branches. The user is required to supply up to 10 input/output examples which describe the program they wish to create, and programs generated in our intermediate language can be directly and automatically converted to Java or C code. Our neural network is trained on a corpus of synthetic, self-generated examples, the initial population of which is biased using one sample human-useful program. When given a new I/O target pair, the neural network is used to generate a search space which we exhaustively iterate through to a given search depth to find a matching program. In detail, our approach works as follows:

- We use a genetic programming approach to generate a training corpus of programs, based on a seed program which reflects some of the common abstract features believed to be useful in human-required programs. This seed program could be supplied by a human as an over-specified initial program.
- We train a neural network with the resulting corpus, such that the input layer is provided with input/output examples, and the output layers must generate the corresponding program by selecting one line of code per output layer. The neural network is able to both recognise programs that it has already seen and infer programs that it has not.
- We use a technique that we term *automated corpus refactoring* in which the neural network re-trains itself by adjusting its own training corpus based on the kinds of programs it was able to locate from that corpus; we demonstrate that this technique can provide significant improvement in the capabilities of the system to find more unseen programs.

Our results show that we are able to automatically generate 60% of a target corpus of unseen programs based only on 10 I/O examples, including counting how many of a specific value appear in an array, and shifting the contents of an array left or right. We believe that our work is the first to demonstrate that a neural network can be trained to output general-purpose programs that include loops and branch statements, starting only from an automatically generated-corpus based a small set of abstract features that useful programs tend to have. We provide all of the source code for our system, along with instructions on how to repeat our experiments[1].

In the remainder of this paper we first survey related work in Sect. 2, then present our approach in Sect. 3. In Sect. 4 we evaluate our system on both abstract program learning and a specific set of human-useful programs such as searching and array reversal. We then conclude and discuss future work in Sect. 5.

---

[1] https://bitbucket.org/AlexanderWildLancaster/automaticrefactoringsynthesis.git.

2   Background

Program synthesis has long been studied in computer science; in this section we discuss the most relevant research in genetic programming, inductive programming, and neural code synthesis and imitation.

Genetic programming (GP) applies a paradigm of mutation and crossover, seen in biological reproduction, to source code in order to formulate a particular program. A wide range of research has examined topics from improving efficiency to the ability to navigate noisy landscapes and generality of solution [3]. The genetic tools provided by this research have also shown adoption in real-world commercial applications in the sub-field of genetic improvement [12] (GI). However, despite its successes, there are also clear limitations in its use for synthesising programs starting from no initial code. The work "Why We Do Not Evolve Software? Analysis of Evolutionary Algorithms" [16] presents arguments against the current state of the art in genetic algorithms, and the work "Neutrality and Epistasis in Program Space" [13] explores why this may be. Specifically, GP and hence GI rely on finding paths in the fitness landscape of program space from a starting position to the desired functionality. If a program's functionality precludes this incremental path-finding, perhaps because it is a function which cannot 'partially succeed' and must be fully implemented to show success, genetic methods cannot navigate towards it in program space and instead must rely on pure chance to find it. This is more likely to occur in the cases this paper investigates, which have very low numbers of user provided specification-examples, and therefore very low granularity in terms of success/failure metrics. This work focuses instead on using neural techniques to interpolate between learned and recognised functionalities within program space, which does not require a navigable fitness landscape. We show that genetic methods remain critical, however, in the generation of the training corpus used by the neural network, to guide the exploration of program space in a humanly-useful direction.

Inductive programming has been successfully used for a variety of code synthesis tasks, most notably in the FlashFill approach to spreadsheet function generation [8]. In this work, a set of examples is provided by a user, and a sequence of inductive logic passes are applied to incrementally reduce the search space of possible programs which match the examples in a broadly similar way to SMT solving [4,5]. This approach depends heavily on the use of a highly restricted and specialised language over which to search, often with the inductive logic passes being designed specifically with that language in mind. These approaches can synthesise functions very quickly and without training data, but rely on carefully crafted programming languages with associated inductive logic rules, making them hard to generalise to a broader class of synthesis problems.

Neural networks have been applied to the code sythesis problem in two different ways: imitation and synthesis. Neural program imitation works by encoding a program itself as a set of weights in a neural network – literally training a neural network to imitate a program. This has been demonstrated in work such as the Neural Turing Machine [6], the Neural GPU [10] or the Differentiable Neural Computer [7]. These examples show that, from a large number of pure

I/O examples and with no prior knowledge of what any other program looks like, a resulting 'program' can be learned which has high accuracy though remains probabilistic. The main drawbacks are the volume of I/O examples needed (tens of thousands) which arguably are no easier to generate than the algorithm itself; the lack of generality such that the encoded program can correctly operate on longer input lengths that those it was originally trained on; and the lack of scrutability since the program cannot be output as conventional source code, instead being encoded opaquely within the weights of a neural network.

Neural program synthesis, by comparison, trains a neural network on a set of programs by showing it the source code and corresponding I/O pairs, then attempts to generate the source code for unseen programs by issuing new I/O pairs. This is usually done by having the neural network identify a search region in which the program is likely to appear (for example by selecting which operators are most likely) and then searching exhaustively through this region. This approach has the benefit that the neural network outputs source code which can be examined, and that generated programs are both deterministic and tend to generalise across different input sizes. The downside is that a training corpus must be generated which is in some way informative of reaching useful unseen programs. To date, neural program synthesis has been applied to highly simplified programming languages and has used uniform random sampling of the program space to generate a training corpus (and approach that scales for simple languages) [1,14]. We explore the application of the neural synthesis approach to a far more general programming language; given the non-viability of random sampling in the resulting search space for this language, we propose a novel solution to the corpus generation problem for training, by using weighted genetic sampling combined with iterative automatic refactoring of the neural network's own training corpus based on its self-assessed success.

3   Methodology

In this section we describe the overall architecture of our system. This involves first generating a training corpus, using a synthesis system similar to a genetic algorithm, which uses a fitness function to select parents to reproduce with mutation. This corpus is then used to train a neural network, using the program's behaviour (its I/O mappings) as features, and source code as output labels. The neural network is then able to recognise seen algorithmic behaviour and return source code which can reproduce that behaviour. Rather than simply read off the highest-ranked program, we select N options for each line, and search through a set of programs, to account for imperfections in the neural network's outputs.

3.1   Simplified Language

We designed a simplified C-like programming language, generated functions of which can easily be converted into Java or C-code with a cross-compiler. We designed this language to allow rapid test/execute cycles when generating a training corpus and then searching through a projected search space given by our neural network. This is possible because the language is directly interpreted, rather than compiled to disk and then executed, and allows us to run around 23,500 programs per second.

Control	Arithmetic	Array
IF VAR GREATER THAN ZERO	ADD	VAR = ARRAY_INDEX
IF VAR1 EQUAL VAR2	SUBTRACT	ARRAY_INDEX = VAR
ELSE	MULTIPLY	ARRAY_INDEX += VAR
LOOP	DIVIDE	
NO-OP	MODULO	
	LITERAL (1,0,-1)	
	INCREMENT	

Fig. 1. The operators available in our simplified language.

To simplify the design of our neural network, we map our language onto the output neurons using a uniform set of possibilities per line. In detail, we logically imagine that each line of a program can have the same $1,332$ different options, derived from 15 operators (see Fig. 1), from variable declaration to addition or a loop header. Once a program has been chosen, we check to see if it is syntactically coherent and automatically correct programs that are not. In C-like programs this creates two main corrections: cases in which there are too many 'closing braces', and cases in which there are too few (an unterminated loop). For the former case we simple replace hanging braces with a no-op. In the latter case we insert a closing brace at the very end of a program for any un-closed control blocks; in addition, any un-closed loops are converted to conditional blocks rather than loops. By taking this approach to neuron behaviour uniformity, the neural network does not itself have to learn special cases which limit what each line can be based on prior lines, which would create a much more complex network structure (and, we speculate, a more difficult learning problem).

As further restrictions for this study, in all of our tests, we use programs 9 lines long, padded with the NO_OP operator. We allow 6 integer variables to be accessed by our programs, of which two are fixed and unable to be written to. All of our tests involve passing a single array and a single standalone integer into the program. The two fixed integer variables are the input integer and the length of the input array. The program then has read and write access to both the input array and a second array used as output. These limits allow a wide range of functionalities, while still imposing limits to maintain the problem within computationally tractable sizes.

3.2 Neural Network and Search Architecture

Our code synthesis architecture combines a neural network, used to derive an ordered ranking of possible options, with a search process which iteratively tries these ranked programs up to a configurable search depth.

For this particular study we assume every program can take two parameters: an integer array of length 8 as the first parameter, and an integer as the second. We also assume that every program returns an integer array of length 8. Every cell in an array can hold a value between -8 and 8, while the integer parameter can hold a value between 1 and 4. Reducing the range of the integer parameter to only positive non-zero values simplifies the search space, as they can always meaningfully use the parameter to refer to an array index.

While our language is capable of representing much more diverse function specifications and numerical ranges (equivalent to C), we use these restrictions as a first step to simplify the search space and neural network complexity. The crucial extension we are targeting is the ability to use LOOP and IF statements, allowing more complex programs in terms of flow than are possible in other code synthesis approaches. We accept a trade off in terms of program length in return for being able to handle a new class of program.

The neural network is then designed as a standard feed-forward architecture as follows. The input layer uses 1,700 input neurons to take 10 I/O examples concatenated together. The output structure uses 9 layers, one for each potential line of a program; each such layer consists of 1,332 neurons, one for every possible way the respective line could be written (including the possibility of a no-op). Internally we use 8 residual layers, each consisting of two dense layers with a width of 512 and an additive layer skip (shown to improve deep networks [11,15]), and using the ReLu activation function. Dropout was used on all layers, with a probability to keep of 0.75. We used softmax activation for our output layers, and a crossentropy loss function. Our optimizer was the Tensorflow implementation 'RMSPropOptimizer', with learning rate 10^{-5} and momentum 0.9.

The neural network is trained by (automatically) generating a corpus of example programs; the mechanics of this generation are described in detail in the next section. For each generated program in this corpus we randomly generate 10 input/output examples for that program. During training, our randomly generated I/O examples are fed into the neural network's input layer as 170 integer values (each I/O is being composed of 8 values for the input array, one value for the input integer, and 8 values for the output array, this creates 17 values for one I/O example and thus 170 values in total for 10 I/O examples). We choose to encode integers as 10-bit binary numbers for input to the neural network, which was experimentally shown to perform better than using scalar inputs, and so our network has a total of 1,700 input neurons. The network is trained by back-propagating the corresponding output layer neuron values from the actual source code of the corpus program associated with these I/O examples.

Once training is complete, in the testing phase we supply only the 10 I/O examples for a desired program and we use the neural network's probability distribution over its output layer neurons to create a ranked list of programs to search across, from most to least likely. The highest-confidence program would therefore be generated by selecting the highest activity neuron from each output layer. Each layer mapped to a line in the program being generated, and each neuron mapped to one of the 1,332 valid statements which could appear on that line.

The 9 highest-activity neurons, one from each of the 9 output layers, therefore map to 9 statements which then make up the highest-confidence program.

To generate a volume of program space, the N highest ranked neurons are chosen per line, giving N ways that particular line could be written in the sampled program. The search volume would therefore consist of every combination of these options, i.e., $number\_of\_options\_per\_line^{number\_of\_lines}$. For the experiment in this paper, when not otherwise noted, we used 4 options per line for standard programs, and 6 when searching within the human-useful program set.

3.3   Corpus Generation

In a simple DSL, a training corpus for a neural network could be generated by sampling uniformly at random from the space of all possible programs [2]. For our purposes, however, the search space of our more general-purpose language is far too large for uniform random sampling to be effective. When sampled in this way, the resulting corpus of programs is highly repetitive, each program has a high probability of being made up of only (or mostly) lines of code that have no effect, and very few programs contain condition or loop elements (which feature heavily in human-useful programs).

As an alternative to uniform random sampling we designed an approach which combines genetic programming with a set of abstract search biases and a dissimilarity measure. Our generator starts with a seed program, which is an abstract problem reflecting the kinds of search biases that we need; for example a program that uses a loop and a conditional branch, and which reads all of the input array values once and writes each cell of the output array. Starting from this seed program, the genetic algorithm creates iterative populations of mutations. Within a population, we promote code length and an even distributions of all operators, and we penalise writing to loop iterator variables. Finally, mutated programs are only accepted into a population if their are behaviourally dissimilar to the rest of the population. This similarity is measured by feeding 25 randomly generated inputs to each program, and marking the programs dissimilar if any of their output arrays contain a single different value as a result of the inputs. Programs are also rejected if any program reads from or writes to the same memory address in an array twice, further reducing the search space. To gain good learning coverage of flow control, we seed five separate sub-corpuses to form our overall corpus. The first had 0 flow control operators. The second had 1 loop only. The third had 1 loop and 1 CONDITIONAL_GREATER_THAN_0 operator. The fourth had 1 loop and 1 CONDITIONAL_EQUALITY operator. The fifth had 1 loop, 1 CONDITIONAL_EQUALITY and 1 ELSE operator.

The result of this generation process was a diverse set of 10,000 functionally distinct programs, split between the 5 sub-corpuses of 2,000 each. In this work we determine functional similarity by feeding both programs a set 25 randomly generated inputs and checking for any difference. We then split these programs amongst training, testing and validation for the neural network. Training received 8,000 programs, the other two corpuses received 1,000 programs each.

As a result, each corpus' programs were functionally dissimilar, with no program functionality was replicated between corpuses. Note that none of our set of human-useful programs is involved in training the neural network; all such programs are therefore unseen by the system.

3.4 Automatic Corpus Refactoring

Our corpus generation approach tries to train the neural network with a diverse set of programs that facilitate its ability to synthesise human-useful programs. However, corpus generation itself does not necessarily maximise the neural network's internal generality or its use of available model representation space.

We use a novel approach to enhancing the generality and model efficiency of the neural network, by altering the corpus based on the network's own success rate – an approach we term *automatic corpus refactoring*.

The neural network is first trained using the corpus generated as above. It is then asked to locate every program in the training corpus by being given the set of I/O pairs which should result in the given program being found. Because the neural network outputs a ranked list of potential programs, the actual program match may be 10's or 100's of programs down this ranked list. However, during experiments we observed that a *functionally equivalent program* would often exist earlier in the ranking than the exact-match program in the training corpus.

In corpus refactoring, we test to see if such a functionally equivalent program exists earlier in the ranking, and if so we *replace* the training program with this equivalent version. We then retrain the neural network again (with weights re-initialised) based on this new corpus. We can perform this refactoring iteratively, using a new corpus to again replace programs with earlier-found equivalents, until the performance converges to a maximum. As our results demonstrate, refactoring in this form increases performance not just on the training corpus, but also on the testing corpus and on the number of human-useful programs that were correctly constructed – in other words, by adjusting its own training corpus without actually adding any new information, the system is able to find more programs in total than it previously could.

4 Results

This work investigates the effects of automated corpus generation and modification techniques, in the context of trained code synthesis system.

We firstly examine the system's overall code synthesis performance in its intended normal configuration. This allows us to examine its performance, when attempting to solve a human-defined testing corpus of unseen programs. We examine the effects of our automatic refactoring (AR) technique over a set of iterations, to isolate its performance from the initial success of the corpus generation and neural network training steps. AR allows us to improve the performance of a system by adapting its training corpus in response to its current behaviour.

We then investigate the genetic corpus generation approach in further depth, by performing ablation studies on its 'requirements' and fitness function. Following these two studies, we attempt to shed light on the performance gains produced by the AR technique, by examining the changes it makes the corpus.

We evaluate our approach with a set of 'human-useful' programs that the synthesis system is required to find – which we distinguished from the set of programs that the synthesis system finds during its own automated corpus generation phase. For all of our experiments we used Python 3.6.7, Tensorflow 1.12.0 and JVM openjdk 10.0.2 2018-07-17.

4.1 Program Synthesis

To test general program synthesis capability we ran our end-to-end approach 10 times to gain average results. We do this because there are two sources of stochasticity in our approach: the way in which the corpus generation phase works, which is based on randomised mutations; and the way in which the neural

Program name	Without AR	With AR	GP n=60	
Absolute	18.18%	**52.94%**	0.00%	The output array is the absolute value of the elements in the input array
Add one	18.18%	**52.94%**	85.00%	The output array is the value of the elements in the input array plus one
Add param	72.73%	**88.24%**	96.67%	The output array is the value of the elements in the input array plus the parameter integer
All negatives to zero	90.91%	**94.12%**	0.00%	The output array is the maximum of (the value in the input array;zero)
Array length	90.91%	**94.12%**	100.00%	The first value of the output array is the length of the input array, the remaining values are 0
Count param	**90.91%**	88.24%	8.33%	The first value of the output array is the number of times the parameter integer appears in the input array, the remaining values are 0
Iterator up to param	63.64%	41.18%	100.00%	The first N values of the output array are set to their index, the rest are zero, where N is the parameter integer
Keep above param	0.00%	0.00%	0.00%	The first N values of the output array are the corresponding values in the input array, the rest are 0, where N is the parameter integer
Max(value, param)	0.00%	**5.88%**	0.00%	The output array's values are the maximum of either (the input array's corresponding value;the input parameter)
Min(value,param)	0.00%	**5.88%**	0.00%	The output array's values are the minimum of either (the input array's corresponding value;the input parameter)
Modulo 2	0.00%	0.00%	0.00%	The output array's values are the modulo 2 of the values in the input array
Modulo param	90.91%	**94.12%**	21.67%	The output array's values are the modulo parameter of the values in the input array
Multiply by param	90.91%	**94.12%**	0.00%	The output array is the input array, but offset by N rightwards, losing the last value and setting the first value to zero, where N is the input parameter
Negative	54.55%	**94.12%**	1.67%	The output array's values are the negative values of the values in the input array
Offset by one	27.27%	11.76%	66.67%	The output array is the input array, but offset by one rightwards, losing the last value and setting the first value to zero
Offset by param	0.00%	0.00%	0.00%	The output array is the input array offset by N rightwards, losing the last value and setting the first value to zero, where N is the parameter
Return max	0.00%	0.00%	0.00%	The output array's first value is the highest value in the input array, the other values are 0
Return min	0.00%	0.00%	0.00%	The output array's first value is the lowest value in the input array, the other values are 0
Reverse	0.00%	0.00%	0.00%	The output array is the reverse of the input array
Sum values	54.55%	**76.47%**	26.67%	The output array's first value is the sum of all the values in the input array, the other values are zero
Average	38.18%	**44.71%**	25.33%	

Fig. 2. Percentage find rates for two experiment sets, with and without the automated corpus refactoring stage (the first set averaged over 11, and the second over 17 runs). A simple genetic programming algorithm, using the same linguistic constraints, is used as baseline. It can be seen that GP succeeds on simpler problems, but has lower performance when a conditional statement is required.

network is initially configured, which uses randomised starting weights prior to training. We run corpus generation, five rounds of automated corpus refactoring, and then present the input/output examples for our set of (previously unseen) human-useful programs to see how many the system can find.

The results are shown in Fig. 2, detailing both the find rate before any corpus refactoring and also the find rate after the final round of refactoring. For each successfully found program, the neural network has output source code which correctly derives the output from each corresponding input. As an example, for the program "max(value, param)", the array could be $[-5, 3, -2, 3, -4, 1, 5, 8]$, the parameter '1', and the output $[1, 3, 1, 3, 1, 1, 5, 8]$. From these results we can see that our system locates an average of 38% of our human-useful programs as a result of its initial corpus generation process; this rises to an average of 44% (and a maximum of 60%) after five rounds of corpus refactoring. If we examine individual programs in this target set, we see that the majority of find rates tend to increase, while a couple of find rates (for example the offset-by-one program) notably decrease. We speculate that the decreases in some program find rates may be caused by those programs lying outside the generalised space into which the neural network moves during corpus refactoring.

We next examine the find-rate of the training, test and human-useful program set over each iteration of automatic corpus refactoring. These results are shown in Fig. 3 for the training and testing sets, and in Fig. 4 for the human-useful set.

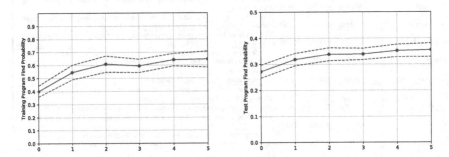

Fig. 3. Success rate on training (left) and test (right) corpus, over each iteration of automatic refactoring, starting from the unmodified corpus, with Standard Deviation

Both the training and test data set show a steady increase in the find-rate of programs from the respective set. For the training set, which shows a find-rate increase from 0.4 to 0.65 (where a value of 1.0 would be all programs found), the process of self-adjusting the training corpus in automatic refactoring clearly shows an enhanced ability to correctly locate more entries in the training corpus. The effect in the test corpus is similar, in this case showing an increase from 0.27 up to 0.36. However, in the case of the test data set the result is much more significant. The increase in find-rate here (i.e., for programs which the system has never seen before) indicates an unexpected phenomena: by having the neural network's training corpus refactored, without adding any data, this allows the neural network to locate more unseen programs than it previously could. It is worth noting that performance decreased in some cases. This is potentially due to the neural network specialising to a particular form of program (the most common) at the expense of others. While this specialisation is overall beneficial, some degradation occurs in certain types of program. We will explore ways to mitigate this effect in future, potentially using a mixture of experts approach employing a set of trained neural networks specialised in different areas.

We see a similar effect in the human-useful programs over successive refactoring iterations, as shown in Fig. 4. Again, all of these programs are unseen by our system during training, but reshaping the training data enables more of them to be successfully synthesised. This suggests that the use of our automated refactoring approach perhaps causes the neural network to become more generalised in its capabilities. However, the data in Fig. 2 provides a more mixed picture: here we see that find-rates for most programs increase after refactoring, but some find rates actually decrease. We explore this further in the next section.

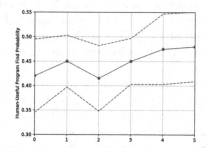

Fig. 4. Success rate on human-useful corpus, over each iteration of the automatic refactoring process, with unchanged corpus as first data point. Corpus size is 20, so each increment of 0.05 corresponds to an average of one program found. 1st Standard Deviation displayed

4.2   Requirements in Corpus Generation

We now examine the effects of the initial requirements on corpus generation. These requirements are used as input to the genetic algorithm to guide its generation of a set of programs on which the neural network is trained. As a consequence of this training, the neural network is then able to find (or not find) a set of previously unseen human-useful programs. The precise nature of these requirements for corpus generation are therefore an important, if indirect, element of how successful our synthesis approach is at finding programs after training.

In this section we examine how the use of different requirements affects synthesis success. Our complete set of requirements, used across all of the experiments reported so far, includes three major categories as follows.

Array Access. This requirement is that all programs containing a loop operator must access every element of the input array. This requirement was included to overcome a perceived problem in the input-access of generated programs. These would often access their inputs in ways which human-written programs rarely would, such as only reading a single element of the input array, or altering their loop iterator and as such skipping elements.

Program Flow. This requirement involved subdividing the corpus into 5 sub-corpuses, each with its own requirement as to how the flow-control operators should be used. The first corpus required all its programs to have no flow-control operators at all. The second corpus required only a single loop operator. The third required a single loop operator and the first type of conditional operator. The fourth required a single loop operator and the second type of conditional operator. The fifth type required a single loop, the first type of conditional operator and an else block. For each of these corpuses, a single "seed" program was supplied. This program was what we considered to be the "maximally simple" implementation of the requirements; as an example of this the loop-only requirement, from the second corpus, would read in all input values, then write them out unchanged to the output array. The seed programs were implemented due to the genetic search's inability to start generation without them.

Genetic Fitness Function. Lastly, our genetic algorithm fitness function rewards particular operator ratios: all operators are expected to be used at least once, with flow control operators in particular weighted twice as highly as others. This was done to promote the use of flow-control, while penalising operators repetition. This was necessary to move away from the "maximally simple" seed programs to those with more commonly useful features.

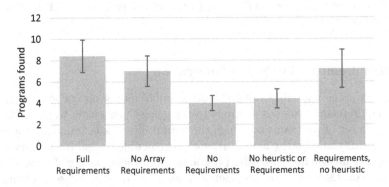

Fig. 5. Average performance for sets of corpuses with varying requirements for constituent generated programs.

We examine the effects of the above requirements by selectively switching them off during corpus generation and comparing how many of our human-useful program set is found as a result. The results are shown in Fig. 5, in which each experiment was run 5 times and we average the data.

The first test shows our full set of requirements, as used in the earlier experiments reported in this section. This achieves the highest performance of any experiment, finding an average of 8.4 programs ($\sigma = 1.5$) from our human-useful target set. The second experiment removes the array access requirement, but keeps the program flow and fitness function heuristics. This performs slightly worse, achieving an average of 7 human-useful programs ($\sigma = 1.4$), indicating that most of our programs are in an area of the total search space in which the input array is uniformly accessed. In the third experiment we removed both the array access requirement and the program flow corpus generation technique, leaving only the fitness function heuristics. This resulted in the worst overall success, with only an average of 4 programs found from our set ($\sigma = 0.71$).

We then removed all requirements and the fitness function heuristics, which actually shows a slight increase in performance with an average of 4.4 ($\sigma = 0.98$) programs found. Finally, we experiment with only using the array access and program flow requirements but remove the fitness function heuristics, which results in the second-best performance overall – indicating that these requirements are more important to success than the fitness function heuristics.

Altogether, these results support the hypothesis that achieving good performance on the human-useful corpus requires a set of corpus generation biases that are reflective, at a very abstract level, of the typical form of useful programs. The way in which these abstract requirements are communicated to a synthesis system in a human-natural way is a key area of future work.

4.3 Effects of Corpus Refactoring

In this section we examine the effects of automated corpus refactoring in more detail, to better understand why it enables more programs to be found without adding any new data to the system. We characterise this as not adding new data because, even though the training corpus is modified, it is modified only as a result of the neural network's own output from the initial training corpus; the only thing being 'added' is therefore the neural network's apparent preference for which precise form of a target training program to use, but this preference is itself entirely derived from the original training corpus and the neural network's inherent behaviour. We therefore attempt to better understand why this effect occurs, in so far as is possible with the black-box nature of neural networks.

In broad terms, the use of feeding output of one neural network as training labels to another has been demonstrated previously in teacher-student distillation network training [9]; in our case however we believe the success is in fact due to an interplay between the network and the search process. We analyse this effect using the entropy shown by output layers before and after automatic refactoring. These experiments help to verify whether or not the neural network is 'self-generalising' as a result of its search process, or if in fact it is specialising to certain kinds of program in which it tends to become an expert.

In our experiments we measure the entropy of each output layer of our neural network, where each layer corresponds to one line of code. As discussed in Sect. 3.2, each output layer of the network can select from one of a fixed set of possible operations for that line of code – where each option is represented by one neuron. The highest-activated neuron in an output layer is taken as the network's best guess for this line of code. We hypothesise that one of the reasons for corpus refactoring finding extra programs is that the network becomes better generalised in its representation of algorithms. We test this theory by examining the entropy of each output layer – in other words, across all programs, how 'specialised' is each output layer to always choosing the same operation for their line of code, versus their ability to represent a balanced spread of output options. The more balanced the spread is for each output layer, without losing the ability to synthesise programs, the more generalised the neural network may be.

We use the Theil inequality metric to measure the 'inequality' of each line. Maximum inequality (only one option ever used) would be minimum entropy (perfectly predictable). To compute this we find the probability of every option for every line being chosen, across all the programs in the training corpus. If every option were chosen with equal probability, they would each be the average, μ, which is equivalent to $1/N$, where N is the number of options per line.

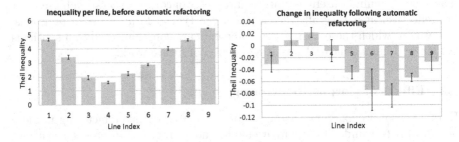

Fig. 6. Reverse entropy of operator distributions by line, as measured by the Theil index. Lower values imply a more even distribution of operator use for a particular, therefore higher entropy.

Figure 6 shows the results of this experiment. On the left we see the entropy of each output layer before any refactoring has taken place, and on the right we see entropy after five refactoring iterations. We see a clear trend towards a more balanced ability for each output layer to select a broader range of options, supporting our hypothesis that our refactoring process may aid in generalising the capacity of the neural network.

We can also infer from these experiments that program length becomes more consistent after refactoring. This is to say, if we count the number of non-empty lines (which can appear on any line post-refactoring), we tend towards a closer average across all programs (the length goes from 7.11 lines with a standard deviation of 1.82, to a line average of 7.78 with a standard deviation of 1.41). This suggests that the refactoring process tends to choose longer forms of programs to effectively specialise the network towards programs of a certain length. This is an unexpected duality: as a result of corpus refactoring our network seems to train towards specialising to a certain length of program, which simultaneously generalising itself within that program length by increasing the ability for different lines to take more diverse operations.

5   Conclusion

We have presented an investigation into combining automated corpus generation using a genetic algorithm, with a neural network search technique, to synthesise code in a simplified general-purpose language when given a set of I/O challenges describing the intention of the program.

Our corpus generation is based on a set of highly abstract requirements which align the set of self-generated training programs with roughly the features found in human-useful programs. Our neural network then automatically refines this corpus based on measures of its own success by locating alternative implementations of each program which proved to be higher-ranked in the neural network's own prediction. Together, this technique is able to locate up to 60% of our human useful target programs (which include the synthesis of looping and conditional branch statements) – none of which appeared in the training data.

Our future work will proceed in two main directions: firstly to further explore how initial corpus generation can be easily directed by non-experts when a particular I/O example cannot be synthesised; and secondly to expand the range of program types that we can synthesise to include those that feature function composition and object instantiation/use. We also intend to further investigate the properties of the neural network itself, to explore how well it generalises in its recognition capabilities to I/O examples of different lengths to those in training, and how the effects of automatic corpus refactoring may be further exploited.

Acknowledgements. This work was supported by the Leverhulme Trust Research Project Grant *The Emergent Data Centre*, RPG-2017-166.

References

1. Balog, M., et al.: Deepcoder: Learning To Write Programs. ICLR (2017)
2. Chen, X., et al.: Towards synthesizing complex programs from input-output examples. ICLR, pp. 1–31 (2017)
3. Dabhi, V.K., Chaudhary, S.: Empirical modeling using genetic programming: a survey of issues and approaches. Nat. Comput. **14**(2), 303–330 (2015)
4. Feng, Y., et al.: Program synthesis using conflict-driven learning, pp. 420–435 (2017)
5. Feser, J.K., Chaudhuri, S., Dillig, I.: Synthesizing data structure transformations from input-output examples. In: Proceedings of the 36th ACM SIGPLAN Conference on Programming Language Design and Implementation. PLDI 2015, pp. 229–239 (2015)
6. Graves, A., et al.: Neural turing machines. CoRR, pp. 1–26 (2014)

7. Graves, A., et al.: Hybrid computing using a neural network with dynamic external memory. Nature **538**(7626), 471–476 (2016)
8. Gulwani, S.: Automating string processing in spreadsheets using input-output examples. In: ACM SIGPLAN Notices, vol. 46, no. (1), p. 317 (2011)
9. Hinton, G., Vinyals, O., Dean, J.: Distilling the knowledge in a neural network, pp. 1–9 (2015). http://arxiv.org/abs/1503.02531
10. Kaiser, L., Sutskever, I.: Neural GPUs Learn Algorithms. ICLR, pp. 1–9 (2015)
11. Kawaguchi, K., Bengio, Y.: Depth with nonlinearity creates no bad local minima in ResNets, pp. 1–14 (2018)
12. Petke, J., et al.: Genetic improvement of software: a comprehensive survey. IEEE Trans. Evol. Comput. **22**(3), 415–432 (2018)
13. Renzullo, J., et al.: Neutrality and epistasis in program space, Gi, pp. 1–8 (2018)
14. Vijayakumar, A., et al.: Neural-guided deductive search for real-time program synthesis from examples. ICLR (2018)
15. Wu, S., Zhong, S., Liu, Y.: Deep residual learning for image steganalysis. Multimedia Tools Appl. **77**(9), 10437–10453 (2017)
16. Yampolskiy, R.V.: Why we do not evolve software? Analysis of evolutionary algorithms. Evol. Bioinform. Online **14**(1), 1176934318815906 (2018)

A Search-Based Approach to Generate MC/DC Test Data for OCL Constraints

Hassan Sartaj[1,2]([✉]) [iD], Muhammad Zohaib Iqbal[1,2], Atif Aftab Ahmed Jilani[1,2], and Muhammad Uzair Khan[1,2]

[1] Quest Lab, National University of Computer and Emerging Sciences, Islamabad, Pakistan
{hassan.sartaj,zohaib.iqbal,atif.jilani,uzair.khan}@questlab.pk
[2] UAV Dependability Lab, National Center of Robotics and Automation (NCRA), Islamabad, Pakistan

Abstract. Automated generation of test data is an important and challenging activity in Model-based Testing. This typically requires solving of constraints, written in Object Constraint Language (OCL), specified on models in order to obtain solutions that can be used as test data. Test data generation techniques in the literature discuss various coverage criteria for test generation to achieve a sufficient level of coverage. One of the recommended criteria is modified condition/decision coverage (MC/DC) that is a requirement of different safety standards, such as DO-178C. In this paper, we propose a search-based strategy that utilizes case-based reasoning (CBR) to reuse the already generated test data and generate new test data that provides MC/DC coverage of OCL constraints. To evaluate the performance of the proposed approach in solving MC/DC constraints, we perform an empirical evaluation using AVM without CBR, AVM with CBR, and use Random Search (RS) as a baseline for comparison. We use 84 OCL constraints from four case studies belonging to different domains with varying size and complexity. The experimental results show that our proposed strategy of reusing already generated test data is better as compared to generating test data without using previous test data.

Keywords: SBSE · Model-based testing · MC/DC · OCL · Test data generation

1 Introduction

Model-based Testing (MBT) allows complete automation of software testing activities and is being applied for scalable testing of industrial applications [29]. In such testing, models of the system or its context are typically used to automatically generate test cases and test data for the system under test (SUT). The model-based test data generation strategies focus on the generation of data by solving the various constraints (e.g., guards) on the models or solving the

© Springer Nature Switzerland AG 2019
S. Nejati and G. Gay (Eds.): SSBSE 2019, LNCS 11664, pp. 105–120, 2019.
https://doi.org/10.1007/978-3-030-27455-9_8

corresponding invariants. Object Constraint Language (OCL) [22] is the OMG standard for specifying constraints and invariants on models and is being widely used [4]. The current state-of-the-art in generating test data corresponding to OCL constraints for model-based testing is by using search-based strategies (e.g., in [2,3]).

This paper reports some of the work that we are doing with our industry partner, who is a large avionics systems developer. A major objective in developing such systems is to comply with the international safety standard of DO-178C [11], which is the prevailing standard for avionics systems. Around seventy percent of the overall objectives of DO-178C focus on verification. As per DO-178C, an important consideration for the highest critical level avionics application is to test the application based on the Modified Condition/Decision Coverage (MC/DC) criterion. The MC/DC criterion subsumes a number of other structural coverage criteria (including statement coverage, branch coverage, and condition coverage) and is considered as one of the most stringent coverage criteria to achieve. Empirical evidence from previous studies also suggests that the MC/DC criterion is more effective in terms of fault detection than other structural coverage criteria [33,34].

When using MBT for testing of avionics systems, a major challenge being faced is the automated generation of test data corresponding to MC/DC criterion [28]. The current OCL test data generation strategies are focusing on generating *one* solution corresponding to a constraint. However, for MC/DC coverage, a number of solutions are required to cover the OCL constraint. For example, consider the OCL constraint shown in Listing 1.1, To obtain MC/DC coverage we need to solve the combinations of true and false values that are required to achieve the MC/DC criterion.

An obvious strategy to obtain MC/DC coverage is to refactor the OCL constraints and re-execute the OCL data generator for each of the refactored constraints. Automated solving of non-trivial OCL constraints written for industry systems is a time-consuming task. For instance, it can take up to 15 min to solve a constraint. With hundreds of constraints in a reasonably sized system, the cost of generating test data for MC/DC using such a strategy gets very high [17].

In this paper, we propose a search-based strategy that utilizes case-based reasoning (CBR) [19] to reuse the already generated test data and generate new test data that provides MC/DC coverage of OCL constraints. The strategy defines the OCL constraints reformulation for MC/DC criterion and then applies the CBR concept in Alternating Variable Method algorithm (AVMc) to reuse the previous solution. To assess the proposed approach, we perform an empirical evaluation of 84 OCL constraints from four case studies varying in nature and size. One of the case studies is an industrial case study of a Ground Control Station for an Unmanned Aerial Vehicle. The other two case studies, EU Rental [12] and the Royal and Loyal [31] are widely referred in OCL literature and are considered as academic benchmarks. The fourth case study is a subset of UML meta-model for State Machines [23]. For the experiment, we compare AVMo with AVMc and use Random Search (RS) as a baseline for comparison.

The experimental results show that AVMc performs significantly better when compared with the original AVMo in terms of the ability to efficiently solve OCL constraints. To summarize, the main contributions of this paper are:

- We propose a search-based strategy that uses existing test data to generate new test data corresponding to the MC/DC criterion.
- We devise a strategy for reformulating OCL constraints in order to achieve the MC/DC criterion, especially dealing with negations of OCL expressions involving collections.
- We conduct an extensive empirical evaluation consisting of 84 OCL constraints from four case studies varying in nature and size.

The remaining portion of this paper is organized as follows: Sect. 2 presents our proposed strategy to include MC/DC criterion in OCL test data generation approach, Sect. 3 provides the empirical evaluation. Section 4 provides related work, and Sect. 5 concludes the paper.

2   Strategy to Achieve the MC/DC Criterion

To generate test data according to the MC/DC criterion, multiple solutions are required corresponding to a constraint. For example, consider a constraint as an expression $C = p \vee q$, where p and q are the clauses of the constraint. There are four combinations of possible outcomes, two each for p and q (TT, TF, FF, FT). The idea of the MC/DC is to select the subset of all possible combinations that have a direct impact on the outcome value of the entire constraint. In the case of C, these combinations are (FF, TF, FT). To identify this subset, the first step is to reformulate the original constraint in order to obtain more constraints that satisfy the MC/DC criterion. During reformulation, a special consideration needs to be given to negation of expressions involving OCL collections and handling negation of logical expressions. The final step is to apply the concept of case-based reasoning to optimize the process of constraint solving for MC/DC criterion. Following, we further discuss these steps of our proposed strategy.

Listing 1.1. OCL constraint on Account class

```
context Account inv: self.accountNumber.oclIsUndefined()=false and
                     (self.isActive=true or self.balance<1000)
```

2.1   OCL Constraint Reformulation for MC/DC

To reformulate an OCL constraint for MC/DC, we first identify the truth value combinations that are required for MC/DC coverage of a given OCL constraint. For this purpose, we use the pair-table approach as suggested by Chilenski and Miller [10]. For example, consider the OCL constraint on a class *Account* shown in Listing 1.1. For simplicity, we transform the predicate of the constraint to an equivalent Boolean form by assigning each clause a unique identifier. In this example, the resultant Boolean expression is $p \wedge (q \vee r)$.

Table 1. Example pair table

#	pqr	Res	p	q	r
1	TTT	T	5		
2	TTF	T	6	4	
3	TFT	T	7		4
4	TFF	F		2	3
5	FTT	F	1		
6	FTF	F	2		
7	FFT	F	3		
8	FFF	F			

Table 2. Negation of collection operations

#	Collection operation	Negation
1	$forAll(p)$	$exists(not\ p)$
2	$exists(p)$	$forAll(not\ p)$
3	$one(p)$	$select(p) \rightarrow size() <> 1$
4	$includes(N)$	$excludes(N)$
5	$select(p)$	$select(not\ p)\ or\ reject(p)$
6	$select(p) \rightarrow isEmpty()$	$select(p) \rightarrow notEmpty()$
7	$reject(p) \rightarrow isEmpty()$	$reject(p) \rightarrow notEmpty()$
8	$select(p) \rightarrow size() = C$	$select(p) \rightarrow size() <> C$
9	$select(p) \rightarrow size() < C$	$select(p) \rightarrow size() >= C$
10	$select(p) \rightarrow size() > C$	$select(p) \rightarrow size() <= C$

The pair table provides a number of potential pairs for each clause and we need to select minimum subsets of pairs that cover all clauses. The minimum subsets of pairs that cover all required combinations for the given example are $\{2, 6\}$, $\{2, 4\}$, and $\{3, 4\}$ as shown in Table 1. These pairs represent the combinations TTF, TFT, TFF, and FTF. To achieve MC/DC, the given predicate in a constraint has to be solved so that all the truth combinations contained in the minimum subset are solved. Therefore, for each false value of the combination, a clause in the given predicate is negated. For example, to satisfy the combination TTF for a constraint $p \wedge (q \vee r)$, the constraint provided to the solver is reformulated with a negated r, i.e. $p \wedge (q \vee \neg r)$.

2.2 Handling Negation for OCL

OCL constraints consist of different types of clauses i.e., the clauses using relational operators and the clauses using OCL collection operations. The negation of relational operators is done by either adding *not* operation or simply inverting the relational operator e.g., $<$ is converted to $>=$. The negation of various OCL collection operations is not straightforward because their negation affects a subset or whole collection. To negate *forAll(p)* we need to make predicate (i.e., p) false for the whole collection and change this operation to *exists(not p)* as shown in Table 2 (row 1). In the case of *exists(p)* operation (row 2), the complete collection must be negated. Thus, *exists(p)* is converted to *forAll(not p)* with the negated predicate. In the case of *one(p)* operation, which requires exactly one instance to satisfy the predicate, it is transformed using *select(p)* with *size()* operation but with size not equal to one (row 3). The negation of *includes(N)* operation is converted to *excludes(N)* and vice versa (row 4). The operation *select(p)* is changed to *select(not p)* or *reject(p)* and vice versa (row 5). Furthermore, *select(p)* and *reject(p)* operations when applied with *isEmpty()* operation, they are negated to *notEmpty()* (row 6 and 7). In the same way, when *select(p)* is used along with *forAll(p)*, *exists(p)* and *one(p)*, their corresponding negations are applied. Moreover, when *size()* operation is used with *select(p)*, which means a specified number of instances within a collection should satisfy the predicate. So in the case of *select(p)* with *size()* operation, the Boolean operation used with *size()* is negated (rows 8–10).

2.3 Logical Operations Reformulation

To obtain the exact truth value as required by the minimum subset from the pair table, only negating a given clause is not sufficient as the solver may still skip solving the required clause. This is because the existing heuristics for some logical operations such as *or*, *xor*, and *implies* are developed to optimize the search in a way that they favor solving of the 'easiest' clause. For example, for the predicate "*A* or *B*", the heuristic to calculate the branch distance (as discussed in [2]) is: If $(d(A) <= d(B))$ then solve *A* otherwise solve the *B* clause. Even if the clause *B* is negated, the generated test data may not solve clause *B* because the negation of a clause may make it even harder to solve. The heuristics for *xor* and *implies* also suggest the same. To make sure that the resultant test data contains values corresponding to each required combination of MC/DC, our strategy performs a second pass to reformulate the constraint.

In the case of 'or' operator, the strategy changes this operator to 'and' operator between the negated clauses. For the case of 'implies' operator, first, a logically equivalent expression containing the basic operators (i.e. *and*, *or* and *not*) is obtained and then 'or' operator is converted to 'and' operator. For example, *a* implies *b* is converted to a logically equivalent expression which is: *not* (*a*) or *b*.

Listing 1.2. MC/DC constraints

```
C1: context Account inv: self.accountNumber.oclIsUndefined()=false and
                (self.isActive=true and self.balance>=1000)         --TTF
C2: context Account inv: self.accountNumber.oclIsUndefined()=false and
                (self.isActive=false and self.balance<1000)         --TFT
C3: context Account inv: self.accountNumber.oclIsUndefined()=false and
                (self.isActive=false and self.balance>=1000)        --TFF
C4: context Account inv: self.accountNumber.oclIsUndefined()=true and
                (self.isActive=true and self.balance>=1000)         --FTF
```

Similarly, in the case of 'xor' operator, it is also transformed to its logically equivalent expression and then the conversion from 'or' to 'and' operator is performed. For example, *a* xor *b* is converted to logically equivalent expression which is: (*a* or *b*) and *not* (*a* and *b*). For the example predicate shown in Listing 1.1, the conversion corresponding to the four required combinations (i.e., TTF, TFT, TFF, and FTF) that results in the MC/DC constraints to be solved by the OCL solver as shown in Listing 1.2. The MC/DC constraint C1 in Listing 1.2 corresponding to the combination TTF has the third clause negated and transformed logical operator (i.e., or → and). In the same way, the constraints C2, C3, and C4 are obtained after applying MC/DC.

2.4 Applying Case-Based Reasoning

To solve MC/DC constraints, we adapt the concept of case-based reasoning (CBR) [19]. We apply CBR in the context of MC/DC constraints to reuse the previous solution. CBR provides a well-suited mechanism to reuse solutions to previously solved problems while solving a current problem that is similar to the already solved problems.

To apply the concept of CBR in the context of OCL constraints, we define some terminologies. Let $C = \{C_1, C_2, C_3, \ldots, C_n\}$ be the collection of MC/DC constraints to solve and all previously solved solutions in repository are: $S = \{S_1, S_2, S_3, \ldots, S_{n-1}\}$, where n is the number of OCL constraints. When the constraint C_1 is solved, its solution S_1 is stored in a repository for future use. Therefore, the size of the solutions repository is one less than the total size of MC/DC constraints. To store a solution in the repository, a constraint, a predicate and the resultant data (solution) of the constraint is required. A solution is represented as a tuple: $S_k = (C_k, P_k, data)$. Let $P_s = \{P_{s_1}, P_{s_2}, P_{s_3}, \ldots, P_{s_{n-1}}\}$ be the list of predicates of OCL constraints corresponding to each solution in the repository. Each predicate in the repository has multiple clauses and it is represented as $P_{s_i} = \{c_{s_1}, c_{s_2}, c_{s_3}, \ldots, c_{s_m}\}$. For the current constraint to solve, the target predicate is represented as $P_t = \{c_{t_1}, c_{t_2}, c_{t_3}, \ldots, c_{t_m}\}$, where m is the total number of clauses in a predicate.

To identify the suitable previous solution to reuse, the similarity must be measured between the target predicate and already solved predicate. The similarity score between the two predicates is calculated by using Eq. 1. Where, $d\left(c_{t_j}, c_{s_{ij}}\right)$ is the similarity score between target clauses and a clause from the repository. The higher the similarity score between the two predicates the more the solution corresponding to the predicate is suitable to reuse. Since a predicate has a number of clauses, the similarity score between the two clauses is calculated by using Eq. 2.

$$d\left(P_t,\ P_{s_i}\right) = \sum_{j=1}^{m} d\left(c_{t_j},\ c_{s_{ij}}\right) \tag{1}$$

$$d\left(c_{t_j},\ c_{s_{ij}}\right) = \begin{cases} 1, & c_{t_j} = c_{s_{ij}} \\ 0, & c_{t_j} \neq c_{s_{ij}} \end{cases} \tag{2}$$

According to Eq. 2, if the two clauses are the same, the similarity score between them is 1 and 0 otherwise. For the example MC/DC constraints shown in Listing 1.2, the similarity score between constraints C3 and C4 is one because the third clause is the same. After calculating the similarity score of each solution in the repository, the possible set of closest solutions are obtained.

Reusing Previous Solution. Typically, a local search algorithm starts the search by using a random individual. To optimize search for reusing the closest previously solved solution, the initial seed needs to change. Once a set of possible closest and already solved solutions is obtained, we need to pick one nearest solution as an individual to start the search.

Let $N_s = \{N_{s_1}, N_{s_2}, N_{s_3}, \ldots, N_{s_x}\}$ be the list of nearest possible solutions having size x that are obtained after calculating the similarity score. It is possible that two or more nearest solutions in N_s have the same similarity score and in that case, the problem is which one to select. To handle this problem, we need to calculate the fitness of each nearest solution and then select the solution with minimum fitness. We use the fitness function developed by Ali et al. [3] to solve the OCL constraints. The fitness function determines how far the solution of the constraint is from evaluating to *true*. For example, if for the constraint is C: $x > 0$, there are two potential candidate solutions i.e., S_1: $x = -125$ and S_2: $x = 0$, the solution S_2 is less far from satisfying C as compared to S_1. Therefore, the fitness of S_2 is better than that of S_1. because it is very close to evaluate the constraint C to *true*. The fitness of each nearest solution in N_s corresponding to the target constraint is $f_{s_n} = \{f_{s_1}, f_{s_2}, f_{s_3}, \ldots, f_{s_x}\}$. Let S_c be the closest solution from the set N_s with minimum fitness f_{s_c} which is calculated as $f_{s_c} = \min(f_{s_n})$. Now, according to the original behavior of a local search algorithm, a random individual is generated. Let S_r be a random individual with fitness f_{s_r}. The target closest solution is obtained by using Eq. 3.

$$S_T = \begin{cases} S_c, & f_{s_c} < f_{s_r} \\ S_r, & f_{s_c} \geq f_{s_r} \end{cases} \tag{3}$$

According to Eq. 3, if the fitness f_{s_c} of the closest previous solution S_c from N_s is less than that of the random solution S_r, the solution S_c is selected. Otherwise, the search is started from a random solution S_r. Since it is possible that an individual generated randomly can be a suitable option to start the search, so we also check the fitness of a random individual.

2.5   Identifying Conflicting Constraints

The combinations obtained for MC/DC are not always solvable and are, at times, infeasible [26]. For example, if the required combination is FF for the constraint, $x \geq 10$ or $x \leq 25$, it is considered as an infeasible combination to solve. Conflict can occur in those constraints in which two or more clauses containing primitive type attribute are dependent. We consider a clause as a dependent if the same attribute is used in multiple clauses. For example, the two clauses in the predicate $x \geq 10$ or $x \leq 25$ are dependent because the same attribute 'x' is used in both clauses.

Therefore, first, a conflict is identified by analyzing dependency among clauses. If two or more clauses are dependent, fitness values are examined after a certain number of fitness evaluations. We set the number of fitness evaluations to 1000, which is half of the total search budget. If a constraint is non-conflicting regardless of the complexity, its fitness should improve as the search proceed. If fitness does not improve after a specified number of fitness evaluations, the constraint is marked as a conflicting constraint and the search process is stopped for this constraint. Finally, we also manually inspect the conflicting constraint for confirmation.

3   Empirical Evaluation

In this section, we present the empirical evaluation of our proposed approach. The main objective is to evaluate the performance of our proposed strategy to use the previous solution in solving MC/DC constraints. For the evaluation, we selected the original version of Alternating Variable Method (AVMo) that solves each constraint individually using Ali et al. [3] approach. We select AVM because the final constraints after MC/DC contain a number of conjunctions, disjunctions, and negations for which AVM has shown better performance than (1+1) EA in the original experiment [2,3]. AVM is a local search algorithm that starts the search by selecting one problem variable and tries to maximize its fitness. When the fitness is improved for the selected variable, the AVM tries to solve the next variable and this process continues until the complete problem is solved or the search budget exceeds. We apply our proposed strategy to reuse the previous solution in AVM and is referred to as AVMc. We use Random Search (RS) as a comparison baseline. Our evaluation addresses the following research question.

RQ1: Is reusing the previous solution to solve constraints (AVMc) better than individual constraints solving (AVMo)?

- **RQ1.1:** Is AVMc better than AVMo in success rates?
- **RQ1.2:** Is AVMc better than AVMo in iteration counts?
- **RQ1.3:** Is AVMc better than AVMo in time to solve OCL constraints?

We primarily evaluate the performance of the algorithms in terms of success rates. In cases where success rates are not sufficient to significantly differentiate between the algorithms, we perform analysis using iteration counts. We also compare algorithms based on the time to solve OCL constraints.

3.1   Experiment Design and Settings

We perform an experiment using four distinct case studies and analyze the results as per the guidelines given in [6]. One case study is industrial that represents a Ground Control Station (GCS) for an Unmanned Aerial Vehicle. Two case studies, EU-Rental [12] and the Royal and Loyal [9,31] are widely referred in OCL literature and are considered as a benchmark. The fourth case study comprises of the OCL constraints used in a subset of UML meta-model for State Machines [23].

In total, there are 402 OCL constraints in all case studies. Out of 402 constraints, we select constraints that have more than one predicate and that produce a Boolean result (a requirement for solving a constraint [3]) for our experiment. This leads to 84 OCL constraints. The included OCL constraints have varying complexity with predicates ranging from two clauses to constraints with seven clauses. Each OCL constraint transforms into multiple constraints when MC/DC criterion is applied.

As search algorithms are random in nature, therefore, we set the number of runs to 100, i.e., each algorithm is executed 100 times for each constraint.

The maximum number of iterations for each run is set to 2000 iterations because it has been used to solve OCL constraints in the previous empirical studies such as Ali et al. [3]. The experiment is executed on 15 independent machines, having at least quad-core 1.2 GHz processors with at least 1 GB RAM, and Linux and Windows operating systems.

To compare success rates (which is a dichotomous data), we apply the Fisher Exact test and calculate the Odds Ratios to check the extent of improvement. In the cases where success rates are not statistically significant, we compare based on the number of iterations a search algorithm takes to solve a constraint. We apply the Wilcoxon test to compare the search algorithms and use Vargha-Delaney $\hat{A}_{12}$ measure [30] to calculate the magnitude of improvement. The significant level is set at 0.05 as per the accepted practice in the domain [2,3].

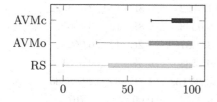

Fig. 1. Success rates for GCS case study

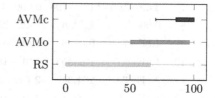

Fig. 2. Success rates for EUR case study

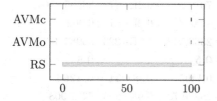

Fig. 3. Success rates for SM case study

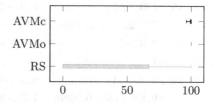

Fig. 4. Success rates for RnL case study

3.2 Results and Analysis

To answer RQ1.1 and RQ1.2, for industrial (GCS) case study, from Fig. 1 we can see that the median success rate achieved by AVMc, AVMo, and RS are 98%, ≈80%, and ≈68% respectively. To analyze the results statistically, we refer to Table 3. In the case of AVMc vs. AVMo, for 24 out of 30 constraints the results are significant (i.e., p-value < 0.05). The results of effect size measure (Odds ratio and $\hat{A}_{12}$) show that for 22 out of 24 constraints AVMc is better than AVMo. When comparing AVMo with RS, the results are significant for 28 out of 30 constraints and for 15 out of 28 AVMo is better than RS. The comparison between AVMc and RS shows that for 27 out of 30 constraints the

Table 3. Statistical results for GCS case study

CN	AVMc vs. AVMo		AVMo vs. RS		AVMc vs. RS	
	p-value	OR/A	p-value	OR/A	p-value	OR/A
1	**0.000012**	**0.3986**	**2.6E−13**	**0.669**	**0.0532**	**0.5444**
2	**0.8449**	**0.4954**	**5.7E−74**	**0.9246**	**1.6E−6**	**0.6116**
3	**0.335**	**0.5225**	**7.9E−33**	**0.7782**	**1.6E−11**	**0.6568**
4	**0.0846**	**0.4599**	7.5E−35	301.2494	7.5E−35	301.2494
5	**0.1764**	**0.4686**	**0.081**	**0.5405**	**0.1232**	**0.4647**
6	0.00018	2.0599	1.7E−29	0.0242	4.4E−15	0.0498
7	3.6E−106	127.4298	0.00012	1.6782	5.8E−140	213.8522
8	0.0043	1.7226	7.4E−27	0.0388	7.8E−16	0.0669
9	1.2E−7	0.0188	9.4E−33	321.8789	1.2E−13	6.0629
10	1.5E−37	10.3353	1.3E−15	0.2588	6.5E−7	2.6751
11	3.1E−33	264.3433	**2.6E−10**	**0.3715**	1.3E−33	267.8885
12	8.4E−29	7.0351	3.4E−16	0.2512	0.0025	1.7676
13	7.6E−26	21.7076	1.3E−15	3.8677	4.3E−70	83.9588
14	9.5E−26	32.1866	3.8E−190	4420.632	1.6E−292	142285
15	1.3E−28	78.7383	8.3E−139	2709.393	4.3E−237	213333
16	4.6E−94	47.4575	1.5E−74	707.692	6.4E−273	33585.276
17	7E−22	3.5238	1.9E−119	0.0007	6.2E−51	0.0023
18	2.5E−24	15.6491	1.1E−131	2363.542	1.9E−223	36987.353
19	**1**	**0.5**	**1**	**0.5**	**1**	**0.5**
20	4.8E−34	6.1659	8.3E−37	0.1495	**0.00031**	**0.4264**
21	**9.1E−196**	**0.9968**	1.3E−295	16220.735	6.9E−293	5397.908
22	0.0112	1.6089	8.4E−35	0.0034	8.1E−24	0.0054
23	**3E−59**	**0.815**	**7.3E−56**	**0.1987**	**0.00028**	**0.5829**
24	9.9E−13	9.8444	0.0026	1.7893	1.3E−23	17.6148
25	**0.1711**	**0.532**	**1E−40**	**0.8128**	**2.4E−11**	**0.6566**
26	0.00015	2.5521	4.1E−8	0.2204	**5E−14**	**0.677**
27	5.2E−30	31.8636	6.6E−28	0.0339	**5.2E−54**	**0.1924**
28	**7.7E−76**	**0.87**	8E−50	441.5571	8E−50	441.5571
29	1.9E−30	224.076	3.3E−14	2.8472	1.6E−72	637.9834
30	**6E−147**	**0.9688**	9.6E−123	1577.4113	9.6E−123	1577.411

[a]Bold text values indicate the results obtained based on the iterations count and when a statistically significant difference is not observed.

Table 4. Overall comparison results for all case studies

CS	AVMc vs AVMo		AVMc vs AVMo (Time)		AVMo vs RS		AVMc vs RS	
	Significant	ES	Significant	ES	Significant	ES	Significant	ES
GCS	24	22	25	12	28	15	27	21
EUR	26	26	29	22	32	31	32	32
SM	10	3	9	5	7	7	9	9
RnL	8	8	8	5	9	9	9	9

[a]Significant results count show the number of times p-value < 0.05 and the effect size (ES) count show the number of times an algorithm is better.

results are significant and for 21 out of 27 AVMc is better than RS based on effect size measure.

Due to space limitation in the paper, we provide a summarized analysis of the results for EUR, SM, and RnL case studies in Table 4. Therefore, we refer to this table for the discussion on the results of these case studies. However, the detailed results are available in an online public repository[1].

For EUR case study, when comparing AVMo with AVMc based on the success rate, we can see from Fig. 2 that the median success rate achieved by AVMc, AVMo, and RS are $\approx$100%, $\approx$65%, and $\approx$10% respectively. In the case of AVMc vs. AVMo, for 26 out of 34 constraints the results are significant (p-value < 0.05) and for all 26 constraints AVMc is better than AVMo based on effect size measure (Table 4). When comparing AVMo with RS, the significant difference is obtained for 32 out of 34 constraints and for 31 out of 32 constraints the effect size suggests that AVMo is better than RS. The comparison between AVMc and RS shows that for 32 out of 34 constraints the results are significant and for all cases, AVMc is better than RS based on effect size measure.

For SM case study, from boxplot in Fig. 3, we see that both AVMo and AVMc are able to achieve a 100% median success rate. In the case of RS, for some constraints, it achieves approximately a 100% success rate and sometimes its success rate is close to zero. Table 4 shows that in the case of AVMc vs. AVMo, for all 10 constraints the results are statistically significant. The effect size measure suggests that for three constraints AVMc is better than AVMo. When comparing AVMo with RS, except for the constraint number 1, 3 and 6, the results are statistically significant and for the remaining seven constraints the effect size shows that AVMo is better than RS. The comparison between AVMc and RS shows that except for the constraint number 1 results are significant and according to effect size AVMc is better than RS for all constraints.

For RnL case study, if we compare search algorithms performance based on success rate, from boxplot in Fig. 4, we can see that both AVMo and AVMc are able to achieve $\approx$100% median success rate. In the case of RS, for some constraints, it achieves $\approx$65% success rate, however, in most cases, the success rate is close to 0. From statistical results presented in Table 4, we can see that for AVMc vs. AVMo, for eight out of 10 constraints the results are statistically

---

[1] https://github.com/hassansartaj/ssbse19

significant. The effect size measure shows that for all eight constraints, AVMc is better than AVMo. When we compare AVMo and AVMc with RS, we can observe that for nine out of 10 constraints, the results are statistically significant and for all nine constraints both AVMc and AVMo are better than RS according to the effect size measure. Based on the above-mentioned discussion on four case studies, we conclude that AVMc outperforms both AVMo and RS based on success rates (RQ1.1) and iteration counts (RQ1.2).

To answer RQ1.3, we compare the time taken by executing AVMc and AVMo on various case studies (as shown in Table 4, column 3). The comparison between AVMc and AVMo for GCS case study shows that for 25 out of 30 constraints the difference between the time taken to solve constraint with AVMc is significantly (p-value < 0.05) better than the time taken to solve constraint with AVMo. For EUR case study, for 29 out of 34 constraints AVMc performs significantly better than AVMo. In the case of the SM case study, for 9 out of 10 constraints AVMc takes significantly lesser time than AVMo. Similarly, for RnL case study, for 8 out of 10 constraints the results are significantly better than AVMo. Moreover, the actual time taken by AVMc including the seed time is less as compared to AVMo. For some constraints AVMc takes approximately half time from a total of AVMo. We report the detailed time analysis results for all case studies at online repository (see Footnote 1). The results include a statistical comparison (p-values and effect size), the total time to solve each constraint and the initial seed selection time for AVMc. Therefore, based on the time analysis, we conclude that reusing the previous solution as the initial seed, as we do in AVMc, improves the performance of constraints solving.

3.3   Threats to Validity

A potential threat to validity is the generalization of the results. To minimize the threat to external validity, for our experiment, we selected four case studies from various domains with different size and complexity. We used 84 OCL constraints from all the case studies. We selected constraints that contain predicate with the number of clauses ranging from two to seven. The selected constraints were representative of various cases with different complexity levels. We compare AVMo using Ali et al. [3] approach with AVMc that uses our proposed strategy to reuse the previous solution. It is not feasible to compare our approach with the approaches that are not targeting OCL constraint solving and constraint coverage, as these cannot be directly applied in our context. The approach by Hemmati et al. [17] is the most relevant approach of MC/DC solving of OCL state machine constraints and uses the (1+1) EA approach of Ali et al. [3]. Our approach is an improved strategy of reusing solutions while solving a constraint for MC/DC. If other strategies of OCL constraint solving evolve, our approach will be applicable to these approaches as well. We do not claim that our results are generalizable for all cases, but this threat is largely common among all empirical studies. Construct validity threat occurs when the relationship between cause and effect cannot be determined. To reduce construct validity threat, we used the same stopping criterion for all algorithms and it was fixed up to 2000 iterations. We also used various measures such as time, success rates, and iteration counts that are considered suitable for the comparison among search algorithms. Conclusion validity threat is related to the effect of treatment on the outcome of results. To reduce conclusion validity threat, we ran each constraint 100 times. Moreover, to measure statistical significance, we used the Fisher exact when comparing based on success rate and Wilcoxon test when the comparison is performed based on iterations count. We also calculate the effect size using the Odds ratio and Vargha-Delaney $\hat{A}_{12}$ measure [30]. Finally, the search algorithms we used in our experiment do not require explicit parameter setting. Therefore, there is no potential threat to the internal validity of our experiment.

4   Related Work

In the work related to code-based approaches, there are approaches that generate test data for different coverage criteria, such as branch coverage [15,16], path coverage [18], and multiple conditions coverage [13] and modified condition/decision coverage (MC/DC) criterion [7,33,34]. Godboley et al. [14] try to enhance MC/DC coverage using code transformation approach. Li et al. [20] uses combinatorial testing to achieve MC/DC and then conducts an empirical evaluation to access the efficiency and effectiveness of MC/DC in terms of faults detection. There are some code-based test case generation approaches that target multiple coverage criteria and use the concept of solutions archiving. Rojas et al. [27] used the concept of solutions archiving to enhance the performance of the whole test suite generation. Panichella et al. [25] proposed an archive-based algorithm (DynaMOSA) to efficiently generate test cases. The major advantage of our approach over the above-mentioned approaches is that the generated test data can be used for the application using any programming language.

In the work related to specification-based approaches, a test data generation approach was proposed that solves constraints [2,3] using search techniques. Moreover, to improve test data generation, a work targeting boundary value analysis was proposed by Ali et al. [5]. There are approaches [1,8,24] that use OCL constraints for generating test data. For solving constraints there are approaches that use Boolean specification [32] and state-based specification [21]. The main limitation of these approaches is that they do not support the MC/DC criterion. Hemmati et al. [17] applied the MC/DC criterion on guard conditions present in the state machine. Their experiment results highlight the limitations of the search budget, search space, and execution time. Whereas our approach significantly improves the performance of MC/DC constraints solving.

5   Conclusion

An important step in the model-based testing of systems is generating test data from constraints written in Object Constraint Language (OCL). The existing test data generation approaches from OCL focus on generating one solution corresponding to a constraint. If a constraint has more than one clauses, there is a possibility that test data is generated corresponding to only a subset of the clauses. Test data generation techniques in the literature discuss various coverage criteria for test generation to achieve a sufficient level of coverage. For safety-critical applications, a commonly used criterion is Modified Condition/Decision Coverage (MC/DC) which requires the coverage of individual clauses of a constraint. The goal of this work is to improve the OCL test data generation by including support for MC/DC criterion. For this purpose, we propose a search-based strategy that utilizes case-based reasoning (CBR) to reuse the already generated test data and generate new test data that provides MC/DC coverage of OCL constraints. To evaluate the performance of the proposed approach in solving MC/DC constraints, we perform an empirical evaluation using AVM without CBR (AVMo), AVM with CBR (AVMc), and use Random Search (RS) as a baseline for comparison. We use 84 OCL constraints from four case studies belonging to different domains with varying size and complexity. The experimental results show that our proposed strategy of reusing already generated test data is better as compared to generating test data without using previous test data.

References

1. Aichernig, B.K., Salas, P.A.P.: Test case generation by OCL mutation and constraint solving. In: Fifth International Conference on Quality Software (QSIC 2005), pp. 64–71. IEEE (2005)
2. Ali, S., Iqbal, M.Z., Khalid, M., Arcuri, A.: Improving the performance of OCL constraint solving with novel heuristics for logical operations: a search-based approach. Empir. Softw. Eng. **21**(6), 2459–2502 (2016)
3. Ali, S., Iqbal, M.Z., Arcuri, A., Briand, L.C.: Generating test data from ocl constraints with search techniques. IEEE Trans. Softw. Eng. **39**(10), 1376–1402 (2013)
4. Ali, S., Yue, T., Zohaib Iqbal, M., Panesar-Walawege, R.K.: Insights on the use of OCL in diverse industrial applications. In: Amyot, D., Fonseca i Casas, P., Mussbacher, G. (eds.) SAM 2014. LNCS, vol. 8769, pp. 223–238. Springer, Cham (2014). https://doi.org/10.1007/978-3-319-11743-0_16
5. Ali, S., Yue, T., Qiu, X., Lu, H.: Generating boundary values from OCL constraints using constraints rewriting and search algorithms. In: 2016 IEEE Congress on Evolutionary Computation (CEC), pp. 379–386. IEEE (2016)
6. Arcuri, A., Briand, L.: A practical guide for using statistical tests to assess randomized algorithms in software engineering. In: 2011 33rd International Conference on Software Engineering (ICSE), pp. 1–10. IEEE (2011)
7. Awedikian, Zeina, K.A., Antoniol, G.: MC/DC automatic test input data generation. In: Proceedings of the 11th Annual Conference on Genetic and Evolutionary Computation, pp. 1657–1664. ACM (2009)
8. Benattou, M., Bruel, J.M., Hameurlain, N.: Generating test data from OCL specification. In: Proceedings of ECOOP Workshop Integration and Transformation of UML Models (2002)
9. Cabot, J.: OCL repository (2014). https://github.com/jcabot/ocl-repository

10. Chilenski, J.J., Miller, S.P.: Applicability of modified condition/decision coverage to software testing. Softw. Eng. J. **9**(5), 193–200 (1994)
11. Ferrell, T., Ferrell, U.: RTCA DO-178C/EUROCAE ED-12C (2017)
12. Frias, L., Queralt Calafat, A., Olivé Ramon, A.: EU-rent car rentals specification (2003). http://hdl.handle.net/2117/97816
13. Ghani, K., Clark, J.A.: Automatic test data generation for multiple condition and MCDC coverage. In: Fourth International Conference on Software Engineering Advances, ICSEA 2009, pp. 152–157. IEEE (2009)
14. Godboley, S., Prashanth, G., Mohapatro, D.P., Majhi, B.: Increase in modified condition/decision coverage using program code transformer. In: 2013 IEEE 3rd International Advance Computing Conference (IACC), pp. 1400–1407. IEEE (2013)
15. Gupta, N., Mathur, A.P., Soffa, M.L.: Automated test data generation using an iterative relaxation method. ACM SIGSOFT Softw. Eng. Notes **23**(6), 231–244 (1998)
16. Gupta, N., Mathur, A.P., Soffa, M.L.: Generating test data for branch coverage. In: Proceedings of the Fifteenth IEEE International Conference on Automated Software Engineering, ASE 2000, pp. 219–227. IEEE (2000)
17. Hemmati, H., Arefin, S.S., Loewen, H.W.: Evaluating specification-level MC/DC criterion in model-based testing of safety critical systems. In: 2018 IEEE/ACM 40th International Conference on Software Engineering: Software Engineering in Practice Track (ICSE-SEIP), pp. 256–265. IEEE (2018)
18. Lakhotia, K., Harman, M., McMinn, P.: A multi-objective approach to search-based test data generation. In: Proceedings of the 9th Annual Conference on Genetic and Evolutionary Computation, pp. 1098–1105. ACM (2007)
19. Leake, D.: Case-Based Reasoning: Experiences. Lessons and Future Directions. MIT Press, Cambridge (1996)
20. Li, D., Hu, L., Gao, R., Wong, W.E., Kuhn, D.R., Kacker, R.N.: Improving MC/DC and fault detection strength using combinatorial testing. In: 2017 IEEE International Conference on Software Quality, Reliability and Security Companion (QRS-C), pp. 297–303. IEEE (2017)
21. Offutt, J., Liu, S., Abdurazik, A., Ammann, P.: Generating test data from state-based specifications. Softw. Test. Verif. Reliab. **13**(1), 25–53 (2003)
22. OMG: Object constraint language specification v2.4. Object Management Group Inc. (2014). http://www.omg.org/spec/OCL/2.4/
23. OMG: UML. unified modeling language specification, version 2.5.1. Object Management Group Inc. (2017). http://www.omg.org/spec/UML/2.5.1/
24. Packevicius, S., Krivickaite, G., Barisas, D., Jasaitis, R., Blazauskas, T., Guogis, E.: Test data generation for complex data types using imprecise model constraints and constraint solving techniques. Inf. Technol. Control. **42**(2), 131–149 (2013)
25. Panichella, A., Kifetew, F.M., Tonella, P.: Automated test case generation as a many-objective optimisation problem with dynamic selection of the targets. IEEE Trans. Softw. Eng. **44**(2), 122–158 (2018)
26. Rajan, A., Whalen, M.W., Heimdahl, M.P.: The effect of program and model structure on MC/DC test adequacy coverage. In: Proceedings of the 30th International Conference on Software Engineering, pp. 161–170. ACM (2008)
27. Rojas, J.M., Vivanti, M., Arcuri, A., Fraser, G.: A detailed investigation of the effectiveness of whole test suite generation. Empir. Softw. Eng. **22**(2), 852–893 (2017)
28. Spitzer, C., Ferrell, U., Ferrell, T.: Digital Avionics Handbook. CRC Press, Boca Raton (2014)

29. Utting, M., Legeard, B.: Practical Model-Based Testing: A Tools Approach. Elsevier, Amsterdam (2010)
30. Vargha, A., Delaney, H.D.: A critique and improvement of the CL common language effect size statistics of McGraw and wong. J. Educ. Behav. Stat. **25**(2), 101–132 (2000)
31. Warmer, J.B., Kleppe, A.G.: The Object Constraint Language: Getting Your Models Ready for MDA. Addison-Wesley Professional, Boston (2003)
32. Weyuker, E., Goradia, T., Singh, A.: Automatically generating test data from a boolean specification. IEEE Trans. Softw. Eng. **20**(5), 353–363 (1994)
33. Woodward, M.R., Hennell, M.A.: On the relationship between two control-flow coverage criteria: all JJ-paths and MCDC. Inf. Softw. Technol. **48**(7), 433–440 (2006)
34. Yu, Y.T., Lau, M.F.: A comparison of MC/DC, mumcut and several other coverage criteria for logical decisions. J. Syst. Softw. **79**(5), 577–590 (2006)

Bio-Inspired Optimization of Test Data Generation for Concurrent Software

Ricardo F. Vilela[1(✉)], Victor H. S. C. Pinto[1], Thelma E. Colanzi[2], and Simone R. S. Souza[1]

[1] Institute of Mathematical and Computer Sciences,
University of São Paulo (ICMC-USP),
Trabalhador São-carlense Avenue, 400 - Center,
São Carlos, SP 13.566-590, Brazil
{ricardovilela,victor.santiago}@usp.br, srocio@icmc.usp.br
[2] Informatics Department, State University of Maringá,
UEM - Av. Colombo, 5790 - Zona 7, Jd. Universitário, Maringá 87020-900, Brazil
thelma@din.uem.br

Abstract. Concurrent software includes a number of key features such as communication, concurrency, and non-determinism, which increase the complexity of software testing. One of the main challenges is the test data generation. Techniques of search-based software can also benefit concurrent software testing. To do so, this paper adopts a bio-inspired approach, called BioConcST, to support the automatic test data generation for concurrent programs. BioConcST uses a Genetic Algorithm (GA) and an evolutionary strategy adapted to accept genetic information from some bad individuals (test data) in order to generate better individuals. Structural testing criteria for concurrent programs are used to guide the evolution of test data generation. An experimental study was carried out to compare BioConcST with an elitist GA strategy (EGA) in terms of adequacy of testing criteria for message-passing and shared-memory programs. Twelve concurrent Java programs were included and the results suggest BioConcST is a promising approach, since in all the testing criteria evaluated, it achieved a better coverage and the effect-size measure was large in most cases.

Keywords: Concurrent software testing · Structural testing · Search-based software testing · Genetic algorithm · Test data generation

1 Introduction

Software testing is an expensive and non-trivial activity which, in general, is carried out on the basis of the tester's experience. In the past, a great effort to systematize this activity was undertaken and different testing techniques, criteria and tools have been proposed [1].

© Springer Nature Switzerland AG 2019
S. Nejati and G. Gay (Eds.): SSBSE 2019, LNCS 11664, pp. 121–136, 2019.
https://doi.org/10.1007/978-3-030-27455-9_9

Concurrent software testing poses new challenges that require specialist strategies to deal with the communication and non-determinism of these programs. The use of the same input in different executions does not guarantee that the program will follow the same sequence of instructions owing to the non-deterministic behavior that makes the testing activity challenging. In addition, concurrent programs may have a significant degree of synchronization among the processes or threads (syncs) and this must be checked during the testing activity. Structural testing criteria were drawn up for concurrent programs, including a test model, coverage criteria and testing tools that address the question of message-passing and shared-memory communication paradigms. These criteria are useful for a manual selection of test data in order to determine the test requirements of the concurrent programs under test (SUT). These test requirements include, for instance, to test all possible syncs, assuring the coverage of specific aspects of concurrent programs and, therefore, contributing to deal with challenges in this software domain. However, the manual analysis of these programs is a complex and error-prone task, even for a tester with exceptional expertise, since non-determinism is a factor that makes this activity hard and time-consuming.

The generation of test data is a problem that involves a large set of choices or decisions. For a traditional program, the input domain can be infinite and different test sets can present good solutions. The same problem happens in the context of concurrent programs adding the necessity of finding a good test set to execute also all possible synchronizations and communications. Hence, test data generation for concurrent program can be treated as an optimization problem to be tackled by search techniques, which might be guided by testing criteria based on features of concurrent programs. Genetic Algorithm (GA) is a meta-heuristic widely used to address the problem of test data generation, because it has a generic form and efficient search mode. Moreover, studies involving automatic test data generation for concurrent programs are still fairly recent [8,20].

This paper proposes a bio-inspired approach, named BioConcST, defined to support the generation of automatic test data for concurrent programs. BioConcST involves employing evolutionary strategies that lead to a dynamic search by avoiding an early convergence in the search space and prevents the generation of test data being restricted to the local maximum. In the context of this work, local maximum represents a region of the program where a large number of test requirements are concentrated, but they are not necessarily the most important for testing purposes. Our approach selects test data where there is a low code coverage (bad candidates) to improve the test set over the generations. The candidates (i.e. the test data) that are able to meet a large number of test requirements (e.g. high code coverage) are not always effective in making the software fail since the faults are usually grouped into specific parts of the program [9]. If the test data go through a particular part of the program, there is a risk that faults will not be revealed. The aim is to identify key test requirements, such as synchronization edges that have not yet been executed, the use of shared variables, and the messages exchanged, which may lead to an improvement in the generation of new individuals by genetically recombining the test data.

To the best of our knowledge, BioConcST is the first approach for the generation of test data for concurrent programs that considers both concurrent communication paradigms (shared-variables and message-passing). BioConcST was evaluated experimentally and compared with an elitist approach that always prioritizes the best individuals in the generations. We analyzed eight testing criteria in twelve programs that use message passing or shared memory in the process/thread communication. In the case of all testing criteria, there is a statistically significant difference between the samples evaluated and BioConcST was superior in all analyses that were conducted.

The paper is structured as follows: Sects. 2 and 3 provide background and related work; Sect. 4 describes the BioConcST approach; Sect. 5 describes an experimental study conducted to evaluate BioConcST and finally, Sect. 6 summarizes the conclusions and makes suggestions for future work.

2   Concurrent Software Testing: Basic Concepts

Concurrent programming provides features that increase the efficiency of the execution time, avoids idle resources, and reduces computational costs [3]. Interaction between the processes/threads takes place through two different activities: communication and synchronization. Communication occurs through the data exchanged and the synchronization establishes an order of execution for the processes/threads, and thus creates the semantics of the application. Shared-variable and message-passing are the concurrent paradigms used for the interaction between processes or threads. When the processes/threads only have separate address spaces, communication and synchronization take place through message-passing. It is assumed that, while waiting for a message, the receiver is already making a logical synchronization with the transmitter. In this study, we examine the exchange of messages by *send/receive* primitives, following the syntax: *send (Message, Receiver Address)* and *receive (Message).*

Concurrent software testing focuses in detect errors related to communication, parallelism, and synchronization. Thus, the testing criteria are defined to find the errors of these categories and also to test sequential aspects. A test model, data flow criteria and a testing tool (ValiPar) for Java concurrent programs with message-passing and shared-memory paradigms are defined in [17]. The family of testing criteria for shared-memory and message-passing [17,18], adhered to in this study, are presented below.

- **all-nodes (AN)**: requires that all nodes (statements) be executed at least once by the test sets.
- **all-edges (AE)**: all edges (control-flow) must be executed at least once by the test sets.
- **all-sync-edges (ASE)**: all synchronization edges (synchronization flow) must be executed at least once by the test sets. These edges denote the synchronization between the threads (or processes) of the program.
- **all-shared-uses (ASU)**: the test sets must execute paths that cover all shared-memory communication associations. Shared-memory communication

association refers to shared-variables and it is defined as a triad formed of a definition point, use point and shared-variable.

- **all-m-uses (AMU)**: test sets must execute paths that cover all message-passing 'communication associations'. Message-passing 'communication association' refers to message-passing and it is defined as a triad formed by the definition point, use point and variable sent in a communication.
- **all-intra-message-uses (AAU)**: test sets must execute paths that cover all intra-m-c-use and intra-m-p-use associations. The purpose of this criterion is to reveal faults in the message-passing communication of different threads of the same process. The intra-m-c-use and intra-m-p-use associations take note of the m-use of data before they have been sent by a message and then the respective c-use (computational use of a variable) and p-use (predicative use of a variable) of the same data, after they have been received by the target thread in the same process.
- **all-inter-message-uses (AEU)**: test sets must execute paths that cover all inter-m-c-use and inter-m-p-use associations. This criterion aims to reveal faults in the message-passing communication of different threads belonging to separate processes. The inter-m-c-use and inter-m-p-use associations include the m-use of data before they have been sent by a message and then the respective c-use and p-use of the same data after they have been received by the target thread, in a separate process.
- **all-uses (AU)**: require that all kinds of data-flow association must be executed at least once by test sets. The purpose of this criterion is to test all possible use of the variables in the program.

3   Search-Based Software Testing for Concurrent Software

Bio-inspired optimization techniques [12], such as GA, are becoming important for several research areas including software testing. When applied to test data generation, GA is usually divided into two categories: (1) coverage-based evaluation function, where the evaluation is performed based on the coverage of each test data; and (2) goal-oriented evaluation function, where the function is specified according to a goal which is usually the coverage of a particular element. These approaches are usually employed for sequential programs [6,14] that only focus on the data flow and/or execution flow of the programs under test. Some related works that have explored bio-inspired techniques in the context of concurrent programs are described next.

Chicano et al. [2] conducted a comparative study that included five metaheuristic algorithms to support the detection of errors in Java concurrent programs. Their main purpose was to evaluate the applicability of space-state search techniques in the context of concurrent software. The results suggest that metaheuristic algorithms are a more effective way of finding safety property violations than the classical, deterministic and 'complete search' algorithms that are generally used in the explicit-state model checking domain. Despite this, the approach uses an expensive technique that may be infeasible for large programs and also does not conduct a dynamic analysis of program execution.

Hrubá et al. [4] adopt a strategy to apply a multi-objective GA to the test-and-noise configuration search problem (TNCS) for multi-threaded programs. According to the authors, this technique is able to provide TNCS solutions that cover a significant number of distinct interleaving schemes and can achieve stable results even with repeated executions. The approach also finds devices to mitigate the influence of non-deterministic factors and extends the search to less common patterns of behavior. The gathered data, prevented the approach from being adversely affected by the degeneration problem and was able to obtain settings of tests and noise that improve the efficiency of the testing process. However, the approach does not take into account the data flow of shared variables and fails to address the problem of message passing programs.

Tian and Gong [20] devised an evolutionary method to test data generation for concurrent programs. GA is used for producing test data that are designed for the coverage of multiple paths, which is caused by message-passing in concurrent programs. Empirical results indicate that the proposed method is more efficient than a random generation. However, the authors removed the factor of non-determinism when applying their approach and, hence, this approach does not cover all aspects of the concurrent applications.

Rojas et al. [13] investigate the effectiveness of whole test suite generation, through search-based techniques, under different perspectives of software testing. A key analysis carried out verifies whether or not whole generating suites could be optimized by only targeting coverage goals not already covered. This hedging strategy can be efficient to prioritize those test data that perform coverage goals not yet achieved. Nevertheless, it cannot be applied to concurrent programs due to non-determinism, because a test data can achieve a coverage goal in a given execution, but it cannot be guaranteed in future executions. This makes it difficult the individual fitness evaluation.

Steenbuck and Fraser [19] proposed a coverage criterion for shared memory programs that enforce concurrent execution of combinations of shared variable access points with different schedules and a search-based approach in test case generation for this coverage criterion. The results were satisfactory for the identification of defects related to data race conditions and deadlocks. However, the approach presents limitations in the detection of the other types of faults, in particular, those related to the data flow of variables of the concurrent programs.

Based on the context presented, we noticed that there is no scientific evidence on how test data generation can be performed for concurrent programs taking into account the main paradigms of communication, message passing and shared memory. In addition, important aspects such as data flow of communication and non-determinism are not explored in the identified studies.

4   BioConcST: Bio-Inspired Optimization for Concurrent Software Testing

Our approach uses GA to create a population of candidate solutions (i.e. a set of test data), guided by a fitness function which uses information from concurrent software testing criteria. In this optimization problem, the best solutions are not necessarily grouped in the same region of the search space. In BioConcST, the search process is dynamic and seeks possible best solutions far from the best current solution. Thus, our search includes mechanisms that seek to extend to a global search, prioritizing individuals with high and low fitness values.

To illustrate this scenario, a program that calculates two methods - Greatest Common Divisor (GCD) and Least Common Multiple (LCM) is utilized. This program calculates these methods from three numbers (x, y, z) by following 4 processes (one master M and three slave processes $(S1, S2, S3)$). M sends the inputs to the slaves to calculate the GCD or LCM value: $S1$ receives the values of x and y; $S2$ receives the values of y and z. $S1$ and $S2$ send the results to process M. $S3$ will only be executed if the returned values do not represent the end result. When this is the case, $S3$ receives the values sent by $S1$ and $S2$ so that it can calculate the end result for GCD or LCM. The input arguments of GCD/LCM program are given as follows: **(i)** the value that defines the method required for computing (0 for GCD or 1 for LCM); **(ii)** the value of x; **(iii)** the value of y; and **(iv)** the value of z.

Suppose the test input $t1 = \{0\ 9\ 18\ 6\}$. A timestamp of this execution (GCD) is illustrated in Fig. 1. This figure shows a space-time diagram in which vertical lines represent the execution of four processes $P0; P1, P2$ and $P3$. The interaction between processes is represented by arrows from a *send event* to a *receive event*, where these interactions represent sync-edges to be covered during the testing activity. This test input must execute 50% of the code statements (coverage for all-sync-edges criterion) to calculate the GCD (because neither all sync-edges are covered). On the other hand, if the input test $t2 = \{1\ 5\ 5\ 5\}$ for the calculation of the LCM, it does not execute the $S3$ process, since the value returned from the $S1$ and $S2$ slaves are enough to obtain the final result (Fig. 1 (LCM)). Therefore, $t2$ has a lower coverage for the all-sync-edges criterion (24.5%) although it is able to cover parts of the code not covered by $t1$. $t1$ appears to be better than $t2$ for the next generations because it is able to achieve greater coverage. However, when only the preliminary best inputs are taken into account and the test inputs with low coverage are ignored, important test information of the program might be overlooked with the risk that it will no longer be discovered in the search space.

An overview of our bio-inspired optimization approach to concurrent software testing is shown in Algorithm 1. The BioConcST algorithm requires as input a concurrent program under test (SUT) and the information about its communication paradigm (message-passing or shared-memory). As output, the program provides an appropriate test set that consists of the selected test data in the optimization process.

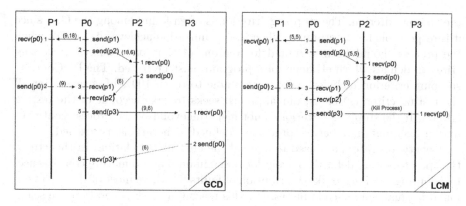

Fig. 1. Timestamp of GCD/LCM program.

Algorithm 1 BioConcST Algorithm

Require: Concurrent program under test **SUT**
Require: Communication paradigm **CP**
Ensure: Optimized Test Suite **TS** $= (td^1, td^2, ..., td^n)$, td : test data

1: **procedure** OPTIMIZETESTSUITE(SUT, CP)
2:      $TS \leftarrow InitializeRandomPopulation$
3:      POPEVALUATION(TS)
4:      **while** StopCondition is not TRUE **do**
5:          $Parents \leftarrow$ SELECTPARENTS(TS, TS_{size})
6:          **for** $P_1, P_2, \in Parents$ **do**
7:              $Ch_1, Ch_2 \leftarrow$ CROSSOVER($P_1, P_2, C_{method}, C_{rate}$)
8:              CHILDREN.PUSH(Ch_1, Ch_2)
9:              CHILDREN.PUSH($Mutation(Ch_1, M_{method}, M_{rate})$)
10:             CHILDREN.PUSH($Mutation(Ch_2, M_{method}, M_{rate})$)
11:         **end for**
12:         POPEVALUATION($Children$)
13:         $TempPOP.Push(GetBestSolution(Children))$
14:         $TempPOP.Push(GetWorstSolution(Children))$
15:         $TempPOP.Push(Tournament(Children))$
16:         $TS \leftarrow$ REPLACE($TS, TempPOP$)
17:     **end while**
18: **return** TS
19: **end procedure**

In the first stage (line 2) a random population of test data is generated, which will be the starting-point for optimizing the problem. The population consists of an individual (or chromosomes) that correspond to the test data (or test inputs) of the program under testing. The test data consists of one or more input parameters, each parameter being regarded as a gene in our approach. For instance, consider a program that has three integer values as input parameters. Each input parameter can be regarded as a gene, and thus the set formed by the three input values makes up a chromosome.

In the next stage (line 3), a 'fitness evaluation' of the population is carried out so that the individuals can be categorized in terms of their ability to achieve a test goal (for instance, a test goal must comply with a specific testing criterion). The stages of the fitness evaluation are described in lines (3–10) of Algorithm 2.

In the optimization process, a stopping criterion for the algorithm must be defined. It is important to note the difference between the stopping criterion and the testing criterion. The stopping criterion is often found among the GAs since it is responsible for determining when the optimization achieves its goal or when the process should be interrupted for reasons of time or resources. A testing criterion defines which elements of a program must be tested. The BioConcST' stopping criterion includes a population able to reach 100% of coverage for all the testing criteria, that is, our approach seeks to take account of the testing criteria. If the stopping criterion is not met, the evolutionary process continues until a maximum number of (previously defined) generations, is reached.

Genetic operators are used to expand the current population. In this study, the operators were defined to avoid local maximum and premature convergence, by adopting the Pareto-like distribution of faults [9] where most of the faults are found in small source-code pieces. For this reason, in each generation, we select the best and the worst solution (or test data), while the rest of the individuals are selected by tournament.

To broaden the search for individuals, two types of genetic operators are used for recombination (C_{method}). When two individuals are selected for recombination, following a rate value (C_{rate}), a random method defines which one will be used for recombination. The purpose of this strategy is to make the search more dynamic during the generations. The first recombination method is the single-point crossover, whereby after recombination, two new child individuals are generated. In the second method, a random value is chosen for each parent (range of 0 to 1), and then a chromosome gene is randomly selected and modified (Eq. 1). This method can allow greater diversity in the search, since it accepts a small degree of randomness in the process of recombination, unlike the first method. The mutation also occurs by means of different operators (M_{method}), following a previously defined rate (M_{rate}). In the former, a gene is selected and a random value is redefined for that gene. Another type selects two genes in the same chromosome and thus inverts the values between the genes.

$$Gene = \alpha * Parent_1 + (1 - \alpha) * Parent_2 \qquad (1)$$

A child population is generated from the genetic operators and a fitness assessment is necessary to measure the aptitude of the new individuals. Following this, the best and worst individuals of this population are selected to form the new generation, and the other individuals are selected by tournament. As a result, the optimization process is iterated until the stopping criterion is reached. An optimized test set is obtained after the generation cycles.

The evaluation of individuals in our context defines the suitability of a test input regarding the elements achieved by this test data. The method used to evaluate individuals from a population is shown in Algorithm 2.

Algorithm 2 Population Evaluation

Require: Population of individuals TS

```
 1: procedure POPEVALUATION(TS)
 2:     for each test data td do
 3:         InstFile ← VALIPAR INST(SUT)
 4:         ElemReqList ← VALIPAR ELEM(InstFile)
 5:         for execution ← 0; execution <10; do
 6:             TraceFile ← VALIPAR EXEC(td, InstFile)
 7:             Increment(execution)
 8:         end for
 9:         Coverage ← VALIPAR EVAL(TraceFile, ElemReqList)
10:         Fitness_td ← FITNESSFUNCTION(Coverage, CP)
11:         FitnessPop ← Fitness_td
12:     end for
13: return FitnessPop
14: end procedure
```

Since the fitness assessment of each individual depends on the type of communication paradigm of the SUT, we define two fitness functions based on the testing criteria pertaining to the communication paradigm. The fitness function is formed of other functions that determine the coverage of each testing criterion, as shown in Eq. 2, where TC represents the testing criterion. Every criterion follows the same function structure. The dividend of the fraction is formed of the covered elements of the TC, such that "i" represents one of the executions from the test data. Each test data is executed ten times so that different synchronization sequences can be identified and the effects of non-determinism reduced. In this way, the sum of all different elements identified during the runs is obtained. In turn, the fraction divisor comprises the total number of elements required for a program. Certain criteria are more powerful in terms of strength and for this reason, they should be given priority during the software testing. Additionally, the value obtained in Eq. 2 is standardized according to its corresponding weight. The weights were defined according to the strength of each criterion [7]. Table 1 shows the weights defined for each testing criteria in accordance with the communication paradigms.

$$f(TC) = \left(\sum_{i=1}^{10} \frac{CoveredElements^i}{TotalElements} \right) \times Weight_{TC} \qquad (2)$$

Table 1. Normalization of criteria weight.

	Criteria weight							
	AN	AE	AU	AEU	AAU	ASE	AMU	ASU
Message passing	5	5	30	15	15	15	15	-
Shared memory	10	10	40	-	-	20	-	20

The fitness value of an individual is made up of all included criteria. Equation 3 shows the fitness function for the testing criteria of message-passing programs, in which the following testing criteria are covered: all-nodes (AN), all-edges (AE), all-uses (AU), all-inter-message-uses (AEU), all-intra-message-uses (AAU), all-sync-edges (ASE), and all-m-uses (AMU). A fitness function has also been established for the testing criteria for shared-memory programs (Eq. 4), and the following testing criteria are included: all-nodes (AN), all-edges (AE), all-uses (AU), all-sync-edges (ASE), and all-shared-uses (ASU).

$$Fitness_{MP} = f(AN)+f(AE)+f(AU)+f(AEU)+f(AAU)+f(ASE)+f(AMU) \tag{3}$$

$$Fitness_{SM} = f(AN) + f(AE) + f(AU) + f(ASE) + f(ASU) \tag{4}$$

Some functionalities from the ValiPar testing tool [11] are employed in Algorithm 2 to obtain information about the test, such as: testing requirements, testing execution and evaluation. Each test data is run ten times to reduce the effects of non-determinism and to execute separate synchronization edges. While not ensuring that all edges will be covered, this provides more information about the test and greater reliability for the fitness evaluation.

5   Experimental Evaluation

An experimental study was conducted to evaluate our approach in terms of testing adequacy criteria. Concurrent programs that use message passing and shared variable paradigms were subjected to BioConcST and the Elitist Genetic Algorithm (EGA). Our choice was based on the contrast between the approaches. While the former allows some worse individuals to survive through the generations, the latter does not do it. With this in mind, our objective was to investigate whether the assurance of recombination of those individuals contributes to the selection of the test set in concurrent programs [16]. The results of these approaches were compared in the same conditions with the aim of determining whether BioConcST is more efficient and effective than EGA in providing coverage with regard to the testing criteria required for concurrent software.

We began by formulating the H hypothesis: BioConcST reaches coverage above the EGA, relative to the adequacy of concurrent testing criteria. We evaluated H for each test criterion in relation to the programs under test. With the null hypothesis the test sets of BioConcST reach a coverage equal to EGA. The following hypotheses were defined on the basis of each communication paradigm.

Null hypothesis (H_0): There is no difference, between the test sets of BioConcST and EGA, with regard to the coverage of the testing criteria ($H_0 : BioConcST = EGA$).

Alternative hypothesis (H_1): There is a difference between the test sets of BioConcST and EGA, with regard to the coverage of the testing criteria ($H_1 : BioConcST \neq EGA$).

5.1   Study Subjects: Concurrent Programs

The subjects were extracted from the TestPar[1] benchmark making a total of 12 java concurrent programs (Table 2). The table includes some features of the subjects. Some programs such as Greatest Common Divider (GCD) and Token Ring have different versions since they have different implementation features. The second column displays the communication paradigm (Par.) adopted by each subject: Message Passing (MP) or Shared Memory (SM). The third column shows the number of processes (Pr) and the number of threads (Th). The fourth column shows the number of synchronization edges (Sync-edges) for each program. The number of definitions (Defs) is shown in the fifth column. The required c-use and p-use elements are listed in the sixth column, while the intra-m-uses and inter-m-uses elements are arranged in the seventh column. Finally, the uses of shared variables (s-uses) are given in the eighth column. Note that the message passing programs do not have shared variables, and shared memory programs do not have intra/inter message uses.

Table 2. Concurrent programs selected for the experimental study

Program	Par.	Pr/Th	Sync-edges	Defs.	c-uses/p-uses	Intra/inter-m-uses	s-uses
GCD 1	MP	4/4	33	229	412/54	95/195	-
GCD 2	MP	3/3	16	159	238/54	40/80	-
GCD/LCM	MP	4/3	57	434	676/208	128/384	-
Token Ring 1	MP	4/4	12	238	302/88	8/24	-
Token Ring 2	MP	4/4	12	281	314/72	21/63	-
Token Ring 3	MP	4/4	51	285	388/128	236/726	-
Eratosthenes	MP	4/4	15	380	541/174	6/42	-
Roller Coaster	MP	6/6	206	530	1236/86	1088/4372	-
Producer Consumer	SM	1/5	20	158	226/92	-/-	36140
Cigarette Smokers	SM	1/5	42	59	92/48	-/-	5136
Matrix	SM	1/13	192	552	484/24	-/-	127152
Jacobi	SM	1/5	532	364	967/160	-/-	277092

5.2   Experimental Setup

In the configuration of the algorithms, the same parameters were defined for both systems and there was an attempt to make a fair evaluation between them (except the selection method because they are specifically designed for each approach). In a previous study [21], we conducted a systematic mapping study to find evidence about the configuration of GA parameters for test data generation and a suggestion of parameters configuration was done. We use this suggestion to define the initial configuration of the experiment. Pilot experiments were

---

[1] http://testpar.icmc.usp.br/benchmarks.

performed to calibrate the algorithms using parameter values adopted in the literature. The population size was fixed to a higher than the required value provided by the benchmark documentation. The number of executions was set to obtain a significant sample of analyzes, taking into account that each SUT is executed at least a thousand times. The number of generations as well as mutation and crossover probabilities were set up after an algorithm convergence analysis. Hence, these parameter values have been defined after the identification of fitness stability. The settings are shown in Table 3.

Table 3. Experimental configuration

	BioConcST	EGA
Number of generations	10	10
Runs/executions	10	10
Population size	10	10
Mutation probability	0.3	0.3
Crossover probability	0.7	0.7
Selection method	Tournament	Elitism

The activities involved in the experiment were carried out by a virtual machine in an isolated way, without the interference of other processes that could affect the results. The settings of the virtual machine are as follows: **(i)** Processor: Quad-core; **(ii)** Memory: 8 GB RAM; **(iii)** Operating System: Ubuntu 14.04.1 LTS; and **(iv)** JavaRuntime Edition: build 1.7.0 71b14.

5.3   Analysis of Results

In our analysis of the adequacy of testing criteria, we conducted normality tests in our samples to determine the distribution of the data and define an adequate statistical mean test. The Shapiro-Wilk test was employed for the normality test and this resulted in a p-value greater than 0.05, which suggests that our sample does not have a normal distribution pattern. For this reason, we opted for a Kruskal-Wallis non-parametric mean test. In addition, we applied the Bonferroni multiple comparison tests, which allow the samples to be divided into groups when there is a significant statistical difference.

Figure 2 shows the results obtained by BioConcST and EGA with regard the coverage of the testing criteria. Figure 2-A shows the results of coverage for shared-memory programs. The analysis found significant differences between all the evaluated criteria and, therefore, the Null Hypothesis (H_0) can be rejected with regard to the difference between the approaches, where BioConcST shows a better criteria adequacy for this type of paradigm. The results for message-passing programs (Fig. 2-B) also showed a significant difference in all seven of the analyzed testing criteria, with a p-value less than 0.05. Thus, the null hypothesis

(H_0) can be rejected with regard to the equality of coverage of criteria between the approaches investigated. BioConcST achieved better results for message-passing programs.

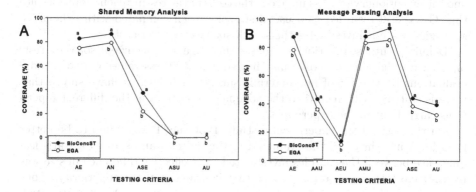

Fig. 2. Coverage for the test set generated by BioConcST and EGA in relation to the testing criteria for shared-memory (A) and message-passing (B). The letters (a) and (b) in the results represent the grouping of the samples, where there is a significant statistical difference when different letters are in the same testing criterion.

The Vargha-Delaney Effect Size measure was used to evaluate the magnitude of the difference estimated by the statistical test. Table 4 shows the results[2] of the effect size and the magnitude levels for all the testing criteria including the message-passing and shared-memory paradigms. The magnitude levels for all the criteria were large, except for ASU which was evaluated as medium. These results corroborate that BioConcST is superior to EGA when assessed by most of the selected criteria for concurrent programs.

Table 4. Gathered data from Vargha-Delaney Effect Size measure

		AN	AE	AU	AEU	AAU	ASE	AMU	ASU
Message passing	**Effect size**	1.0	1.0	1.0	1.0	1.0	1.0	1.0	-
	Mag. level	Large	Large	Large	Large	Large	Large	Large	-
Shared memory	**Effect size**	1.0	1.0	1.0	-	-	1.0	-	0.7
	Mag. level	Large	Large	Large	-	-	Large	-	Medium

5.4   Discussion

Concurrent programs are usually complex and carry out large tasks that involve a high computational cost; for this reason, the testing of these programs is more

---

[2] The experimental package is available in: http://bit.do/eNfts.

complex than when conducted by conventional applications. When a genetic algorithm is adopted, each individual evaluation requires one execution of the program under test, i.e., the costs also mainly depends on the complexity of the program under testing. A large population in GA entails in long execution time and the evolutionary process increases the costs of the testing even more. Despite this, GA is still regarded as a useful strategy when compared with exhaustive strategies, since it investigates the search space at a lower cost.

Defining a fitness function is a major challenge for concurrent software testing, because the same test data may have different fitness values in two or more evaluations as a result of non-determinism. Nevertheless, we have shown that there is stability with regard to the adequacy of criteria in the different repetitions carried out in the experiment.

On the basis of the experimental study, BioConcST was found to be better than EGA in light of all the evaluated testing criteria and showed a statistical difference between the samples investigated. The effective difference in size was high for most of the criteria, a factor that is evidence of the superiority of our approach for message passing and shared memory programs. As we have noted, the control flow criteria are more trivial to cover than the other testing criteria, mainly because these criteria have a lower number of testing requirements. The data flow testing criteria included a large number of test requirements, which created difficulties for both approaches of test data generation.

We believe that most of these data flow elements are not directly linked to the program input, but rather to the synchronization sequence executed by the test input. This problem has already been investigated and can be solved using reachability or model checking techniques [5], but they require a high computational cost caused by expensive of these techniques.

A critical issue that emerged from the results was the low coverage for certain criteria. Although BioConcST is superior, the coverage of test requirements is still low. This became more apparent for the shared-memory testing criteria. The results demonstrated that only providing test data for concurrent testing might not be sufficient and other information is required to meet these test requirements and ensure the test activity can become more optimized.

Regarding threats to validity, the experimental study was performed using only Java programs using paradigms of message exchange and shared memory. These programs are relatively small but have been chosen from existing works in this area and consider the main features of competing programs and therefore we believe that our results can be generalized. Another threat is related to the configuration of genetic algorithms. In this case, we chose to set the default values between the approaches so that the results were not affected by this configuration.

6   Conclusion and Suggestions for Future Work

This paper presents BioConcST, a bio-inspired optimized approach for automatic test data generation for concurrent programs. The approach was evaluated using

12 Java concurrent programs with communication through message-passing and shared-memory. Our study evaluated how a dynamic search through a genetic algorithm can lead to the generation of test data adequate to the concurrent testing criteria. The results show the superiority of our approach to all testing criteria investigated in both communication paradigms. The results showed that the generated test data presented good coverage for the testing criteria. Some critical points should be explored when optimizing this problem. For example, checking other information to be addressed to the test data generation process to improve test coverage, such as similarity between the test run and test requirement not yet achieved; eliminating non-executable test requirements and identifying synchronization sequences not yet achieved from the executions.

Taking into account the need for more empirical studies about test data generation for concurrent software, we intend to investigate the following topics in further research:

- Perform an optimization that is guided by other types of objectives such as paths, synchronization sequences, and faults. Evidence is found that multi-objective search is superior compared to a standard GA for test generation of Java programs [10];
- Compare BioConcST to other methods, for instance Random Search because this method presents good results for test data generation [15]; and
- Develop experimental studies to evaluate the effectiveness for revealing faults of test data generated by BioConcST approach.

Acknowledgement. This study was financed in part by the Coordenação de Aperfeiçoamento de Pessoal de Nível Superior - Brasil (CAPES) - Finance Code 001 and National Council for Scientific and Technological Development (CNPq).

References

1. Bertolino, A.: Software testing research: achievements, challenges, dreams. In: 2007 Future of Software Engineering, FOSE 2007, Washington, DC, USA, pp. 85–103. IEEE Computer Society (2007)
2. Chicano, F., Ferreira, M., Alba, E.: Comparing metaheuristic algorithms for error detection in Java programs. In: Cohen, M.B., Ó Cinnéide, M. (eds.) SSBSE 2011. LNCS, vol. 6956, pp. 82–96. Springer, Heidelberg (2011). https://doi.org/10.1007/978-3-642-23716-4_11
3. Grama, A., Karypis, G., Kumar, V., Gupta, A.: Introduction to Parallel Computing, 2nd edn. Addison-Wesley Longman Publishing Co., Inc., Boston (2003)
4. Hrubá, V., Křena, B., Letko, Z., Pluháčková, H., Vojnar, T.: Multi-objective genetic optimization for noise-based testing of concurrent software. In: Le Goues, C., Yoo, S. (eds.) SSBSE 2014. LNCS, vol. 8636, pp. 107–122. Springer, Cham (2014). https://doi.org/10.1007/978-3-319-09940-8_8
5. Konnov, I., Veith, H., Widder, J.: On the completeness of bounded model checking for threshold-based distributed algorithms: reachability. Inf. Comput. **252**, 95–109 (2017). https://doi.org/10.1016/j.ic.2016.03.006

6. Mairhofer, S., Feldt, R., Torkar, R.: Search-based software testing and test data generation for a dynamic programming language. In: Proceedings of the 13th Annual Conference on Genetic and Evolutionary Computation, GECCO 2011 (2011)

7. Melo, S.M., Souza, S.R.S., Souza, P.S.L.: Structural testing for multithreaded programs: an experimental evaluation of the cost, strength and effectiveness. In: Proceedings of the 24th International Conference on Software Engineering & Knowledge Engineering (SEKE 2012), pp. 476–479 (2012)

8. Nistor, A., Luo, Q., Pradel, M., Gross, T.R., Marinov, D.: Ballerina: automatic generation and clustering of efficient random unit tests for multithreaded code. In: International Conference on Software Engineering (2012)

9. Ostrand, T.J., Weyuker, E.J.: The distribution of faults in a large industrial software system. SIGSOFT Softw. Eng. Notes **27**(4), 55–64 (2002)

10. Panichella, A., Kifetew, F.M., Tonella, P.: Automated test case generation as a many-objective optimisation problem with dynamic selection of the targets. IEEE Trans. Softw. Eng. **44**(2), 122–158 (2018)

11. Prado, R.R., et al.: Extracting static and dynamic structural information from Java concurrent programs for coverage testing. In: Latin American Computing Conference (2015)

12. Rai, D., Tyagi, K.: Bio-inspired optimization techniques: a critical comparative study. SIGSOFT Softw. Eng. Notes **38**(4), 1–7 (2013)

13. Rojas, J.M., Vivanti, M., Arcuri, A., Fraser, G.: A detailed investigation of the effectiveness of whole test suite generation. Empir. Softw. Eng. **22**, 852–893 (2017)

14. Scalabrino, S., Grano, G., Di Nucci, D., Oliveto, R., De Lucia, A.: Search-based testing of procedural programs: iterative single-target or multi-target approach? In: Sarro, F., Deb, K. (eds.) SSBSE 2016. LNCS, vol. 9962, pp. 64–79. Springer, Cham (2016). https://doi.org/10.1007/978-3-319-47106-8_5

15. Shamshiri, S., Rojas, J.M., Fraser, G., McMinn, P.: Random or genetic algorithm search for object-oriented test suite generation? In: Annual Conference on Genetic and Evolutionary Computation (GECCO 2015), pp. 1367–1374 (2015)

16. ShiZhen, ZhouYang, C.T.: Comparison of steady state and elitist selection genetic algorithms. In: Proceedings of International Conference on Intelligent Mechatronics and Automation, pp. 495–499 (2004)

17. Souza, P.S., Souza, S.R., Zaluska, E.: Structural testing for message-passing concurrent programs: an extended test model. Concurr. Comput. **26**, 21–50 (2014)

18. Souza, P.S., Souza, S.S., Rocha, M.G., Prado, R.R., Batista, R.N.: Data flow testing in concurrent programs with message passing and shared memory paradigms. In: Proceedings of the International Conference on Computational Science (2013)

19. Steenbuck, S., Fraser, G.: Generating unit tests for concurrent classes. In: IEEE International Conference on Software Testing, Verification and Validation (2013)

20. Tian, T., Gong, D.: Test data generation for path coverage of message-passing parallel programs based on co-evolutionary genetic algorithms. Autom. Softw. Eng. **23**, 1–32 (2014)

21. Vilela, R.F., Souza, P.S.L., Delamaro, M.E., Souza, S.R.S.: Evidence on the configuration of genetic algorithms for test data generation (portuguese). In: Proceedings of XIX Ibero-American Conference on Software Engineering (2016)

Revisiting Hyper-Parameter Tuning
for Search-Based Test Data Generation

Shayan Zamani[(⊠)] and Hadi Hemmati

Department of Electrical and Computer Engineering,
University of Calgary, Calgary, Canada
{shayan.zamani1,hadi.hemmati}@ucalgary.ca

Abstract. Search-based software testing (SBST) has been studied a lot in the literature, lately. Since, in theory, the performance of meta-heuristic search methods are highly dependent on their parameters, there is a need to study SBST tuning. In this study, we partially replicate a previous paper on SBST tool tuning and revisit some of the claims of that paper. In particular, unlike the previous work, our results show that the tuning impact is very limited to only a small portion of the classes in a project. We also argue the choice of evaluation metric in the previous paper and show that even for the impacted classes by tuning, the practical difference between the best and an average configuration is minor. Finally, we will exhaustively explore the search space of hyper-parameters and show that half of the studied configurations perform the same or better than the baseline paper's default configuration.

Keywords: Search-based software engineering · Test data generation · Hyper-parameter · Tuning · Replication

1 Introduction

Since the early days of search-based software engineering (SBSE), the topic of search-based software testing (SBST) has been continuously studied and improved [20]. There are now several great publicly available SBST tools such as EvoSuite for unit testing Java programs that are continuously being maintained and improved [10]. SBST has even gone far beyond academia and started to be deployed in large scale, e.g., in Facebook [19].

In general, SBST techniques reformulate a test generation problem, e.g., maximizing branch coverage of unit tests, to an objective function and employ a meta-heuristic search technique to optimize the objective. Examples of these meta-heuristic search techniques are hill climbing, simulated annealing, and evolutionary algorithms [17]. Evolutionary Algorithms, like Genetic Algorithm (GA), are among the most common techniques that have been used in SBST, so far. However, there are debates on whether using evolutionary algorithms or keep generation test data with random methods [22].

© Springer Nature Switzerland AG 2019
S. Nejati and G. Gay (Eds.): SSBSE 2019, LNCS 11664, pp. 137–152, 2019.
https://doi.org/10.1007/978-3-030-27455-9_10

A GA starts with a set of initial population to search through the search space. Then it evolves the candidate solutions by permuting the encoded solutions with genetic and natural selection operations [20], in several iterations, until it finds the optimal solution or exhausts the search budget. Therefore, the choice of the objective function, the chromosome encoding format, and GA's input parameters (SBST's hyper-parameters) such as population size, crossover rate, mutation rate, etc. can have a significant impact on the effectiveness of the SBST technique [14]. For instance, it has been illustrated in previous work that the coverage of EvoSuite for a class varies with the values of GA's hyper-parameters [4].

Therefore, finding an optimal configuration of hyper-parameters could potentially, improve the SBST's effectiveness, significantly. In general, there are many parameters to be tuned for a GA. For example, Grefenstette used six parameters to tune its GA, namely, Population Size, Crossover Rate, Mutation Rate, Generation Gap, Scaling Window and Selection Function [16]. However, in another paper, 19 different operators or parameters are listed that contribute in the performance of a given GA and it is suggested that one should take into account the permutation of all these 19 parameters' values [14].

Although the tuning problem is being studied in other areas frequently [5–8], there are not many successful reports of tuning techniques in SBST. Arcuri et al. tried to find a tuned setting for EvoSuite that works better than its default for a collection of classes (SF100). However, the resulting branch coverage after tuning was less than the default configuration's results [4]. Therefore, it is quite important for researchers in the field, as well as practitioner, to know whether tuning is needed before using a SBST technique for test data generation and if so how much improvement a tuning method could potentially bring.

In this paper, we partially replicate Arcuri and Fraser's paper titled "Parameter tuning or default values? An empirical investigation in search-based software engineering", which was published in Empirical Software Engineering journal in 2013 [4]. The paper is one of the very few studies on the hyper-parameter tuning of SBST techniques. It includes three case studies, where the first one focuses on illustrating the impact of tuning. The two other case studies then investigate the effectiveness of a proposed tuning method (which showed no improvement compared to default settings). In our study, we only focus on the impact of tuning, thus only the first case study of their paper (from now on called "the baseline paper") will be (partially) replicated.

In particular, we focus on the first two research questions of the first case study, in the baseline paper, where the main findings are:

– "Different parameter settings cause very large variance in the performance"
– "Default parameter settings perform relatively well, but are far from optimal".

Here we argue that the conclusions are taken from the set of 20 handed picked classes, which do not represent the entire project's classes. We exhaustively study the impact of tuning, with the similar hyper-parameter search space as the baseline paper (1,200 different configurations), on 117 classes of three random projects from the very same SF100 and show that different parameter settings do NOT have the significant impact that is claimed. We show this first by looking into all classes vs. a handpicked set and second by measuring improvements using the raw coverage (the number of extra branches covered when using a different configuration) rather than a relative measure used in the baseline paper. Together we show that the impact of tuning is much less than the reported ones. In addition, we show that the true impact is limited to the maximum improvement ranges (called "potentials" in this paper) in the project-level, which are 64% of class-level potentials. Finally, we analyze the distribution of the entire 1,200 configurations of hyper-parameters in terms of their effectiveness and show that half of the configurations are performing at least as well as the default configuration. This means that even a randomly selected configuration would have a 50% chance to be better than the default setting, but the issue is the improvements are minor (maximum 12 extra branches per project), anyways.

The main contributions and findings of this paper are as follows:

- Running an exhaustive search with over 2 million configuration/class pair evaluations, to study the impact of hyper-parameter tuning.
- Replicating the previous study on tuning and showing (clarifying) that, in contrary to the reported results, on average, different parameter settings cause no change in coverage at all on most (81%) classes.
- Showing that, in some cases, a relative coverage measure may not be the best metric to explain the potentials of tuning. Tuning for only 12 extra branches per project would be reported as 52% average improvement per class using the relative coverage.
- Showing that half of the possible configurations perform as well or better than the default configuration, but overall, the practical improvements are insignificant in most cases.

2   Empirical Study

In this section, we will explain the details of our experiment design and results.

2.1   Objective and Research Questions

Our objective is to revisit the previous study on the impact of tuning on SBST, by partially replicating our baseline paper, introduced in the introduction section. Our main hypotheses are that (a) not all classes in a project are significantly sensitive to parameter tuning, (b) the improvement of coverage is magnified in previous studies, and (c) most configurations are already good and don't leave much room for improvement in the SBST context. To investigate the above hypotheses, we design the following research questions:

- **RQ1:** *What portion of classes in a project would be sensitive to hyper-parameter tuning?*
  The idea of this question is to first identify classes that won't be affected at all no matter what configuration will be used.

- **RQ2:** *To what extent code coverage of classes within a project may change, when the hyper-parameters of SBST techniques change?*
  Knowing the answer to RQ1, we now need to know how much potential improvement one can gain by tuning, to decide whether tuning is even worthwhile (if the portion of sensitive classes is small the potentials are negligible, tuning is not justifiable).
- **RQ3:** *How are different hyper-parameter configurations (including the default from the baseline paper) compared in terms of their resulting code coverage?*
  The goal of this RQ is to dig deeper into the effectiveness of different configurations and see where a default configuration sits comparing to a median setting.

2.2   Experiment Design

Subjects Under Study: We have selected three random projects from the SF100 Java benchmark (which is a well-known dataset in SBST and have been used in the previous work. It is also the same source for our baseline paper [4]), namely, JSecurity, Geo-Google, and JOpenChart. We made sure that the sizes of our selected projects are around or greater than the median project size within SF100, which is 35 classes [11], per project, so that we don't study only the trivial projects, by chance. In addition, we checked that the average number of branches per class in our selected projects are around the median value of SF100 projects, which is 18 branches (See Table 2). Therefore, by considering these two measurements, we believe that our random selected classes are representative of other SF100 projects.

The summary of SF100 projects' properties is available in the Table 1 from the information available in [11]:

Table 1. Summary of SF100 projects statistics

	Min	Median	Average	Max
# of Classes per Project	1	35	87.84	2189
# of Branches per Class	0	18	33.20	2480

Table 2. Statistics of randomly selected projects from data in [11]

Project	# of Classes	# of Branches	Average # of Branches per Class
JSecurity	72	998	13.86
Geo-Google	52	1344	25.84
JOpenChart	38	693	18.24

SBST Tool: In order to evaluate the tuning techniques, we use the well-known open source SBST tool, EvoSuite [10,12]. EvoSuite is also the tool that was used in the baseline paper [4]. EvoSuite accepts Java bytecode of a class and creates a test suite that maximizes different criteria (e.g., branch coverage) using a Genetic Algorithm for optimization [13]. The GA parameters it employs are configurable. If no specific parameter is passed to EvoSuite, it will use a default setup that we refer to as "EvoSuite defaults" or the "baseline paper defaults". EvoSuite defaults have been selected by following guidelines, best practices, and experimentation, and have shown to be quite good and reasonable in the previous study [4].

Measurements: In this study, we use code (branch) coverage as our test adequacy measure, to be consistent with our baseline paper [4]. In addition to the raw coverage data (number of the covered branches as well as their percentages), we also report "Relative Coverage", which is suggested [2] and used in the baseline paper [4]. The rationale of using the relative coverage in the baseline paper was that "using the raw coverage values for parameter setting comparisons would be too noisy. Most branches are always covered regardless of the chosen parameter setting, while many others are simply infeasible".

Therefore, for a given configuration with resulting branch coverage equal to b on class c, we report Relative Coverage rc(b, c) as defined below:

$$RelativeCoverage = \frac{b - min}{max - min}$$

where b is the number of covered branches, and min and max are the minimum and maximum number of branches covered in the class c over all experimented configurations.

During the experiments, we report both raw coverage and the relative coverage and discuss this choice of metric.

Among all classes within a project, there are some classes that have the same coverage for any configuration at any iteration, and their max and min values are the same. We call them as **insensitive classes**.

Experiment Procedure: The experiments investigate the sensitivity of the three projects under study, in terms of branch coverage, when the GA hyper-parameters changes. Basically, we define a set of limited values per GA parameter (in EvoSuite) and run an exhaustive search over this search space. We then run EvoSuite per configuration and calculate branch coverage for all classes within each project.

The search space consists of the combination of 5 most important parameters of GA in EvoSuite, i.e. population size, crossover rate, elitism rate, selection function, and parent replacement check. In the tuning literature, there are some cases in which more parameters are considered to be tuned [14,16]. However, due to the extreme cost of exhaustive search and to be consistent with our baseline paper, we limit the tuning to these five parameters.

In the following, there is a brief explanation of the parameters of our interest to be tuned:

1. Crossover Rate: It is the probability with which two candidates selected from the parent generation are crossed over.
2. Population Size: This parameter indicates how many individuals exist in each generation and due to mutation and crossover operations the population remains constant while evolving.
3. Elitism Rate: This parameter determines how many or what percentage of top individuals are exempted from any crossover or mutation during evolution and are directly passed to the next generation without any modification.
4. Selection Function: This parameter specifies the mechanism with which individuals of a population are selected for the purpose of reproduction operations. In oppose to the other mentioned parameters, this one is not numerical and is a nominal variable. Three types of known selection methods are roulette wheel selection, tournament selection, and rank selection.
   In the roulette wheel selection method, individuals with more fitness score are more probable to be selected.
   In tournament selection, based on the tournament size a number of individuals are selected uniformly and this method does not weight the selection probability regarding fitness score.
   Rank selection considers fitness score into its selection method; however, unlike roulette wheel selection, the probability is not proportional to fitness score, rather it is based on the rank of individuals.
   Therefore, the fittest individuals do not dominate the selection like what happens in the tournament approach.
5. Parent Replacement Check: If this parameter is considered in the genetic algorithm, it checks the two off-springs, which are generated in the reproduction phase, against their parents. If they do not show an improvement in fitness score compared to at least one of their parents, they are not included in the next generation, and the algorithm continues with the parents in the next generation [4].

Following the baseline paper (the settings from its first case study) [4], we also have limited the values per parameter to a small discretized sub-samples, as follows:

- Crossover rate: 0, 0.2, 0.5, 0.75, 0.8, 1 (6 cases)
- Population size: 4, 10, 50, 100, 200 (5 cases)
- Elitism rate: 0, 1, 10%, 50% (4 cases)
- Selection: roulette wheel, tournament with size either 2 or 10, and rank selection with bias either 1.2 or 1.7 (5 cases)
- Parent replacement check: activated or not (2 cases)

Thus, the search space under exploration in this study includes $6 \times 5 \times 4 \times 5 \times 2 = 1,200$ different combinations of GA parameters, used by EvoSuite.

During an experiment, we take a pair of one configuration and one class, each time, and evaluate this pair's coverage using EvoSuite, with a search budget of two minutes, which is a realistic amount in practice and was used in the baseline paper as well. In order to address randomness, we repeat each evaluation 10 times. The average coverage of these repetitions is then reported as the pair's coverage.

There are 177 classes in total, in the three projects under study. Considering 10 repetitions of evaluating these classes on a search space of 1,200 configurations, where each evaluation takes two minutes, this analysis would take $177 \times 10 \times 1200 \times 2$ minutes equals to more than 8 years, on a single core machine. Therefore, we used computer clusters to run this amount of computation in parallel. The clusters in use were ComputeCanada (Graham with 32-core instances and Cedar with 48-core instances) and Cybera (8-core instances), which are all Linux-based systems, summed up to 360 nodes.

Note that all the scripts and output results are publicly available[1].

2.3 Results

In this section, we will report and explain the results of the experiments per research question.

RQ1 (Insensitive Classes): As discussed in Sect. 2.2, a large proportion of classes within a project may be insensitive to hyper-parameter tuning, which affects the usefulness of tuning in practice. In RQ1, we report this proportion per project in our study. Looking at Table 3 we see that 86% (73 out of 85), 95% (53 out of 56), and 50%(18 out of 36) of classes were insensitive to hyper-parameter tuning in our three projects. The number of classes that we observed in the projects are different from what is presented in Table 2 which were taken from [11]. This is due to the reason that the projects are still changing, and versions are different. The high number of insensitive classes in each project highlights that although tuning SBST techniques for some classes may be useful (see RQ2), the coverage of most classes in a given project will not be affected by tuning. Thus, applying an umbrella tuning on all classes of a project may not be effective, and the impact of tuning may be only limited to a small portion of the project.

Table 3. The proportion of insensitive classes per projects.

Project	#Classes	#Insensitive Classes	Proportions
JSecurity	85	73	0.86
Geo-Google	56	53	0.95
JOpenChart	36	18	0.50
Total	177	144	0.81

---

[1] https://github.com/sea-lab/EvoSuiteTuning.

This is in contrary with this generic claim from the baseline paper [4]: "Different parameter settings cause very large variance in the performance". The issue with that claim is that it is based on the 20 manually selected classes, where the tuning was indeed effective. The justification for this selection is given as "We, therefore, selected classes where EvoSuite used up its entire search budget without achieving 100% branch coverage, but still achieved more than 80% coverage." Though this might be a fine selection criterion to detect the sensitive classes, the problem is that the conclusions are generic and do not consider the significant number of insensitive classes.

In fact, our study on 177 classes shows that a blanket tuning over all classes of a project will NOT have a very large variance in the SBST technique's performance. Insensitive classes are mainly the ones that are trivial and easy for the SBST tool to evaluate. The analysis of insensitive classes in the projects under study shows that 85% (123 out of 144) of them have branch coverage more than 0.9 while 4% (6 out of 144) of them are very difficult to cover and their branch coverage is lower than 0.2, regardless of the configuration. Figure 1 summarizes the distribution of classes per project, over the coverage range.

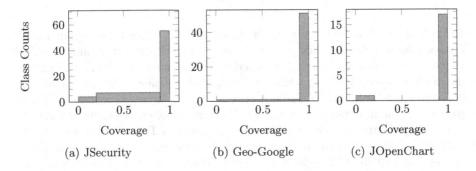

(a) JSecurity   (b) Geo-Google   (c) JOpenChart

Fig. 1. Distribution of 144 insensitive classes in 3 projects, over the coverage range.

So our conclusion is that tuning will NOT make a big difference in the coverage of the entire project. So, in the SBST context, the tuning effort should be focused only on the sensitive classes. Obviously, this first requires a systematic approach to detect such classes, before tuning, and second a metric that only considers those classes when evaluating the improvements, which we discuss more in RQ2.

> On average, more than 81% (144 out of 177) of classes in three projects under study were insensitive to 1,200 different configurations of GA hyper-parameters.

RQ2 (Evaluation Metric): As discussed in the RQ1 results, the coverage of most classes in a project are indifferent to the hyper-parameter configuration of

Table 4. Sensitive classes in the projects under study, and their coverage in terms of the number of covered branches and the relative coverage.

Project	Class Names	Branch	Covered Branches			Relative Coverage		
			Median	Worst	Best	Median	Worst	Best
JSecurity	DefaultWebSessionFactory	75	55.6	50.40	58	0.71	0.54	0.78
	AbstractSessionManager	89	65.4	58.67	70.8	0.48	0.24	0.67
	DefaultSessionManager	33	21	16.50	25.4	0.52	0.33	0.71
	MemoryAuthenticationDAO	24	20.75	9.50	24	0.81	0.15	1.00
	AbstractAuthenticator	47	28.4	21.60	29	0.96	0.56	1.00
	SimpleAuthorizationContext	57	52	51.25	53	0.38	0.28	0.50
	ThreadContext	24	17	16.67	18.25	0.17	0.11	0.38
	DAOAuthenticationModule	12	5	5.00	10	0	0.00	1.00
	DefaultSessionFactory	9	5	5.00	6.2	0	0.00	0.30
	MemorySessionDAO	24	22.8	21.75	24	0.60	0.25	1.00
	DelegatingSession	20	17	17.00	17.6	0	0.00	0.20
	ModularAuthenticator	18	8	8.00	8.6	0	0.00	0.20
	SimpleSessionEventSender	18	18	17.60	18	1.00	0.80	1.00
	ActiveDirectoryAuthenticationModule	14	7	6.50	7	1.00	0.75	1.00
	SimpleAuthenticationEventSender	29	28	27.20	28	1.00	0.60	1.00
	WebUtils	15	15	14.75	15	1.00	0.75	1.00
	LdapAuthenticationModule	27	16	15.75	16	1.00	0.75	1.00
	AnnotationAuthorizationModule	13	8.6	8.00	9	0.60	0.00	1.00
Average		30.44	22.81	20.62	24.32	0.57	0.34	0.76
Geo-Google	AddressToUsAddressFunctor	30	22	8.5	22	1.00	0.21	1.00
	GeoAddressStandardizer	38	27	23.6	28.5	0.87	0.64	0.97
	MappingUtils	8	6.1	5.4	6.6	0.37	0.13	0.53
Average		25.33	18.37	12.5	19.03	0.74	0.33	0.83
JOpenChart	CoordSystemUtilities	92	70.4	39.8	89.33	0.69	0.25	0.96
	RadarChartRenderer	22	2	2	6.00	0.00	0.00	0.20
	CoordSystem	71	65.2	59.6	69.00	0.75	0.37	1.00
	DefaultChart	20	6	5.8	15.80	0.07	0.05	0.72
	BarChartRenderer	16	7.6	4	11.80	0.40	0.14	0.70
	InterpolationChartRenderer	17	12	8.75	13.40	0.67	0.40	0.78
	AbstractChartDataModel	37	27.8	22.75	31.40	0.62	0.16	0.95
	DefaultChartDataModelConstraints	30	28.8	22.2	30.00	0.89	0.29	1.00
	StackedChartDataModelConstraints	54	51	46.8	51.00	1.00	0.58	1.00
	LineChartRenderer	17	12	9.2	13.40	0.60	0.32	0.74
	PieChartRenderer	14	2	2	5.60	0.00	0.00	0.36
	StackedBarChartRenderer	18	13.6	7.8	15.80	0.66	0.08	0.88
	PlotChartRenderer	11	9.6	7	10.00	0.93	0.50	1.00
	DefaultChartDataModel	34	34	32.6	34.00	1.00	0.72	1.00
	AbstractRenderer	7	6.2	3.5	7.00	0.84	0.30	1.00
	ChartEncoder	9	4.8	3	6.00	0.60	0.00	1.00
	Legend	12	11.6	10.25	12.00	0.87	0.42	1.00
	AbstractChartRenderer	16	15.00	14.8	15.00	1.00	0.80	1.00
Average		27.61	21.08	16.77	24.25	0.64	0.30	0.85
Overall		31.14	23.48	19.73	25.87	0.67	0.34	0.86

the SBST technique. In this section, we will assess the potential of the remaining sensitive classes to improve their branch coverage by SBST tuning, with two metrics: number of covered branches and relative coverage. Then, we will discuss how useful are these metrics, in this context.

Table 4 reports the number of total branches per class (the Branch column) and summarizes the branch coverage as the number of covered branches vs. relative coverage (explained in Sect. 2.2). For each category, it reports the median, the worst, and the best numbers overall $1{,}200 \times 10$ configuration evaluations, per class. The last row of each project summarizes all columns per project.

Following the relative metric, suggested in the baseline paper, we can conclude that the range of relative coverage per class is huge when looking at the best vs worst relative coverage (On average 42%, 50%, and 55% in JSecurity, Geo-Google, and JOpenChart projects, respectively). However, if we look at the raw coverage numbers the range between the best and the worst configuration, with respect to the number of covered branches are pretty small (3.7, 6.53, and 7.48 in JSecurity, Geo-Google, and JOpenChart projects, respectively). These numbers can be minimal for some classes, e.g., in the JSecurity project, there are 8 classes (out of 15 classes) where the difference between the best and the worst configurations is less than one branch (which practically can be called an insensitive class).

In other words, although the relative coverage metric shows a great potential (52%) for improvement using a tuning technique, the actual raw numbers reveal that the practical impact is limited to a few branches (on average 6.14 extra). This is equal to $(6.14/31.14)$ 19.7% improvement on raw branch coverage. Although even the 6.14 extra branches might be among buggy ones and thus a good tuning would in fact result in extra bug detection, but the point we make here is that the measurement should be reflective of the real-world effect. If the raw potential is 19.7% (regardless of how many more bugs potentially can be detected by such a tuning) we should not say the potential is 52%. This artificially exaggerates expectations from a tuning method.

Another point is that the impact of tuning is not going to be on the scale of the range of coverage as reported above (The Best - The Worst). In practice, choosing the worst configuration is rare. Even a random configuration would be better than the median results in 50% of the times. Thus, a more reasonable comparison is to set the expectations for improvement between the best and the median, not the worst. Following this approach, the improvement in raw branch coverage per class would be even smaller ($25.87 - 23.48 = 2.39$ branches, equals to $2.39/31.14 = 7.7\%$ potential coverage improvement for each class).

Therefore, we can conclude that although using relative coverage can avoid noises in the results, in some cases, it exaggerates the effectiveness of SBST tool tuning while there are only a few extra branches to be covered.

Following the above discussion, in RQ3, we will look deeper into the distribution of configurations and their corresponding results.

> Looking at relative coverage are not always helpful in terms of measuring tuning potentials. On average, an extra 6 branches on a total of 31 branches in sensitive classes would be reported as 52% improvement in relative coverage – In addition, the potential improvement on raw branch coverage when comparing the best and the median is just 2.39 branches, per class.

RQ3 (Distribution of Configurations): In RQ2, we listed the best/ worst/ median configurations for each sensitive class of projects under study. When it comes to tuning an SBST tool on a project scale, the problem changes a bit. The goal is no longer finding the best configuration per class. It is rather finding one single tuned configuration that works the best over all classes of the project. Note that these two (the class-level and the project-level best configurations) are different. In many cases, It might not be possible to have a configuration that works best for all classes.

Therefore, it is obvious that it might not be possible for a tuning method to be as good as the best configuration as reported in RQ2. So, we define a "Maximum/Minimum" configuration as the best/worst possible configuration in a project-level, as the configuration that results in the highest total branch coverage over all classes in the project. This follows the baseline paper's definition of "optimal" (equal to our "Maximum") configuration, as well.

Now to see the real impact of tuning, in Table 5, we report the Maximum and Minimum results per project. We also report the Best and Worst from RQ2 aggregated on a project-level to show that these two measures are different.

Overall, we can observe that the range of feasible coverage (Maximum - Minimum) of a given project is quite smaller than the range of potential coverage reported in RQ2. Looking at Table 5, the feasible ranges of coverage for projects JSecurity, GeoGoogle, and JOpenChart are only 54, 86, and 52 (on average 64) percents of the potential ones, reported in RQ2, respectively.

Thus, when it comes to assessing the impact of tuning, we have to measure it with raw coverage measures and look at the feasible coverage range bounds.

In practice, a typical SBST tool would have a default configuration, which tuning's goal is to improve its performance. So the next question is to see how EvoSuite default setting performs in comparison to others in the search space.

The current values of EvoSuite default configuration for the hyper-parameters of our interest are as follows:

- Crossover rate: 0.75
- Population size: 50
- Elitism rate: 1
- Selection: rank selection with bias either 1.7
- Parent replacement check (activated)

Table 5. The number of branches per project, the class-level and project-level potential ranges of covered branches, and the median and default performance.

| Project | Total | Project-level Potential Range | | Class-level Potential Range | | Median | Default |
		Maximum	Minimum	All Best	All Worst		
JSecurity	1093	828.20	792.33	843.85	777.13	818.0	822.6
Geo-Google	1408	1371.6	1354.8	1372.1	1352.5	1370.0	1370.3
JOpenChart	795	667.8	579.55	697.53	562.85	644.0	639.7

Looking at last two columns of Table 5, we will see that although the default configuration of EvoSuite is working well and is very close to the Maximum (optimal) coverage of each project (only misses less than 11.66 branches, on average), the median covered branches of all configurations is also very close (missing only 11.86 branches, on average), and performs even better than default for the JOpenChart project.

This suggests that 50% of configurations in our 1,200-member search space, i.e. 600 configurations, are working with a performance very close to or better than the default, which means one has at least 50% chance to select a configuration as good or better than the default, randomly, without any tuning. In Fig. 2, the entire distribution of configurations and their yielded coverage is illustrated, for all three projects.

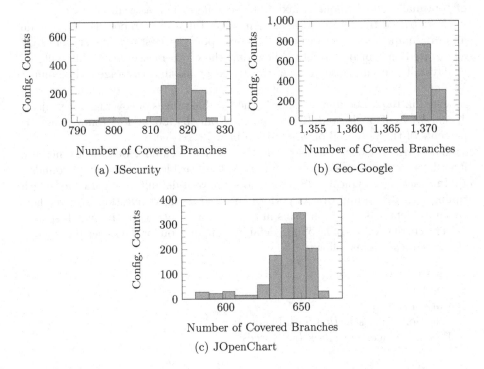

(a) JSecurity

(b) Geo-Google

(c) JOpenChart

Fig. 2. Distribution of 1,200 configurations in the search space over coverage, per project.

Tuning in practice is done on the entire project level, which on average has a 36% less potential for improvement compared to what was reported in RQ2 – As the observed median coverage suggests, half of the configurations are performing as well or better than the default configuration.

2.4   Threats to Validity

In terms of construct validity, the metrics that we used in our experiments are the number of covered branches and relative coverage which both are very common metrics in the context of software search-based testing to illustrate branch coverage. In RQ2, we compared the results of these two metrics and avoided the relative coverage reported in the baseline paper.

Regarding conclusion validity, we address the randomness of the SBST coverage results by repeating each experiment 10 times with different random seeds and taking averages. Note that since we do not directly compare different techniques and only show the ranges a statistical significant test was not applicable.

To minimize internal validity, we replicated the baseline paper as much as possible. We used the same tool, dataset, and hyper-parameters. The only part which was slightly different was that we used the current default values of Evo-Suite, whereas the baseline paper used the default values at the time. Although the overall results are not that different, we wanted to make sure that we use the best default the tool comes with when comparing it with median setting results. In addition, one possible threat is changing the default setting from what is used in [4] to what is used in the current version of EvoSuite (i.e. 1.0.6). Our assumption is that given the wealth of projects that use EvoSuite, over the years from the publishing time of the baseline paper, the new baseline has improved and provides even better results (or at least equal) to those reported in the baseline paper. So it is safe to focus only on the new version of EvoSuite defaults.

Regarding external validity, more empirical studies are needed to generalize the results. Our results are limited to SF100 (not even covering that all). So we need to replicate the study on more SF100 projects and beyond. In addition, we are limited to GA-based SBST (the EvoSuite implementation). Therefore, more experiments are needed where other GA or non-GA-based SBST tools are studied, with respect to the tuning impact. However, given the extreme cost of this type of study, our results are very valuable. The replication nature of the paper is also indirectly helping on the generalization of this type of studies.

3   Related Works

One of the most influential works in tuning in the context of search-based software testing is the empirical study of effect of tuning evolutionary algorithms on *test data generation* tools [3], which was extended later on in the baseline paper for our study [4]. Their preliminary work focuses on 20 random Java classes and uses the relative coverage metric. They noted that there is a high variance of coverage when a different configuration is set for the SBST tool [3]. Later, knowing that tuning is effective for improving the coverage, they applied response surface methodology tuning method on 10 large-scale projects with 609 classes in total to assess only 280 configurations. But, the raw coverage of the tuned configuration was found to be less than default coverage. They reported that the tuning method in use was not working in the SBST context [4]. Later, Kotelyanskii et al. replicated this study using Sequential Parameter Optimization Toolbox (SPOT) method and confirmed that the default setting for EvoSuite is performing well, and tuning cannot outperform it [18]. In contrast, in our study, we studied 177 Java classes from three projects on all settings rather than on a few ones.

While the aforementioned papers are the closest ones in terms of the context of our study, there are many other papers that used and confirmed their finding about effectiveness of tuning in other applications of SBSE. For example, in the configuration of Software Product Lines problem based on stakeholder needs, two meta-heuristics were evaluated with different hyper-parameter settings. It was found that the performance of algorithms depends on the hyper-parameter settings [21]. Parameter tuning of machine learning approaches to solving *software effort estimation* problem has been also studied, and it was shown that parameter settings make a difference in the results of machine learning performance [23]. In addition, it was found that tuning machine learning defect predictors can improve the performance, and it can even change the decisions on what are the important factors of software development [15]. In another study on 6 *clone detection* tools that are used widely, it was shown that tool configuration can improve the performance [24]. In our study, however, we claim that this dependency to the hyper-parameter settings in the context of our interest doesn't change the results significantly and is limited to covering only a few more branches.

4   Conclusion and Future Work

This paper revisits the problem of hyper-parameter tuning in SBST, studied in a previous publication. Studying 177 Java classes from 3 random projects from SF100, we observed that 81% of classes are insensitive to tuning. Moreover, the evidence from this study implies that the relative coverage improvement, used in the baseline paper, may unhelpfully exaggerate the effectiveness of tuning. Exhaustively searching through 1,200 configurations in the hyper-parameters search space, we conclude that not only EvoSuite default but also half of the configurations are covering most of the branches missing only about 12 branches per project compared to the best feasible coverage.

Regardless of the low potentials for tuning observed in this study, the next main observation is that the potentials are much higher in the individual class-levels than the entire project tuning. Thus for future works, we will try to devise a tuning method that looks at the static features of classes and tunes the settings in class-level rather than project-level. Moreover, we will try more GA-based (e.g., EvoMaster [1]) and non-GA-based SBST (e.g., [9]) techniques to confirm our findings and will extend our study to more projects from SF100 and beyond.

Acknowledgement. This work is partially supported by the Natural Sciences and Engineering Research Council of Canada [RGPIN/05108-2014].

References

1. Arcuri, A.: Evomaster: evolutionary multi-context automated system test generation. In: Proceedings of the 2018 IEEE 11th International Conference on Software Testing, Verification and Validation (ICST), pp. 394–397, April 2018
2. Arcuri, A., Briand, L.: A practical guide for using statistical tests to assess randomized algorithms in software engineering. In: Proceedings of the 33rd International Conference on Software Engineering, pp. 1–10 (2011)
3. Arcuri, A., Fraser, G.: On parameter tuning in search based software engineering. In: Cohen, M.B., Ó Cinnéide, M. (eds.) SSBSE 2011. LNCS, vol. 6956, pp. 33–47. Springer, Heidelberg (2011). https://doi.org/10.1007/978-3-642-23716-4_6
4. Arcuri, A., Fraser, G.: Parameter tuning or default values? an empirical investigation in search-based software engineering. Empir. Softw. Eng. **18**, 594–623 (2013)
5. Burke, E.K., Hyde, M.R., Kendall, G., Ochoa, G., Ozcan, E., Woodward, J.R.: Exploring hyper-heuristic methodologies with genetic programming. In: Mumford, C.L., Jain, L.C. (eds.) Computational Intelligence. Intelligent Systems Reference Library, vol. 1, pp. 177–201. Springer, Heidelberg (2009). https://doi.org/10.1007/978-3-642-01799-5_6
6. Craenen, B.G.W., Eiben, A.E.: Stepwise adaption of weights with refinement and decay on constraint satisfaction problems. In: Proceedings of the 3rd Annual Conference on Genetic and Evolutionary Computation, pp. 291–298 (2001)
7. Crawford, B., Soto, R., Monfroy, E., Palma, W., Castro, C., Paredes, F.: Parameter tuning of a choice-function based hyperheuristic using particle swarm optimization. Expert Syst. Appl. **40**(5), 1690–1695 (2013)
8. Feldt, R., Nordin, P.: Using factorial experiments to evaluate the effect of genetic programming parameters. In: Poli, R., Banzhaf, W., Langdon, W.B., Miller, J., Nordin, P., Fogarty, T.C. (eds.) EuroGP 2000. LNCS, vol. 1802, pp. 271–282. Springer, Heidelberg (2000). https://doi.org/10.1007/978-3-540-46239-2_20
9. Feldt, R., Poulding, S.: Broadening the search in search-based software testing: it need not be evolutionary. In: Proceedings of the Eighth International Workshop on Search-Based Software Testing, pp. 1–7 (2015)
10. Fraser, G., Arcuri, A.: Evosuite: automatic test suite generation for object-oriented software. In: Proceedings of the 19th ACM SIGSOFT Symposium and the 13th European Conference on Foundations of Software Engineering (2011)
11. Fraser, G., Arcuri, A.: Sound empirical evidence in software testing. In: 2012 34th International Conference on Software Engineering (ICSE). IEEE (2012)
12. Fraser, G., Arcuri, A.: Whole test suite generation. IEEE Trans. Softw. Eng. **39**(2), 276–291 (2013)
13. Fraser, G., Arcuri, A.: A large-scale evaluation of automated unit test generation using evosuite. ACM Trans. Softw. Eng. Methodol. **24**(2), 8:1–8:42 (2014)
14. Freisleben, B., Härtfelder, M.: Optimization of genetic algorithms by genetic algorithms. In: Albrecht, R.F., Reeves, C.R., Steele, N.C. (eds.) Artificial Neural Nets and Genetic Algorithms, pp. 392–399. Springer, Vienna (1993). https://doi.org/10.1007/978-3-7091-7533-0_57
15. Fu, W., Menzies, T., Shen, X.: Tuning for software analytics: is it really necessary? Inf. Softw. Technol. **76**, 135–146 (2016)
16. Grefenstette, J.: Optimization of control parameters for genetic algorithms. IEEE Trans. Syst. Man Cybern. **16**(1), 122–128 (1986)
17. Harman, M.: The current state and future of search based software engineering. In: Future of Software Engineering (FOSE 2007), pp. 342–357 (2007)

18. Kotelyanskii, A., Kapfhammer, G.M.: Parameter tuning for search-based test-data generation revisited: support for previous results. In: Proceedings of the 2014 14th International Conference on Quality Software, pp. 79–84 (2014)

19. Mao, K., Harman, M., Jia, Y.: Sapienz: multi-objective automated testing for android applications. In: Proceedings of the 25th International Symposium on Software Testing and Analysis, pp. 94–105. ACM (2016)

20. McMinn, P.: Search-based software testing: past, present and future. In: Proceedings of the 2011 IEEE Fourth International Conference on Software Testing, Verification and Validation Workshops, pp. 153–163 (2011)

21. Sayyad, A.S., Goseva-Popstojanova, K., Menzies, T., Ammar, H.: On parameter tuning in search based software engineering: a replicated empirical study. In: Proceedings of Workshop on Replication in Empirical Software Engineering (2013)

22. Shamshiri, S., Rojas, J.M., Fraser, G., McMinn, P.: Random or genetic algorithm search for object-oriented test suite generation? In: Proceedings of the 2015 Annual Conference on Genetic and Evolutionary Computation, pp. 1367–1374 (2015)

23. Song, L., Minku, L.L., Yao, X.: The impact of parameter tuning on software effort estimation using learning machines. In: Proceedings of the 9th International Conference on Predictive Models in Software Engineering, pp. 9:1–9:10 (2013)

24. Wang, T., Harman, M., Jia, Y., Krinke, J.: Searching for better configurations: a rigorous approach to clone evaluation. In: Proceedings of the 2013 9th Joint Meeting on Foundations of Software Engineering, pp. 455–465 (2013)

Short and Student Papers

Towards Automated Boundary Value Testing with Program Derivatives and Search

Robert Feldt and Felix Dobslaw[(⊠)]

Department of Computer Science and Engineering, Division of Software Engineering,
Chalmers University of Technology, Gothenburg, Sweden
{robert.feldt,dobslaw}@chalmers.se

Abstract. A natural and often used strategy when testing software is to use input values at boundaries, i.e. where behavior is expected to change the most, an approach often called boundary value testing or analysis (BVA). Even though this has been a key testing idea for long it has been hard to clearly define and formalize. Consequently, it has also been hard to automate.

In this research note we propose one such formalization of BVA by, in a similar way as to how the derivative of a function is defined in mathematics, considering (software) *program derivatives*. Critical to our definition is the notion of distance between inputs and outputs which we can formalize and then quantify based on ideas from Information theory.

However, for our (black-box) approach to be practical one must search for test inputs with specific properties. Coupling it with search-based software engineering is thus required and we discuss how program derivatives can be used as and within fitness functions.

This brief note does not allow a deeper, empirical investigation but we use a simple illustrative example throughout to introduce the main ideas. By combining program derivatives with search, we thus propose a practical as well as theoretically interesting technique for *automated boundary value (analysis and) testing*.

Keywords: Automated software testing ·
Search-based software testing · Boundary value analysis ·
Information theory · Partition testing

1 Introduction

Software systems increasingly govern our modern society and it is essential that we have effective and efficient ways to avoid that they contain critical faults. An old and natural way for software practitioners to think when creating software tests is to try to identify borders where the behavior of the software should change (the most). Even though such boundary value analysis (BVA) and testing (BVT) based on it is a classic technique in the software testing literature [5],

© Springer Nature Switzerland AG 2019
S. Nejati and G. Gay (Eds.): SSBSE 2019, LNCS 11664, pp. 155–163, 2019.
https://doi.org/10.1007/978-3-030-27455-9_11

and typically a mandatory part of relevant textbooks and certification programs [2,17], there has been only limited progress on how to objectively formalize and define it in a general way.

Boundary value analysis is closely related to partition analysis (PA) which divides the input domain for the software under test (SUT) into sub-domains for which we expect the behavior to be uniform for all inputs within the domains [12]. If the software behaves incorrectly on a sub-domain, the intuition is that it should fail for many or all of its elements. Further, if this holds true, we only need to test one or a few inputs per sub-domain which reduces the testing efforts many-fold. Practical experience also shows that software developers frequently introduce faults at domain borders, for example the common 'off-by-one' errors [11]. Identifying boundaries in the input domain and adding test cases to detect faults at such boundaries is thus often an effective testing strategy.

After the initial papers by White and Cohen [20] and Clarke et al. [5] that introduced and extended the basic method for boundary value analysis and testing[1] it was further refined by a number of authors. Jeng and Weyuker [19] simplified and generalized the approach to also cover discrete-valued inputs and Jeng and Forgacs [13] then proposed a semi-automated approach in which a dynamic search for test inputs is combined with algebraic manipulation of the boundary conditions in order to more efficiently generate test data for BVT.

However, a downside of all of these approaches is that they target numeric real-valued inputs. Discrete-valued inputs are sometimes supported by approximation schemes. Only recently did Zhao et al. [22] consider string inputs and showed how to generate test data to better find problems at borders in code with string predicates. Their basic idea is to introduce a specific string distance metric that is adapted to how strings are typically compared (lexicographically) in string predicates. Since software not only allow for numeric or string inputs, but frequently also complex and structured inputs, it is not obvious how BVA may be generalised or how it facilitates automated testing.

In this research note we argue that a general and sound basis for BVA can be created by considering the information distance between test inputs and their resulting outputs. The information distance is based on Kolmogorov complexity and is thus applicable to any type of object [3] and thereby to any type of software input. Since Kolmogorov complexity is not computable it may seem as though little has been gained. But by approximating it with compression algorithms it has been shown repeatedly and in various domains that these information theoretical metrics can reach state-of-the-art results [4,18]. Furthermore, they can do so without any specific knowledge about the objects features, their importance, or the type of similarity to be considered.

Feldt et al. [10] have previously applied these metrics to measure the distance between software tests and proposed their use to search for test cases. More recently, Feldt et al. [9] generalized these results to search for diverse sets of test cases and Marculescu and Feldt [15] investigated distance metrics in robustness testing. In this research note, we propose a further application

---

[1] Also called domain testing in several papers but less so in recent years.

of these information theoretic measures in software testing: searching for pairs of test inputs for automated boundary value testing based on the normalized compression distance.

In the following we first introduce a short, illustrative example in Sect. 2. Then, in Sect. 3, we introduce a general formalism for the location of boundaries which is inspired by the concept of the classic single-value derivative of a function in (mathematical) calculus. In Sect. 4, we apply our approach to an implementation of the illustrative example specification, and locate boundaries without source-code access, i.e. in a black-box manner. This note closes with a discussion on ways forward and in particular how to use our proposed program derivative in search-based software testing for automated BVA.

2 Illustrative Example: Constrained Sum

We focus on the general situation where there is a given specification and then some software that implements it. Further, we don't have or don't want to access the source code and we seek relevant boundaries for testing. Thus, a black-box, boundary value testing scenario. We here simply call this example (a variant of) the constrained sum problem with the specification:

> **Constrained Sum:** *The software should calculate the sum of two float-ing input values. The result should be returned with one (significant) dec-imal. Negative input values are invalid, as well as any inputs or outputs larger than or equal to 6.*

Figure 1, in Sect. 4, shows a conceptual picture of the boundaries the software engineer had in mind while writing and reasoning about this function for the software system.

3 Difference Quotient and Derivative of a Program

The classic derivative from mathematical calculus is based on comparing the difference between the outputs of a function given as small a change as possible in the inputs. It is typically formally defined in terms of one point, x, and a delta value, h, which together define a second point after summation. The derivative is then the limit as the delta value goes to zero:

$$\lim_{h \to 0} \frac{f(x + h) - f(x)}{h}$$

We argue that this, very general, idea is close to what we want to do in boundary value analysis. We need something akin to a derivative for a software program. A derivative in standard, mathematical calculus measures the sensi-tivity to change of a quantity (often called the function value or the dependent variable) as determined by another quantity (the independent variable). A large (absolute value of a) derivative thus indicates large sensitivity to the input, inde-pendent, variable. Detecting inputs that are highly sensitive to small changes, i.e. nearby inputs for which outputs differ a lot, would thus help us identify boundaries. It is there where we likely should spend more time testing.

However, in contrast to the continuous, single-input functions studied in mathematical calculus, programs in software can have other types than real-valued numbers as inputs and/or outputs. They also commonly have more than one input and sometimes more than one output. The latter problem can be approached in a similar way to how it is done in calculus, i.e. for functions of multiple input values we can define *partial derivatives*. The former problem concerning the restricted domains is more fundamental. How can we construct a new input point from a given input point and a 'delta' value, and what does the 'delta' even mean, e.g. for structured input domains such as graphs, trees or databases?

In order to resolve this we take the alternative viewpoint on defining derivatives, namely the 'difference quotient' over an interval [21]:

$$DQ(a, b) = \frac{f(a) - f(b)}{a - b}$$

The derivative can now be found by letting the input b go towards the input a. Note that the subtract operation '-' here, essentially, acts as a distance function twice, once for the outputs and once for the inputs[2]. For software programs, when neither the inputs nor the outputs might be numbers, we must generalize this and allow for a general distance function for any type of data (inputs and outputs) rather than assuming we can simply use subtraction. Formally we thus define the Program Derivative as follows:

Definition 1. *The Program Derivative (PD) for program P at input a, with output distance function d_o, and input distance function d_i is*

$$PD_{d_o,d_i}(a) = PDQ_{d_o,d_i}(a, b_{min}) \quad = \frac{d_o(P(a), P(b_{min}))}{d_i(a, b_{min})} \quad with$$

$$b_{min} \qquad\qquad = \underset{b, b \neq a}{\arg\min}\, d_i(a, b),$$

where $P(x)$ denotes the output of the program for input x.

The PD and the program difference quotient[3], PDQ, are parameterized on two distance functions: one for the inputs and one for the outputs. They may be the same but need not be; it depends on the types of the inputs and outputs,

---

[2] Subtraction also preserves directionality, however, in the following we focus purely on the distance (the absolute value) rather than on its directionality (which we argue is less clear a concept for arbitrary data types).

[3] We note that for search-based testing the PDQ, used on the right hand side of the PD definition, might be a more fruitful concept than the derivative itself since, for complex and high-dimensional data domains the closest value to another value can be ill-defined, and there can be several directions that are interesting to consider for sensitivity and rates of change (not only the one of the closest 'neighbour').

respectively, and which of the often many possible distance functions for one type are chosen.

Also, note here that for some distance functions d_i and input spaces it might be hard to find a unique b_{min}, i.e. one might find several inputs with the same distance to a. This could either be resolved by randomly selecting one of them or by selecting by largest output distance or in some other way, depending on the use case[4].

The most general choice of distance function is to use the Normalized Information Distance (NID) for both inputs and outputs since it is both universal and general and should capture any important differences [3,18]. We will call this theoretical measure the information difference quotient (IDQ).

By using the 'compression trick' of Cilibrasi and Vitanyi we can approximate the IDQ by substituting a compression function, C, for Kolmogorov complexity [4]. We thus define the Compression Difference Quotient (CDQ) of a program P for inputs a and b:

$$CDQ_C(a,b) = PDQ_{NCD_C,NCD_C}(a,b) = \frac{NCD_C(P(a), P(b))}{NCD_C(a,b)}$$

where NCD is the Normalized Compression Distance [4]. However, we note that if either the inputs or the outputs are numbers, numerical vectors or matrices it may be sensible to use data-type specific distance functions. In general we thus talk about the PDQ_{d_1,d_2} where d_1 and d_2 is by default NCD, but can be any chosen as any suitable distance function.

The program derivative and its quotient thus imply whole families of concrete measures that can be instantiated and then utilized for different testing and analysis purposes. By selecting specific distance functions and calculating the quantities defined by the formulas above, we should be able to detect areas of special interest for software comprehension and quality assurance tasks.

The connection to search-based software testing seems rather direct. For complex and structured data types it might be very hard to define how to maximize and minimize the involved quantities or take 'delta' steps between values. Thus, even though more exact search and optimization approaches might be useful for some programs and distance functions we can always fall back on general, blackbox, meta-heuristic optimization. A good base choice might be an evolutionary search algorithm connected to a data generation framework, e.g. [7], but also alternative search methods can be called for [8,14].

4   Boundary Value Analysis of Constrained Sum

For the purpose of understanding local output differences for the software in our illustrative example from Sect. 2, we applied the CDQ_C on the grid of values in the range covered by $x, y \in [-2, 8]$. For each point in a cell on a grid we

---

[4] Future work should investigate the many alternatives here and if they make any difference in practice.

then sampled a set of surrounding points, calculated CDQ_C, and selected the one with the maximal value[5]. We then color-coded the CDQ_C values in order to visualize the local differences in a two-dimensional plane presented in Fig. 2a. The darker the color of a pixel, the more diverse the outputs of the neighboring inputs it represents according to the applied generic measure. This way, and even without specification, we can learn local functional properties for the software system regardless of its input and output data types (since any data can be dumped to a string and a compressor applied to it).

Figure 2b shows the result of the exact same experiment for another program with the same interface. The plot is clearly dissimilar to Fig. 2a which suggests that it does not implement the specification. When looking more closely we find that the region of similar values in the center is larger, and in fact the second program allows for the sum to be larger or equal to 7. Comparing this to the conceptual image of what we expect the software to do, Fig. 1, it seems clear that there might be some problem with the implementation in Fig. 2b. Further, we might want to reason about the significance of the 'boundaries' outside of the triangle in Fig. 2a.

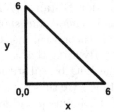

Fig. 1. Boundaries as conceptualized for the constrained sum program.

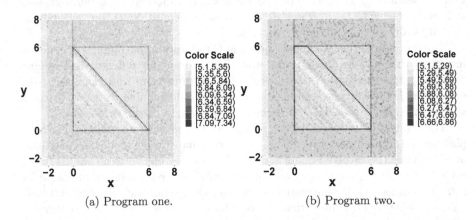

(a) Program one.   (b) Program two.

Fig. 2. Heatmaps of the program derivative values for each cell of a part of the two-dimensional input space for two different implementations of the constrained sum specification from Sect. 2. One program implements the specification (left) and one does not (right). Boundaries of changing behavior are clearly present.

---

[5] In an automated BVA tool we would instead have used search here.

5   Discussion

We have proposed program derivatives to detect boundaries for boundary value analysis and testing. They can be seen as a generalisation of derivatives of single-valued mathematical functions in calculus. While the mathematical derivative and differential calculus of Leibniz and Newton focus on numbers, we propose the use of information distance and the compression trick to generalize this concept to any input and output data types. It can thus be applied to any program. While there have been some proposals for derivatives of specific types of programs such as parsers [16] we know of no as general attempts as the one proposed in this paper.

Since this is only a brief research note there are many avenues for future work. The illustrative example we used here was chosen for simplicity and visualisation potential and as such takes numbers as inputs, which goes against our main motivation. However, the outputs can be of many different types (exceptions were thrown for invalid values, for example) so already on this simple example the NCD allowed comparing values of different types. But future work should also explore the many different ways in which these proposed derivatives and differential quotients can be used in fitness functions and coupled with search-based testing. For example, Marculescu and Feldt [15] proposed a search-based algorithm to find a border between the valid and invalid values of a program under test. We should combine this type of search to 'squeeze' a border with the measures proposed in here to even find other types of borders.

Furthermore, it is not clear that minimizing the denominator in difference quotients is the single possible goal. For constructing sets of interesting test cases we will most likely need a multi-objective formulation that combines diversity of sets of values [9] and derivatives/quotients. Practical work on how to select interesting and relevant distance functions for particular purposes and how to speed up distance calculations are also important and recent advances show promise [6].

A more conceptually intriguing area for future work would be to consider derivatives and quotients of other types of program- and test-related information. As was noted already by Feldt et al. [10], all types of test-related information can be used in information distances and their approximations might have value. They also calculated distances and diversities both on inputs, state information captured in execution traces, and outputs. Alshahwan and Harman later saw promising results when using output diversity [1]. Nevertheless, we propose to investigate the benefits of relating different diversities and distances to each other in more ways than outlined here. For example, we can consider different partial derivatives or relating other quantities, e.g. the derivative of a program's state (output) with respect to one of its inputs (state variables). A lot of future work seems called for.

References

1. Alshahwan, N., Harman, M.: Augmenting test suites effectiveness by increasing output diversity. In: 2012 34th International Conference on Software Engineering (ICSE), pp. 1345–1348. IEEE (2012)
2. Bath, G., McKay, J.: The Software Test Engineer's Handbook: A Study Guide for the ISTQB Test Analyst and Technical Analyst Advanced Level Certificates, 2nd edn. Rocky Nook, Santa Barbara (2012)
3. Bennett, C.H., Gács, P., Li, M., Vitányi, P.M., Zurek, W.H.: Information distance. IEEE Trans. Inf. Theory **44**(4), 1407–1423 (1998)
4. Cilibrasi, R., Vitányi, P., De Wolf, R.: Algorithmic clustering of music based on string compression. Comput. Music J. **28**(4), 49–67 (2004)
5. Clarke, L.A., Hassell, J., Richardson, D.J.: A close look at domain testing. IEEE Trans. Softw. Eng. **4**, 380–390 (1982)
6. Cruciani, E., Miranda, B., Verdecchia, R., Bertolino, A.: Scalable approaches for test suite reduction. In: 41st International Conference on Software Engineering (ICSE). IEEE (2019)
7. Feldt, R., Poulding, S.: Finding test data with specific properties via metaheuristic search. In: 2013 IEEE 24th International Symposium on Software Reliability Engineering (ISSRE), pp. 350–359. IEEE (2013)
8. Feldt, R., Poulding, S.: Broadening the search in search-based software testing: it need not be evolutionary. In: Proceedings of the Eighth International Workshop on Search-Based Software Testing, pp. 1–7. IEEE Press (2015)
9. Feldt, R., Poulding, S., Clark, D., Yoo, S.: Test set diameter: quantifying the diversity of sets of test cases. In: 2016 IEEE International Conference on Software Testing, Verification and Validation (ICST), pp. 223–233. IEEE (2016)
10. Feldt, R., Torkar, R., Gorschek, T., Afzal, W.: Searching for cognitively diverse tests: towards universal test diversity metrics. In: IEEE International Conference on Software Testing Verification and Validation Workshop, ICSTW 2008, pp. 178–186. IEEE (2008)
11. Glass, R.L.: Frequently forgotten fundamental facts about software engineering. IEEE Softw. **3**, 110–112 (2001)
12. Hierons, R.M.: Avoiding coincidental correctness in boundary value analysis. ACM Trans. Softw. Eng. Methodol. (TOSEM) **15**(3), 227–241 (2006)
13. Jeng, B., Forgács, I.: An automatic approach of domain test data generation. J. Syst. Softw. **49**(1), 97–112 (1999)
14. Löscher, A., Sagonas, K.: Targeted property-based testing. In: Proceedings of the 26th ACM SIGSOFT International Symposium on Software Testing and Analysis, pp. 46–56. ACM (2017)
15. Marculescu, B., Feldt, R.: Finding a boundary between valid and invalid regions of the input space. arXiv preprint arXiv:1810.06720 (2018)
16. Might, M., Darais, D., Spiewak, D.: Parsing with derivatives: a functional pearl. In: ACM SIGPLAN Notices, vol. 46, pp. 189–195. ACM (2011)
17. Spillner, A., Linz, T., Schaefer, H.: Software Testing Foundations: A Study Guide for The Certified Tester Exam. Rocky Nook Inc., Santa Barbara (2014)
18. Vitányi, P.M., Balbach, F.J., Cilibrasi, R.L., Li, M.: Normalized information distance. In: Emmert-Streib, F., Dehmer, M. (eds.) Information Theory and Statistical Learning, pp. 45–82. Springer, Boston (2009). https://doi.org/10.1007/978-0-387-84816-7_3

19. Weyuker, E.J., Jeng, B.: Analyzing partition testing strategies. IEEE Trans. Softw. Eng. **7**, 703–711 (1991)
20. White, L.J., Cohen, E.I.: A domain strategy for computer program testing. IEEE Trans. Softw. Eng. **3**, 247–257 (1980)
21. Wikipedia: Difference quotient – Wikipedia, the free encyclopedia (2019). https://en.wikipedia.org/wiki/Difference_quotient. Accessed 20 June 2019
22. Zhao, R., Lyu, M.R., Min, Y.: Automatic string test data generation for detecting domain errors. Softw. Test. Verif. Reliab. **20**(3), 209–236 (2010)

Code Naturalness to Assist Search Space Exploration in Search-Based Program Repair Methods

Altino Dantas[1]([⊠]), Eduardo F. de Souza[1], Jerffeson Souza[2],
and Celso G. Camilo-Junior[1]

[1] Intelligence for Software Group, Federal University of Goiás, Alameda Palmeiras,
Quadra D, Câmpus Samambaia, Goiânia 74690-900, Brazil
`{altinobasilio,eduardosouza,celso}@inf.ufg.br`
[2] Optimization in Software Engineering Group, State University of Ceará, Doutor
Silas Munguba Avenue, 1700, Fortaleza 60714-903, Brazil
`jerffeson.souza@uece.br`
`http://i4soft.com.br`

Abstract. Automated Program Repair (APR) is a research field that
has recently gained attention due to its advances in proposing methods to
fix buggy programs without human intervention. Search-Based Program
Repair methods have difficulties to traverse the search space, mainly,
because it is challenging and costly to evaluate each variant. Therefore,
aiming to improve each program's variant evaluation through providing
more information to the fitness function, we propose the combination of
two techniques, Doc2vec and LSTM, to capture high-level differences
among variants and to capture the dependence between source code
statements in the fault localization region. The experiments performed
with the IntroClass benchmark show that our approach captures differences between variants according to the level of changes they received,
and the resulting information is useful to balance the search between
the exploration and exploitation steps. Besides, the proposal might be
promising to filter program variants that are adequate to the suspicious
portion of the code.

Keywords: Automated Program Repair · Search space exploration ·
Code naturalness

1 Introduction

Automated Program Repair (APR) is a research field that aims to fix buggy
code without human intervention. Search-Based Program Repair algorithms [1]
are based on the generate-and-validate approach, where variations of the original
(bugged) code are generated and then evaluated, mostly, by a test suite. This
evaluation method is time-consuming, might lead the search to plateaus or local

S. Nejati and G. Gay (Eds.): SSBSE 2019, LNCS 11664, pp. 164–170, 2019.
https://doi.org/10.1007/978-3-030-27455-9_12

optimal, and does not provide enough information to the fitness function to accurately differentiate the variants.

There is evidence that using dynamic analysis to capture internal states of the program and then using this information in the fitness function helps to differentiate variants better and improves the search expressiveness [2]. Although promising, this technique is still too costly and given that the search space is usually densely populated by plausible or low-quality solutions, there is still the need for efficient methods. Other approaches using neural network models to evaluate or classify source code in the APR context [3,4] might be used to help to compose the fitness function, but there is no evidence of a relation of those approaches to a fitness evaluation.

Previous research acknowledges that source code has similar properties of natural language and, therefore, the models used to compare natural language suits this new context [5]. Although [6] points out that such models might not be accurate, this research goes one step further and provide an efficient program's variant evaluation through the combination of two techniques, Doc2vec and LSTM, to capture high-level differences among variants (high-order mutations) and to capture the dependence between source code statements in the fault localization region (low-order mutation).

2   Proposed Approach

End-to-end search-based Automated Program Repair techniques comprise several steps with complex tasks involved. Yet, the focus of this proposal is about traversing the program's landscape concerns. Figure 1 presents an overview illustrating what APR aspects are involved with and are impacted by this proposal.

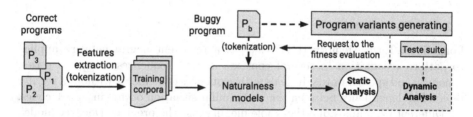

Fig. 1. Our proposal of using code naturalness for Automated Program Repair.

Our approach considers that correct source codes (written in the same programming language as the buggy code) are available in order to perform an automated program repair. Assuming that language models are trained to capture naturalness from scriptures, we rely on that to also assume that they are capable of capturing naturalness from correct source code. The corpus used to train the models are composed of tokens obtained through feature extraction from the correct source codes.

One can use information from the naturalness model in a traditional search-based program repair workflow (dashed lines). As Fig. 1 highlights with the white circle, we propose to use those models to help as a static analysis factor to a fitness function. The model receives a tokenized source code, transformed with the same process as used in training, and it returns information to compound the fitness along with the dynamic factor, which is typically based on a test suite and requires executing the program.

Among the existing ways to capture naturalness information from a corpus, we propose the usage of Doc2vec and LSTM. The motivation to use them, as well as their required inputs and the expected output, is detailed next.

2.1 Doc2vec Model

Doc2vec is an unsupervised machine learning method that learns a fixed feature representation to describe paragraphs and documents [7] throughout the distributions of words and sentences in a corpus. Previous work has proposed metrics to evaluate program variants based on a word embedding [3], but we chose the Doc2vec because it is more appropriate to deal with the whole document.

We employ Doc2vec to encode methods or functions in source codes in the same way it treats paragraphs in documents; thus, our technique obtains a measure of similarity between programs based on their vector representation. Given this information, one might assume that a fix is not so distant from the original bugged code. Besides, one can use this vector representation to investigate the impact of mutation operators, which is typically hard to do using the patch or AST representations.

We developed our proposal upon the Doc2vec provided by the Gensim[1] library in such a way that our model, when trained, receives two source codes and returns how similar they are.

2.2 LSTM Model

Long Short-Term Memory (LSTM) [7] is a recurrent neural network applied to pattern recognition in several contexts as text sequences, temporal series, genomes, and spoken words. It deals with sequences of elements without a regular interval of dependence between them. A similar situation occurs in source codes.

Different from analyzing the whole file, likewise the previous Doc2vec model, we propose to use LSTM to capture data from and generate information for a specific area of the code. Therefore, we train our LSTM model (implemented with the TensorFlow framework[2]) on the corpus of correct programs and then use it to synthesize code patch considering a part of the buggy program as the input sequence. The model receives a sequence of tokens from the suspicious region and generates the sequence it considers more "natural" for that part of the code. The experiment section presents how such an output sequence can be used to evaluate program variants.

---

[1] https://radimrehurek.com/gensim.

[2] https://www.tensorflow.org.

3   Preliminary Empirical Study

We conducted our experiments to answer the following Research Question: **Do naturalness models provide useful information to explore a program's search space?**

Thus, to evaluate our proposal, we used the IntroClass[3] benchmark. Considering this benchmark presents buggy and fixed versions but does not have fault localization data nor the correct patches, we first performed an inspection to generate such data. From the 99 available versions, distributed in six categories (problems), we selected 70 of them. We did not consider fixes achieved only by deletion, changes on the whole file, or empty diff between the bugged and fixed versions.

The tokenization step is as follows: For all 70 versions selected (140, taking the buggy and the correct ones), we removed all headers and comments, separated every relevant token by space (e.g., *vector[i]* became *vector [i]*) and replaced strings with the token "STRRPL" to prevent noise by words unlike to the one from the programming language. Thus, the tokenization process is a feature extraction process in the sense that each token represents a feature. After that, the proposal trained both Doc2vec and LSTM models over the corpora from the correct codes.

Three versions were randomly selected from each problem to test the former model. For each version, 15 variants were generated by applying GenProg's [8] mutation operators and the number of mutations (1, 2, 3) they received clustered those variants. Thus, it was generated 270 variants, and then it was possible to calculate the similarity between the original version and its variants. Such a metric is a unit percentage [0,1].

To the latter, the information of fault localization and a correct patch for all 70 versions were used to process the test and compute the accuracy (Acc) and precision (Prec) metrics. Acc is $\frac{|T \cap Y|}{|T|}$ and Prec is $\frac{|T \cap Y|}{|Y|}$, where T is the set of tokens in the knowing patch fix, and Y is the set of tokens predicted by the model. For this model requires an input sequence of tokens to produce another sequence, different configurations of length for both sequences were verified.

Although training such models might be expensive, it occurs only once, and its results are then used in $\mathcal{O}(1)$ time. A search-based program repair technique could benefit from this while using the information from the models to pre-evaluate a variant, alleviating the time-consuming process of running the test suite.

Experiments' data, scripts, and raw results are available at: https://altinodantas.github.io/sbpr-naturalness.

3.1   Preliminary Results

Figure 2 shows the average similarity grouped by the number of mutations the variants received and the problem they were implemented for. In some cases,

---

[3] https://repairbenchmarks.cs.umass.edu.

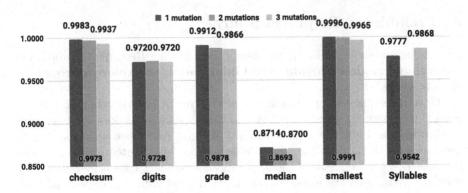

Fig. 2. Similarity between original buggy versions and their variants.

such as *checksum*, *grade*, and *smallest*, the higher the number of mutations, the lower the similarity. This behavior occurs if we assume that applying more perturbations increases the entropy between the original and a variant from it. However, for other problems, fewer mutations produced a lower similarity.

While inspecting the variants, we observed that in some cases, one mutation could have more impact than three mutations. For instance, in the *syllables* problem, a one-mutation variant deleted a **"for"** statement that had the main functionality of the program. Meanwhile, for the same version, a three-mutations variant computed higher similarity because the changes they provoked were not as profound.

This observation is exciting because it provides a method to capture the impact caused by mutation operators without the need of running the variant or the original program against the test suite, which is a time-consuming task. Therefore, a search algorithm could use the similarity to balance the exploration and exploitation, which are two crucial steps to cover a search space adequately. For example, using a threshold on the similarity values, one may enable mutations with more or less impact on the code.

Looking at the reports from the *median* problem, one notices that their values are inferior to the others. We speculate that this behavior is because the *median* has more versions than the other problems. Thus, with more information from the *median* to perform the training phase, the resulting model is more sensible to get differences between versions from that problem. However, a more rigorous investigation is needed.

Moving to the LSTM model evaluation, Table 1 presents the average of Acc and Prec for each configuration considering all versions and problems. Configurations have the format Xin_Yout, where X and Y indicate the number of tokens given as input and number of tokens expected in the output, respectively. As Acc and Prec may be conflicting, the results show, in some sense, which configurations present the best trade-off.

It is possible to notice the configurations with only five tokens in the input, the left part of the table, do not achieve the best values in Acc or Prec.

Table 1. Average of Acc and Prec achieved by LSTM model in all 70 selected versions.

Configuration	Acc	Prec	Configuration	Acc	Prec	Configuration	Acc	Prec
5in_10out	0.25	0.29	10in_10out	0.37	**0.35**	15in_10out	0.35	0.33
5in_20out	0.35	0.28	10in_20out	0.44	0.26	15in_20out	0.43	0.26
5in_30out	0.37	0.24	10in_30out	0.44	0.22	15in_30out	**0.45**	0.20

We might conclude that, on average, for the IntroClass' problems, five tokens are not enough to infer the dependence context due to some statements that are related to others further away.

Rather, since Acc and Prec's trade-off, all the 10-input configurations are not dominated, that is, there is no other configuration with results at least equal to one metric and strictly superior in the other. Notice that 10in_10out achieved the best Prec (0.35). Despite 15in_30out reached the best Acc (0.45) and also may be considered non-dominated, ten tokens to the input seem to be sufficient because increasing the input does not necessarily achieve better accuracy, as the others two 15-input does not overcome the best 10-input in this metric.

It is clear that based on local naturalness, given the faulty location and a correct patch, it was impossible to predict all the tokens needed to a fix. However, at least 37% of those tokens are always found in non-dominated settings; thus, this information could be used to discard variants that present fewer tokens than the model predicts. For instance, one could infer a threshold by analyzing the accuracy of the model over known fixed codes. This makes sense once some mutations are more suitable regarding the region of code they are applied.

Finally, considering the findings presented in this section, we can answer the Research Question saying that: **"yes, naturalness models can provide useful information to be employed by a technique that needs to explore a program's search space"**. From the Doc2vec model, it is possible to get information to control the exploration and exploitation, and from the LSTM it is possible to create a filter on variants that are more suitable to the context of the region pointed by the fault localization.

4   Threats to Validity

The machine learning methods used to infer the naturalness models have a stochastic nature; thus, we performed preliminary training to get the model and decide about the hyperparameters. Nevertheless, fine-tuning the training process may generate different results. Since the investigated benchmark has small C programs, we can not generalize our findings to another programming language. However, previous work [4] presented evidence that LSTM works for real-world programs, including different programming languages. Finally, the results are hugely dependent on the tokenization we adopted.

5   Final Remarks

Several APR methods fix buggy programs by generating and validating variants. However, exploring a program's search space continues to be challenging. Therefore, this paper introduced an approach to generate useful information to explore a program's search space from the naturalness of correct programs. Preliminary results showed the proposal could potentially help APR methods to control their exploration and exploitation steps and filter variants regarding the fault localization data.

Next, we intend to couple our proposal to a search-based APR method. For that, we are working on integrating it to GenProg. Our models will then be used to prevent executing not such promising variants. Then, they will be used to compound the fitness function itself.

Acknowledgements. This study was financed in part by the Coordenação de Aperfeiçoamento de Pessoal de Nível Superior - Brasil (CAPES) - Finance Code 001 and by the Fundação de Amparo à Pesquisa de Goiás (FAPEG).

References

1. Harman, M., Jones, B.F.: Search-based software engineering. Inf. Softw. Technol. **43**(14), 833–839 (2001)
2. de Souza, E.F., Le Goues, C., Camilo-Junior, C.G.: A novel fitness function for automated program repair based on source code checkpoints. In: Proceedings of the Genetic and Evolutionary Computation Conference, GECCO 2018, pp. 1443–1450. ACM, New York (2018)
3. Amorim, L.A., Freitas, M.F., Dantas, A., de Souza, E.F., Camilo-Junior, C.G., Martins, W.S.: A new word embedding approach to evaluate potential fixes for automated program repair. In: Proceeding of the 2018 International Joint Conference on Neural Networks (IJCNN), pp. 1–8, July 2018
4. Roque, L., Dantas, A., Camilo-Junior, C.G.: Programming style analysis with recurrent neural network to automatic pull request approval. In: Proceedings of The 2019 International Joint Conference on Neural Networks (IJCNN). ijcnn.org (2019, to be appear)
5. Hindle, A., Barr, E.T., Su, Z., Gabel, M., Devanbu, P.: On the naturalness of software. In: Proceedings of the 34th International Conference on Software Engineering, ICSE 2012, pp. 837–847. IEEE Press, Piscataway (2012)
6. Jimenez, M., Checkam,T.T., Cordy, M., Papadakis, M., Kintis, M., Le Traon, Y., Harman, M.: Are mutants really natural?: A study on how naturalness helps mutant selection. In: Proceedings of the 12th ESEM, page 3. ACM, 2018
7. Le, Q., Mikolov, T.: Distributed representations of sentences and documents. In: Proceedings of the 31st International Conference on Machine Learning, vol. 32, ICML 2014, pp. II-1188–II-1196. JMLR.org (2014)
8. Le Goues, C., Nguyen, T., Forrest, S., Weimer, W.: Genprog: a generic method for automatic software repair. IEEE Trans. Software Eng. **38**(1), 54–72 (2012)

Dorylus: An Ant Colony Based Tool for Automated Test Case Generation

Dan Bruce(⊠), Héctor D. Menéndez, and David Clark

University College London, London, UK
dan.bruce.17@ucl.ac.uk

Abstract. Automated test generation to cover all branches within a program is a hard task. We present Dorylus, a test suite generation tool that uses ant colony optimisation, guided by coverage. Dorylus constructs a continuous domain over which it conducts independent, multiple objective search that employs a lightweight, dynamic, path-based input dependency analysis. We compare Dorylus with EvoSuite with respect to both coverage and speed using two corpora. The first benchmark contains string based programs, where our results demonstrate that Dorylus improves over EvoSuite on branch coverage and is 50% faster on average. The second benchmark consists of 936 Java programs from SF110 and suggests Dorylus generalises well as it achieves 79% coverage on average whereas the best performing of three EvoSuite algorithms reaches 89%.

Keywords: Search-based testing · Automated test case generation · Ant colony optimisation · Dorylus

1 Introduction

Testing software can be a long and arduous task for developers. It can take up much of the development budget for what may feel like relatively little output. However, it is crucial for checking the correctness and reliability of programs. Automated test generation aims to reduce the burden on the developer by providing test suites that, according to some criterion, effectively test the program. An important part of creating tests for programs is ensuring that much of the program is exercised by the test suite. This has led to the common goal of coverage amongst manual test developers and automation tools alike [6].

Common goals for automatic test generation tools based on coverage are: prioritisation of branches in the generation process [6], infeasibility [2] and traversing branches that depend on complex conditions such as those based on subregions of strings. To deal with these problems we present Dorylus. Dorylus is a search-based optimisation tool capable of generating test data for Java programs. The goal of Dorylus is branch coverage for which it requires only the binary files of the software under test. It uses a two phase search-based optimisation algorithm which prioritises targets to maximise potential coverage.

© Springer Nature Switzerland AG 2019
S. Nejati and G. Gay (Eds.): SSBSE 2019, LNCS 11664, pp. 171–180, 2019.
https://doi.org/10.1007/978-3-030-27455-9_13

It then solves each target as a separate search problem. Rather than focusing on one target at a time, the target being solved changes continually according to its probability of selection. This reduces wasting time on infeasible targets, whilst also allowing prerequisite branches to be covered early in the process. Moreover, only targets immediately reachable from current coverage are considered at any time, creating a dynamic vector of targets.

The contribution of this paper is the Dorylus tool. For any given target the search space of the problem is reduced through a novel lightweight path-based input dependency analysis. This combined with the construction of a probability distribution over numeric inputs and leveraging Levenshtein distance to define distances for string operations, allows rapid convergence on correct inputs. Unlike other techniques, Dorylus considers paths and aims to propagate many unique paths through the program to reach the targets. This path diversity unlocks rare probability predicates, due to many of them being only feasible from a specific rare probability state of the program.

A proof-of-concept qualitative analysis has been performed, comparing Dorylus with EvoSuite to demonstrate its suitability for the problem of test generation. Both tools are tested on 12 programs, 10 of which are taken from the literature, one of these is further modified and one program constructed from interesting code constructs [1]. The results show that on all programs Dorylus at least matched EvoSuite which, on average, covered 95.1% compared with Dorylus' 97.7%. Furthermore, Dorylus was twice as fast on average, reaching maximal coverage in 20.3 s whereas EvoSuite took 41.8 s on average. To test the generalisability of Dorylus, both tools are tested on 936 programs from the SF110 benchmark. For this corpus Dorylus was compared with three algorithms in EvoSuite; whole test suite (WTS), many objective sorting algorithm (MOSA) and many independent objectives (MIO). The results suggest that Dorylus' techniques generalise well as it reaches 79% branch coverage on the corpus, compared with that of EvoSuite who achieves 89%, 86% and 88% with WTS, MOSA and MIO respectively.

2   Dorylus

Dorylus' aim is branch coverage. In order to achieve its goal Dorylus needs two pieces of information from the program that it obtains by instrumenting it. Firstly, the basic blocks that were executed in a given execution, and secondly the values of the operands and the operator at each predicate. This information will guide Dorylus' search aiming for maximum coverage. With the operator's information from a given predicate, Dorylus uses branch distance, as defined by Korel [10], to calculate how far the given test inputs are from executing the unseen branch on the other side of the predicate. Branch distance specifies how far a given predicate is from switching outcomes. For example, given a conditional statement containing the expression $a == 100$, if the outcome is false then the branch distance is $100 - a$. Korel defined such distances for all boolean operations on numeric operands. Branch distance is used for all Java primitives as they are numeric. For string comparisons, Levenshtein distance is used to defined a measure for all core Java boolean string comparison functions. This indicates the number of characters which must be changed (inserted, swapped or deleted) in order to change the outcome of the predicate. Furthermore, as Dorylus operates on bytecode any complex boolean expressions are broken down into atomic components so need not be considered.

Uncovered branches become targets for Dorylus and this list is dynamically updated. A predicate can be observed as the guard of two branches, each labelled as $l_s \rightarrow l_d$ where l_s is the block containing the predicate and l_d is the destination block. Targets are defined as those branches where l_s is covered by the test suite but l_d is not. Therefore, as coverage changes the set of targets to be tackled is updated. When the program is executed, a trace of executed branches and the operands and operators of all executed predicates is given as output. The predicate information can be used to measure branch distance at a given location in the trace. When a test case's trace includes a previously unseen branch, it is added to the test suite.

Once the program is instrumented, some initial inputs are generated uniformly at random and ran on the instrumented program. The traces of these executions define the initial coverage and therefore provide Dorylus with a set of initial targets. Each target is a separate optimisation problem, where the fitness function is branch distance. It is important, however, that even though each search problem is separate, information should be shared between them. Therefore, all test cases that are generated are shared with all targets for which they pass through the guarding predicate. At each target, a novel lightweight dynamic path-based input dependency analysis is carried out to reduce the search space. This analysis identifies parts of the inputs whose mutation affects the outcome of the predicate, thereby drastically reducing the search space of inputs. This must be done on a path basis as depending on the path taken to the guard, different inputs may be included in the variables used in the predicate statement. For primitive numerical types we apply a search process called Ant Colony Optimisation for continuous domains ($ACO_{\mathbb{R}}$) [16]. It creates a probability distribution for each input at each target given the path taken to the guard. This is constructed by maintaining an archive of best performing test cases at each target, diversified by mandating that unique paths must be maintained and may not be removed. $ACO_{\mathbb{R}}$ controls the proximity to the target via Gaussian kernels [16]. When creating a new test case, the kernel is sampled to generate new primitive values. For String input values, rather than attempt to create a distribution, three mutations are defined based on the Levenshtein distance: insert, swap and delete. A guide test case is selected from the target's archive and the string is mutated uniformly at random a number of times according to the branch distance.

Dorylus not only works on simple programs requiring only primitives or strings, but also on more complicated real-world programs. Given a Java class to be tested, Dorylus identifies constructors and all public methods which can be called and labels them as entry points. It looks at the inputs for each method, and uses refection for those containing objects to find the object's constructor and its required inputs. This cycle is repeated until all objects have been deconstructed to primitive and string inputs and a sequence of method calls to instantiate an object of the required type. Initial test cases call a constructor followed by a public method covering all combinations. During the search process, if for a target it appears that there are no inputs affecting the outcome, then the methods of any objects formed by the inputs are searched over. This process identifies state changing methods, such as setter methods, and then searches for the required input values. If it still appears that there are no inputs that affect the target, the process backtracks to previous targets. The aim being to find new paths to the guard predicate which can pass through the guard. When a test case is added to the test suite, the methods it calls and their inputs are sent to each target. Every target then adds a call to the method containing the target to the end of the sequence. This builds up complex sequences of method calls to explore all possible states of the program.

3   Experimental Setup

EvoSuite is a state-of-the-art test generation tool for Java programs [6]. Its aim is to generate unit tests to cover as much of a program as possible, using a genetic algorithm. EvoSuite's search-based approach has featured many improvements over the years with techniques such as dynamic symbolic execution, hybrid search and testability transformations [8]. Furthermore, it has been the winner of a number of test case generation tool competitions [12].

This evaluation tests Dorylus and EvoSuite on a number of programs, and in all instances both were given 2 min to achieve as much coverage as possible. All experiments were carried out 10 times. The choice of 2 min is a tradeoff between coverage and time spent, which has been identified and used in a number of previous studies [7,15]. Three different algorithms within EvoSuite were used; whole test suite (WTS) [6], Multiple Objective Sorting Algorithm (MOSA) [14] and Many Independent Objective (MIO) [2]. In all cases EvoSuite's only coverage criterion was branch coverage, as this is the only criterion included in Dorylus. All other setting of EvoSuite were left to their default values.

There are two corpora on which the tools have been compared. The first corpus consists of 12 programs which demonstrate constructs and programming styles using string inputs. This was selected due to Dorylus being specialised on primitive and string inputs. Furthermore, 10 of these programs have been used widely in the literature to test tools aiming to generate strings that must conform to some constraints, in order to reach parts of the program [1]. Some of the programs exhibit features which can be hard to handle for automated tools. Two programs have been added to the corpus in order to further test the tools. The first addition is to collapse multiple string inputs into a single input which is the split in the program. The other was made by combining different features of the programs to create a hard to cover program. Table 1 shows the complete list of all programs in the first corpus.

The second corpus was selected from the SF110[1] benchmark. SF110 contains 110 Java projects from SourceForge, the first 100 were selected to be statistically representative, the final 10 were the 10 most popular Java projects on Source-Forge at the time [7]. SF110 consists of 23,886 programs, of this Dorylus can handle 8,398, of which 1,000 were chosen uniformly at random to judge the performance of Dorylus and test how well it generalises. If any of the 10 repetitions of a program failed due to a crash in one of the tools, we reran it up to three times. If after these reruns there were still repetitions which had failed, the program was removed from the corpus. Of the 1000 selected programs there were 64 that caused such issues and were therefore removed, leaving a final corpus of 936 classes with an average of 7.6 branches.

4   Results

Table 1 presents the first corpus on which the tools where tested, along with each tools average time and coverage for each program. Dorylus can be seen to be competitive on coverage with EvoSuite, matching coverage on all programs and improving coverage on two. EvoSuite covers an average of 95.1% reaching 100% on all but three programs, whereas Dorylus achieves 100% on all but one program, with an average of 97.7% branch coverage. The programs on which EvoSuite fails to reach 100% coverage are those which require optimisation of sub-regions of inputs. For example, FileSuffix takes two string input parameters, the first being the type of file and the second a file name. The file extension is then taken to be the substring after the last period in the file name. The program then checks the extension against the file type. Coverage of this program is conditional upon being able to generate an input with at least one period, and being able to find the correct substring to be placed after this period (the extension). The correct extension is dependent upon first providing a valid file type, and then matching the given extension with the one defined in the program. Dorylus covers the entire program in under 10 s on average, whereas EvoSuite only reaches 100% coverage on one of the ten repetitions, on average only covering 84.8%. TestProgram is similarly conditional on substring optimisation in addition to having a branch that is only feasible when a certain path is taken through the program. On this class, EvoSuite consistently reached 84.6% coverage and no higher, never covering the branch that required a specific path to be followed. This program emphasises the need for path diversity.

In terms of performance, EvoSuite is far quicker on the simpler programs without nested conditional statements and with many literals present for seeding, for example, in the case of DateParse. As programs get more complex, Dorylus' performance overtakes that of EvoSuite. On the corpus, EvoSuite reaches maximum coverage in a mean time of 41.8 s with a median of 14.5 s, compared with Dorylus' mean time of 20.3 s and median of 7.3 s. As 100% coverage is not attained in three instances for EvoSuite there are three cases of reaching the maximum time of 120 s, Dorylus only reaches the timeout once. An interesting

---
[1] http://www.evosuite.org/experimental-data/sf110/.

Table 1. Results on the first corpus for both EvoSuite and Dorylus. It shows the mean time and coverage for each tool over 10 repetitions on each program.

Program	Branches	EvoSuite WTS		Dorylus	
		Time (s)	Coverage	Time (s)	Coverage
Calc	12	1.1	100%	6.5	100%
Cookie	13	16.6	100%	3.7	100%
Costfuns	20	1.5	100%	3.9	100%
DateParse	39	1.1	100%	31.7	100%
FileSuffix	23	119.6	84.8%	9.6	100%
NotyPevar	8	2.4	100%	1.6	100%
Ordered4	29	37.8	100%	2.1	100%
Pat	39	120	72%	120	72%
Text2Txt	23	10.5	100%	8.0	100%
Title	43	12.4	100%	11.3	100%
DateParse1V	39	58.6	100%	39.4	100%
TestProgram	13	120	84.6%	5.7	100%
Mean	25	41.8	95.1%	20.3	97.7%
Median	23	14.5	100%	7.3	100%

program to mention is DateParse1V, which is DateParse modified so that instead of two string inputs there is only one. This input is then split so that the first three characters become the original input two, and the remaining characters the original input one. The control flow of the program is left unaffected by this change. Despite a small change to the representation, the time taken for Evo-Suite to cover the program jumps from 1.1 s up to 58.6 s. Whereas Dorylus only increases from 31.7 to 39.4 s. DateParse1V demonstrates that Dorylus can be more resilient to representation changes than EvoSuite and is quicker to handle substring optimisation.

In the second corpus there are 936 real-world Java classes upon which the tools were tested, the results for which can be seen in Table 2. All three algorithms within EvoSuite performed similarly, with WTS reaching 89.5%, MOSA 85.7% and MIO 87.6%. Dorylus reached 79.1% in 30.2 s on average. This suggests that the techniques used in Dorylus generalise well, given that EvoSuite is a mature state-of-the-art tool. Interesting to note is the number of programs on which each algorithm achieved higher coverage than the other three. Dorylus outperforms all EvoSuite configurations on 29 programs, suggesting that there is a set of programs on which its techniques are more effective.

However, many of the classes within SF110 are small, with many having no branches at all. As such results for the largest 100 classes of the 936 are also presented. These classes, are substantial with an average of 42 branches and minimum and maximum of 24 and 273 branches respectively. Coverage was much lower, Dorylus reaches 31.29% coverage and EvoSuite 54.56%. However, it can be seen that Dorylus is much quicker on these larger programs. This suggests that it is either failing or stopping the search process early and as such future work will include more randomness in the search in order to continue to improve given more time. As can be seen in Table 2, there are nine classes of the largest 100 on which Dorylus achieves higher coverage than EvoSuite, implying that Dorylus' technique could be used to complement EvoSuite in specific circumstances.

Possible threats to validity include the different implementations of the tools. As previously mentioned, all three algorithms in EvoSuite achieve similar results. It would be worth investigating an implementation of Dorylus in EvoSuite to get a better comparison with less confounding factors.

Table 2. Results on the second corpus for WTS, MOSA, MIO and Dorylus. It shows mean time, coverage and the number of programs where each tool gets the higher coverage than all other approaches.

Classes	Branches	Algorithm	Coverage (%)	Time (s)	Best
All 936	7.6	WTS	89.47	32.6	58
		MOSA	85.66	29.4	44
		MIO	87.58	36.2	19
		Dorylus	79.12	30.2	29
Largest 100	42.4	WTS	54.56	101.9	16
		MOSA	54.28	98.49	27
		MIO	51.85	112.1	4
		Dorylus	31.29	75.67	9

5 Related Work

There are many search-based methods that can be used for automated test generation [11]. What these algorithms have in common is that they obtain solutions guided by a fitness function [9]. The way in which these test cases are created or how the search is guided is what distinguishes these methods from one another. In the context of automated test generation the most prominent search based method used is Genetic Algorithms [4]. A well-known example is the work of Fraser et al. on EvoSuite [5]. EvoSuite produces unit tests for Java programs using a genetic algorithm with some coverage metrics as the fitness functions. It has been tested for both unit testing and system testing and has achieved the highest score compared with state of the art tools for a number of years [12]. Owing to its success a number of algorithms have been integrated into the EvoSuite tool.

Firstly, the Many Objective Search Algorithm (MOSA) uses a multi-objective approach, where every target is an objective [14]. Many test cases are compared based on their performance across all objectives in order to obtain the best performing test cases. In this approach, infeasible branches may cause wasted effort, as targets that have a control dependency on an infeasible branch are infeasible targets, and therefore not worth considering. This improvement was implemented in Dynamic MOSA (DynaMOSA) where targets are updated to only include those immediately reachable from currently covered branches. Dorylus uses a similar design by updating targets dynamically [13]. In doing this, an infeasible region in the control flow graph will only be represented as a single objective, the branch guarded by the infeasible predicate. This approach was proved to be at least as good as the original algorithm [13]. DynaMOSA creates many test cases which are scored according to their position in the Pareto front of all objectives. Conversely, our work aims to prioritise targets in order to speed up exploration of required ancestors before effort is spent on descendants. It is possible for the Pareto front of DynaMOSA to be affected by infeasible targets with very low branch distances, although they will have less impact on performance than on MOSA. Unfortunately we were unable to compare with DynaMOSA as it was not in the release of EvoSuite used in the experiments.

The existing tool most similar to Dorylus is Many Independent Objectives (MIO), in which a population is maintained for each of the objectives [2,3]. MIO was compared against random search, MOSA and whole test suite and found to outperform all three [3]. The goal of MIO is to produce the highest covering test suite in the allotted timeframe. It handles this goal starting with the easiest to solve branches, which provide immediate coverage. This means that where MIO punishes complex and difficult to solve targets, Dorylus puts effort into attempting to solve them unless they are heuristically identified as infeasible. Infeasible branches are implicitly ignored by MIO as it prioritises those targets for whom better performing test cases are being found. Once a plateau is reached for an infeasible branch no new test cases will be found. Dorylus aims to get many paths through to the targets, thereby introducing path diversity. In the case that current members of the archive are unable to affect change on a predicate, Dorylus backtracks to the previous target in order to find new paths. Backtracking can take many steps in order to find new rare probability paths, which are needed to unlock specific regions of code. On the other hand, MIO has a counter for each target which is incremented on every attempt to find a new test case, and resets when a test case is added to the archive. Therefore, if the correct path does not make it to the target, it will implicitly be seen as infeasible and therefore given less attention.

6   Conclusion

We have put forward a new tool to generate input data to cover hard to reach regions of code. It is a search-based method, founded on the ideas of Ant Colony Optimisation, with novel heuristics to assist in unlocking difficult predicates. The concept of a conditional statements dependency on an input variable for a specific path has proved in practice to work well and assist in speed and quality of coverage. Our tool has been compared against EvoSuite, a highly successful test case generation tool. We demonstrated that Dorylus can outperform EvoSuite on programs with complex predicates and code structure. Furthermore, we have shown Dorylus can handle a large number of real-world programs and provide good coverage. Two steps for future work have been identified. Firstly, to incorporate other coverage criterion to improve the effectiveness of the generated test suite. The second step is to combine the approaches of Dorylus with those of EvoSuite to create a hybrid thereby improving EvoSuite's effectiveness on the programs which Dorylus beat it.

References

1. Alshraideh, M., Bottaci, L.: Search-based software test data generation for string data using program-specific search operators. Softw. Test. Verif. Reliab. **16**(3), 175–203 (2006)
2. Arcuri, A.: Many Independent Objective (MIO) algorithm for test suite generation. In: Menzies, T., Petke, J. (eds.) SSBSE 2017. LNCS, vol. 10452, pp. 3–17. Springer, Cham (2017). https://doi.org/10.1007/978-3-319-66299-2_1
3. Arcuri, A.: Test suite generation with the Many Independent Objective (MIO) algorithm. Inf. Softw. Technol. **104**, 195–206 (2018)
4. Campos, J., Ge, Y., Fraser, G., Eler, M., Arcuri, A.: An empirical evaluation of evolutionary algorithms for test suite generation. In: Menzies, T., Petke, J. (eds.) SSBSE 2017. LNCS, vol. 10452, pp. 33–48. Springer, Cham (2017). https://doi.org/10.1007/978-3-319-66299-2_3
5. Fraser, G., Arcuri, A.: EvoSuite: automatic test suite generation for object-oriented software. In: Proceedings of the 19th ACM SIGSOFT Symposium and the 13th European Conference on Foundations of Software Engineering, pp. 416–419. ACM (2011)
6. Fraser, G., Arcuri, A.: Whole test suite generation. IEEE Trans. Softw. Eng. **39**(2), 276–291 (2013)
7. Fraser, G., Arcuri, A.: A large-scale evaluation of automated unit test generation using evosuite. ACM Trans. Softw. Eng. Methodol. (TOSEM) **24**(2), 8 (2014)
8. Galeotti, J.P., Fraser, G., Arcuri, A.: Improving search-based test suite generation with dynamic symbolic execution. In: IEEE 24th International Symposium Software Reliability Engineering (ISSRE), pp. 360–369 (2013)
9. Harman, M., Clark, J.: Metrics are fitness functions too. In: Proceedings of 10th International Symposium on Software Metrics, pp. 58–69. IEEE (2004)
10. Korel, B.: Automated software test data generation. IEEE Trans. Softw. Eng. **16**(8), 870–879 (1990)
11. McMinn, P.: Search-based software test data generation: a survey. Softw. Test. Verif. Reliab. **14**(2), 105–156 (2004)
12. Panichella, A., Campos, J., Fraser, G.: EvoSuite at the SBST 2019 tool competition. In: International Workshop on Search-Based Software Testing (SBST), pp. 29–32 (2019)
13. Panichella, A., Kifetew, F., Tonella, P.: Automated test case generation as a many-objective optimisation problem with dynamic selection of the targets. IEEE Trans. Softw. Eng. **44**(2), 122–158 (2018)

14. Panichella, A., Kifetew, F.M., Tonella, P.: Reformulating branch coverage as a many-objective optimization problem. In: IEEE 8th International Conference on Software Testing, Verification and Validation (ICST), pp. 1–10. IEEE (2015)
15. Panichella, A., Kifetew, F.M., Tonella, P.: A large scale empirical comparison of state-of-the-art search-based test case generators. Inf. Softw. Technol. **104**, 236–256 (2018)
16. Socha, K., Dorigo, M.: Ant colony optimization for continuous domains. Eur. J. Oper. Res. **185**(3), 1155–1173 (2008)

Challenge Paper

Software Improvement with Gin: A Case Study

Justyna Petke[1(✉)] and Alexander E. I. Brownlee[2]

[1] University College London, London, UK
j.petke@ucl.ac.uk
[2] University of Stirling, Stirling, UK
sbr@cs.stir.ac.uk

Abstract. We provide a case study for the usage of Gin, a genetic improvement toolbox for Java. In particular, we implemented a simple GP search and targeted two software optimisation properties: runtime and repair. We ran our search algorithm on Gson, a Java library for converting Java objects to JSON and vice-versa. We report on runtime improvements and fixes found. We provide all the new code and data on the dedicated website: https://github.com/justynapt/ssbseChallenge2019.

Keywords: Genetic improvement · Search-based software engineering

1 Introduction

Genetic improvement (GI) uses automated search to improve existing software [10]. GI-evolved changes have already been incorporated into development [6,7]. Only recently two frameworks emerged that aim to help researchers experiment with GI: Gin [3,11] and PyGGI [1,2]. The new version of Gin provides support for large-scale Java projects, thus we decided to use it for our study.

In this paper we aim to determine whether we can improve various software properties using Gin. We chose Gson for the case study, as it is written in Java and follows the Maven directory structure. The second version of Gin provides utilities for setting up Maven and Gradle projects, so that the user only needs to provide project name and top level directory. This way researchers can quickly test their novel GI strategies on such projects. Several of Gin's utilities are method-based, thus search can be restricted to individual methods.

In this work we use Gin to generate patches for one of the most frequently used methods of Gson. We aim to improve its runtime and fix (injected) bugs.

2 Subject Program

Gson[1] is a Java library for converting Java Objects to JSON and vice-versa. It is used by over 152,000 projects on GitHub, and there have been 39 releases

---

[1] https://github.com/google/gson.

© Springer Nature Switzerland AG 2019
S. Nejati and G. Gay (Eds.): SSBSE 2019, LNCS 11664, pp. 183–189, 2019.
https://doi.org/10.1007/978-3-030-27455-9_14

so far. It can be built with Maven or Gradle, and follows the standard project structure. In this work we use the latest release, that is, gson-parent-2.8.5.

We first ran cloc[2] and the PIT mutation tool[3] to get information about the project. Gson contains 50874 lines of code, 25193 of which are in Java. The test suite achieves 83% line coverage and 77% mutation coverage.

3   Test Suite

The test suite consists of 1051 JUnit tests, 1050 of which are runnable with `mvn test` (1 test is skipped; the total runtime of the remaining 1050 is <10s). Running PIT issued warnings that two tests (`com.google.gson .functional.ConcurrencyTest.testMultiThreadDeserialization` and `com.google .gson.functional.ConcurrencyTest.testMultiThreadSerialization`) leave hanging threads. We ran those tests using Gin's utility, `gin.util.EmptyPatchTester` (which runs all provided unit tests in the input file for a project), and indeed the program did not terminate, unless the `-j` option was added, which runs tests in a separate JVM. Therefore, we fixed those tests by adding a shutDown hook for the ExecutorService instances at the end of each of the two faulty unit tests[4].

4   Methodology

We set out to show how the latest version of the genetic improvement tool, Gin [3], can be used for the purpose of runtime improvement as well as program repair. Therefore, we used the same search algorithm for targeting both objectives: genetic programming; the most frequently used strategy in genetic improvement [10]. Each individual in the population is represented as a list of source code edits.

4.1   Search

Following the famous GenProg algorithm structure [8], for each generation we select two parents from the previous population at random, apply 1-point crossover to create two children, and append both parents and both children to the current population. If the required population size is not divisible by four, we add the original program to the population until we reach the desired number[5]. Finally, we mutate each of the created individuals and calculate their fitness.

Crossover: Crossover takes two parents, i.e., a list of edits, and creates two children: one comprising the first half of edits of parent 1 and the second half of edits of parent 2; the second child containing the remaining edits.

---

[2] https://cloc.org/.

[3] Plugin used: https://github.com/STAMP-project/pitmp-maven-plugin.

[4] Fixed test class is available on the submission's website, in the input folder.

[5] We decided to make this small change following insight that fixes usually require no more that four AST node edits [9].

Mutation: We use two types of mutation operators, which were introduced in Gin [3]. The first type are constrained statement edits, that contain DELETE, COPY, SWAP and REPLACE operations to adhere with the Java grammar. DELETE simply targets a single Java statement for deletion. The remaining three edits target matching pairs of Java statements (e.g. two assignment statements, or two if statements). The second mutation type are Binary and Unary replacement operators. These follow the micro-mutations in [5]: binary operator replacement will replace e.g. == with !=, or <with>; unary operator replacement will replace e.g. ++ with --.

Fitness: For the purpose of runtime improvement, we simply used runtime measured by the system clock, in milliseconds, as fitness. We only allowed individuals that pass all the tests to be considered for mating in the next generation. For the purpose of program repair, we used the number of tests failed as a fitness measure. We only allowed individuals that compile and do not fail more tests than the original program to move to the mating population.

4.2 Setup

For our experiments, due to time constraints, we used 10 generations with population size of 21. For runtime improvement, we ran each test (with 2 s timeout) 500 times and took the total time. This is to off-set the fact that each test case can be run in milliseconds. For program repair this condition is not necessary.

In order to establish which methods to improve, we first ran Gin's utility gin.util.Profiler to establish which methods are the most frequently used. This utility uses hprof[6] to check how often a method appears on the call stack, sampling it every 10 ms. This is a non-deterministic procedure, so we ran each test 10 times to ensure the most frequently used methods are in the output file.

We implemented 4 new classes: gin.util.GP is an abstract class, which also processes input and output; gin.util.GPSimple implements GP search; while gin .util.GPFix and gin.util.GPRuntime extend it, implementing fitness functions.

We ran our experiments on a Lenovo ThinkPad Edge laptop with Intel Core i5-2410M CPU @ 2.30 GHz 4 processor, running 64-bit Ubuntu 18.04.2 LTS.

5   Results

Gin's Profiler revealed that the most frequently used method is com.google. gson.Gson.newJsonReader. However, we did not use it in our experiments as it consisted of only three lines that essentially just instantiated JsonReader and returned it. Thus this method is unlikely to be improvable. Therefore, we opted to target the second most frequently used method: com.google.gson.GsonBuilder .create. This method also contains two addition operators, so it would be interesting to see if the Binary operator could find improvements. Profiler identified 78 tests that cover this method. Overall, Profiler found 585 tests on the

---

[6] https://docs.oracle.com/javase/7/docs/technotes/samples/hprof.html.

hprof call stack (sampled at 10 ms intervals, so not all 1050 tests captured, as expected).

5.1 Runtime Improvement

We first tried the constrained statement edits. The GP run finished in 22 min. 56 improved patches were found. The best individual found improved runtime by 19% on the training set. The best patch found removed one line: `addTypeAdaptersForDate(datePattern, dateStyle, timeStyle, factories);`[7] However, when the mutant was run with `mvn test`, several test cases failed. This shows that the methods used were not enough to capture the desired software behaviour for that method.

We can attribute this to the process the `Profiler` uses to determine the tests associated with a given target method. The `Profiler` samples the call stack at regular intervals, so could conceivably miss some calls. It also excludes parametrised tests. Running on a subset of the tests helps avoid overfitting to any dominant tests in the complete set, but cannot guarantee correct behaviour (insofar as the test suite can measure it). The only solution to this is to treat the limited test set produced by the `Profiler` for a target method as a quick-running surrogate for the whole test set, but one should still evaluate on the whole set at intervals.

We thus ran a second experiment, with all 585 tests identified by the `Profiler` for training. Since we increased the number of tests to 585 from 78, we decreased the number of repetitions of each test by the same fraction ($500/7.5 = 67$), to save time. The experiment finished in 40 min, finding 46 improved patches.

This time Gin was able to find improvements that generalised to the whole test suite of 1050 tests. The best patch improved runtime by 24% on the training set and swapped the following two lines:

`factories.addAll(hierarchyFactories);`

`addTypeAdaptersForDate(datePattern, dateStyle, timeStyle, factories);`

That being said, the improvement is unnoticeable, when tests are run once. This is due to the fact that all tests run in a fraction of a second (1050 tests finish in less than 10 s). Moreover, the 24% improvement amounts to 1.25 s, which could be due to environmental bias, as total execution time was calculated for fitness evaluation purposes.

Even though significant improvements have not been found, there is a key point worth noting. The test suite has a strong impact on the validity of the results of a GI framework. Despite the evolved patch passing all tests, we doubt that this was the intended behaviour of the software, as the `addTypeAdaptersForDate` method uses the `factories` variable. By swapping the statements, the value of the `factories` variable is changed. Thus it is crucial to re-run the full test suite at regular intervals during the search, and before application of GI, it is important to ensure that the test suite is adequate. Generating

---

[7] This mutant can be obtained by running `gin.PatchAnalyser` with the text for the patch found in the output file of GPRuntime.

additional tests on the correctly running original version of the program using a tool such as EvoSuite [4] is also advised.

5.2 Repair

In order to inject faults, we looked at the PIT reports. We found one mutation that was both killed by the existing test suite and could be potentially found by our mutation operators, that is, a change of sign from $+3$ to -3. We thus introduced that mutant and ran our experiment with the 78 tests identified by `Profiler` to cover the `GsonBuilder.create` method. Since we did not repeat test runs, this experiment was quick, running in under 2 min.

The original code segment affected by the mutation was as follows:

```
List<TypeAdapterFactory> factories = new ArrayList<TypeAdapterFactory>(
this.factories.size()+ this.hierarchyFactories.size()+ 3);
```

The mutant looked like this:

```
List<TypeAdapterFactory> factories = new ArrayList<TypeAdapterFactory>(
this.factories.size()+ this.hierarchyFactories.size()- 3);
```

In this case, only the Binary and Unary replacement mutations were used in the GP. Given that we ran the process with 21 individuals and 10 generations, 210 patches were generated overall during the search. 171 of those passed all the tests. The first patch was found in the first generation, and changed the minus sign to a multiplication. This patch passed all 1050 tests. In this case the fix was found quickly because of the limited search space: having limited the possible code mutations that the GP could explore to only mutations that would be likely to fix the bug. To fix a wider range of bugs (i.e. where we do not know the bug *a priori*), the number of edit types would need to be extended to at least the wider range included with Gin and the search would take correspondingly longer.

As in the runtime experiment, we observed that the 78 tests might not be enough to cover all the behaviour, we ran another experiment with the 585 tests identified by the `Profiler`. This time 174 fixes were found in 4 min. This set contained several individuals that contained the required mutation that changed the minus to the plus sign. However, again the first patch found changed minus to a multiplication instead. The question arises whether the fixes found are true fixes, or whether the test suite should be improved.

We also injected another fault, that swaps the following two statements:

```
factories.addAll(this.factories);
```

```
Collections.reverse(factories);
```

Out of 78 tests, just one failed for this mutant. GP search took 41 seconds, this time limited to the constrained statement mutations. No fix was found. We also ran this experiment with 585 tests, to avoid overfitting. No fix was found either. We know the fix is in the search space, so a larger run could potentially produce the desired fix (or different random seeds for mutation selection and individual selection). Given that previous research found that fixes usually contain short mutations, perhaps a different search strategy would have been more effective. The current one almost always increases the size of each mutant by one.

Finally, we introduced a bug that copied the following line right under itself:
`Collections.reverse(factories);`
We ran GP with the 78 tests and 585 tests, as before. In both cases the correct fix was found in the first generation (i.e., deleting the extra line).

6   Conclusions

We showed how Gin can be used for the purpose of program's runtime improvement and repair. It shows how quickly and easily researchers can conduct GI experiments on large Java projects. We added a simple GP search to Gin, and applied it to Gson. Our results show that expression-level changes are possible with Gin that can lead to useful mutations (fixes). There are several future directions. More fine-grained fitness values are possible with Gin, as it captures the expected and actual result of tests. This could guide the search better. From our results a question arises whether GP is the best approach for GI.

We also showed that existing test suites are not enough to capture software behaviour. We pose that Gin can thus be used to test the strength of a given test suite. Gin also provides a utility to generate EvoSuite tests, which could strengthen the test suite, though currently the feature is experimental.

All data for replicability purposes is available on the dedicated website: https://github.com/justynapt/ssbseChallenge2019.

Acknowledgement. The work was funded by the UK EPSRC grant EP/P023991/1 and Carnegie Trust grant RIG008300.

References

1. An, G., Blot, A., Petke, J., Yoo, S.: PyGGI 2.0: language independent genetic improvement framework. In: Proceedings of the 12th Joint Meeting on Foundations of Software Engineering, ESEC/FSE 2017, Tallinn, Estonia, 26–30 August 2019. ACM (2019)
2. An, G., Kim, J., Yoo, S.: Comparing line and AST granularity level for program repair using PyGGI. In: Petke, J., Stolee, K.T., Langdon, W.B., Weimer, W. (eds.) Proceedings of the 4th International Genetic Improvement Workshop, GI@ICSE 2018, Gothenburg, Sweden, 2 June 2018, pp. 19–26. ACM (2018). https://doi.org/10.1145/3194810.3194814
3. Brownlee, A.E.I., Petke, J., Alexander, B., Barr, E.T., Wagner, M., White, D.R.: Gin: genetic improvement research made easy. In: Auger, A., Stützle, T. (eds.) Proceedings of the Genetic and Evolutionary Computation Conference, GECCO 2019, Prague, Czech Republic, 13–17 July 2019, pp. 985–993. ACM (2019). https://doi.org/10.1145/3321707.3321841
4. Fraser, G., Arcuri, A.: Evosuite: automatic test suite generation for object-oriented software. In: Gyimóthy, T., Zeller, A. (eds.) SIGSOFT/FSE'11 19th ACM SIGSOFT Symposium on the Foundations of Software Engineering (FSE-19) and ESEC'11: 13th European Software Engineering Conference (ESEC-13), Szeged, Hungary, 5–9 September 2011, pp. 416–419. ACM (2011). https://doi.org/10.1145/2025113.2025179

5. Haraldsson, S.O., Woodward, J.R., Brownlee, A.E.I., Cairns, D.: Exploring fitness and edit distance of mutated python programs. In: McDermott, J., Castelli, M., Sekanina, L., Haasdijk, E., García-Sánchez, P. (eds.) EuroGP 2017. LNCS, vol. 10196, pp. 19–34. Springer, Cham (2017). https://doi.org/10.1007/978-3-319-55696-3_2
6. Haraldsson, S.O., Woodward, J.R., Brownlee, A.E.I., Siggeirsdottir, K.: Fixing bugs in your sleep: how genetic improvement became an overnight success. In: Bosman, P.A.N. (ed.) Genetic and Evolutionary Computation Conference, Berlin, Germany, 15–19 July 2017, Companion Material Proceedings, pp. 1513–1520. ACM (2017). https://doi.org/10.1145/3067695.3082517
7. Langdon, W.B., Lam, B.Y.H., Petke, J., Harman, M.: Improving CUDA DNA analysis software with genetic programming. In: Silva, S., Esparcia-Alcázar, A.I. (eds.) Proceedings of the Genetic and Evolutionary Computation Conference, GECCO 2015, Madrid, Spain, 11–15 July 2015, pp. 1063–1070. ACM (2015). https://doi.org/10.1145/2739480.2754652
8. Le Goues, C., Nguyen, T., Forrest, S., Weimer, W.: GenProg: a generic method for automatic software repair. IEEE Trans. Softw. Eng. 38(1), 54–72 (2012). https://doi.org/10.1109/TSE.2011.104
9. Martinez, M., Monperrus, M.: Mining software repair models for reasoning on the search space of automated program fixing. Empirical Softw. Eng. 20(1), 176–205 (2015). https://doi.org/10.1007/s10664-013-9282-8
10. Petke, J., Haraldsson, S.O., Harman, M., Langdon, W.B., White, D.R., Woodward, J.R.: Genetic improvement of software: a comprehensive survey. IEEE Trans. Evol. Comput. 22(3), 415–432 (2018). https://doi.org/10.1109/TEVC.2017.2693219
11. White, D.R.: GI in no time. In: Bosman, P.A.N. (ed.) Genetic and Evolutionary Computation Conference, Berlin, Germany, 15–19 July 2017, Companion Material Proceedings, pp. 1549–1550. ACM (2017). https://doi.org/10.1145/3067695.3082515

Author Index

Printed in the United States
By Bookmasters